Question&Answer

COMPANY LAW

Develop your legal skills

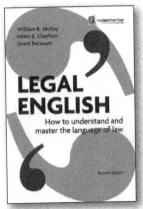

9781408226100

9781447905141

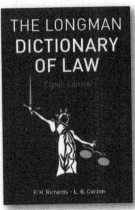

9781408261538

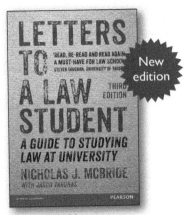

9781447922650

Written to help you develop the essential skills needed to succeed on your course and prepare for practice.

Available from all good bookshops or order online at:
www.pearsoned.co.uk/law

Question&Answer

COMPANY LAW

2nd edition

Fang Ma
University of Portsmouth

Harlow, England • London • New York • Boston • San Francisco • Toronto • Sydney • Auckland • Singapore • Hong Kong
Tokyo • Seoul • Taipei • New Delhi • Cape Town • São Paulo • Mexico City • Madrid • Amsterdam • Munich • Paris • Milan

PEARSON EDUCATION LIMITED
Edinburgh Gate
Harlow CM20 2JE
United Kingdom
Tel: +44 (0)1279 623623
Web: www.pearson.com/uk

First published 2012 (print and electronic)
Second edition published 2016 (print and electronic)

© Pearson Education Limited 2012, 2016 (print and electronic)

ISBN: 978–1-292–06730–8 (print)
       978–1-292–06732–2 (PDF)
       978–1-292–06733–9 (ePub)
       978–1-292–06734–6 (eText)

British Library Cataloguing-in-Publication Data
A catalogue record for the print edition is available from the British Library

ARP impression 98

Front cover bestseller data from Nielsen BookScan (2009–2013, Law Revision Series)

Print edition typeset in 10/13 Helvetica Neue LT W1G by 35
Print edition printed and bound in Great Britain by Ashford Colour Press Ltd

NOTE THAT ANY PAGE CROSS REFERENCES REFER TO THE PRINT EDITION

Contents

Supporting resources

Visit the **Law Express Question&Answer** series companion website at
www.pearsoned.co.uk/lawexpressqa to find valuable learning material
including:

- **Additional essay and problem questions** arranged by topic for each chapter
  give you more opportunity to practise and hone your exam skills.
- **Diagram plans** for all additional questions assist you in structuring and writing
  your answers.
- **You be the marker** questions allow you to see through the eyes of the examiner
  by marking essay and problem questions on every topic covered in the book.
- Download and print all **Before you begin** diagrams and **Diagram plans** from
  the book.

Also: The companion website provides the following features:

- Search tool to help locate specific items of content.
- Online help and support to assist with website usage and troubleshooting.

For more information please contact your local Pearson sales representative or
visit **www.pearsoned.co.uk/lawexpressqa**

Acknowledgements

I would like to thank the team at Pearson, in particular, Zoe Botterill, Gabriella Playford and Hannah Marston, for their support in completing this book. I am grateful for the comments made by reviewers of this book. I also owe my gratitude to my family, friends and colleagues for their encouragement and help in writing this book.

Fang Ma
University of Portsmouth

Publisher's acknowledgements

Our thanks go to all reviewers who contributed to the development of this text, including students who participated in research and focus groups which helped to shape the series format.

What you need to do for every question in Company Law

Books in the *Question and Answer* series focus on the *why* of a good answer alongside the *what,* thereby helping you to build your question answering skills and technique.

This guide should not be used as a substitute for learning the material thoroughly, your lecture notes or your textbook. It *will* help you to make the most out of what you have already learned when answering an exam or coursework question. Remember that the answers given here are not the *only* correct way of answering the question but serve to show you some good examples of how you *could* approach the question set.

Make sure that you regularly refer to your course syllabus, check which issues are covered (as well as to what extent they are covered) and whether they are usually examined with other topics. Remember that what is required in a good answer could change significantly with only a slight change in the wording of a question. Therefore, do not try to memorise the answers given here, instead use the answers and the other features to understand what goes into a good answer and why.

Before answering any exam question in Company Law, it is essential that you read the question very carefully. Students often make the mistake of not addressing the question which is being asked or misunderstanding the question. Try to avoid giving a general answer by writing everything you know about the topic without reference to the particular issues raised in the question. Most of the topics in company law are interrelated because of the pervasive nature of this subject; it is therefore important to plan your answer, for example, by drawing a simple diagram plan. Good planning helps you clearly structure your answer, identify all the key legal issues that are raised in the question and avoid repetition.

In most instances, you need to consider whether the question concerns a private company or a public company because different rules may apply, in particular in the areas of share capital, loan capital, corporate insolvency and corporate governance. Make sure that your answer is well supported and shows good understanding of the relevant law, not just common sense. It is surprisingly common to come across exam answers with little application of case law or statutes such as the Companies Act 2006 and the Insolvency Act 1986. In relation to case law, students tend to give too much detail of the case facts without appropriate discussion of the important legal principles. It should be noted that the cases discussed in the suggested answers in this book are not the only correct or relevant cases. You can use other cases covered in textbooks or lectures to illustrate the same legal principles. In an exam the full case references are not usually required; mentioning the name of the case and the year when it was decided should be sufficient.

Guided tour

What you need to do for every question in Company Law

[sample page text shown in box]

What to do for every question – Identify the key things you should look for and do in any question and answer on the subject, ensuring you give every one of your answers a great chance from the start.

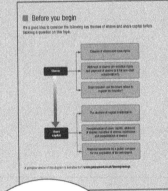

The *Salomon* principles and lifting the corporate veil

How this topic may come up in exams – Understand how to tackle any question on this topic by using the handy tips and advice relevant to both essay and problem questions. In-text symbols clearly identify each question type as they occur.

 Essay question   ? **Problem question**

Before you begin – Use these diagrams as a step-by-step guide to help you confidently identify the main points covered in any question asked. Download these from the companion website to add to your revision notes.

Answer plans and Diagram plans – A clear and concise plan is the key to a good answer and these answer and diagram plans support the structuring of your answers, whatever your preferred learning style.

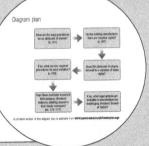

Diagram plan

Answer plan

➜ Consider the legal procedures for the allotment of shares in a private company limited by shares.

➜ Discuss the implications of pre-emption rights.

➜ Examine whether an allotment of preference shares amounts to a variation of class rights.

➜ Assess the procedures required for a variation of class rights.

➜ Evaluate whether Rose and Katie breached their duties as directors by allotting the shares to their family members.

➜ Discuss possible legal actions that Peter can bring against Rose and Katie.

Answer with accompanying guidance – Make the most out of every question by using the guidance to recognise what makes a good answer and why. Answers are the length you could realistically hope to produce in an exam to show you how to gain marks quickly when under pressure.

Answer

This question requires a comparison of a shareholders' agreement and a company's articles of association.[1] The articles of association are internal rule books for the company and govern its internal running whilst a shareholders' agreement is a separate contract between some or all of the shareholders, or between the company and its shareholders.[2]

Articles of associations form a significant part of a company's constitution and must be filed with Companies House. By contrast, a shareholders' agreement is not normally treated as a company's constitution and usually addresses particular issues such as voting, the transfer of shares and the appointment of directors.

[1] This sentence demonstrates that you have identified the main legal issues raised in the question.

[2] The explanations of the articles of association and shareholders' agreements should be the starting point of your answer.

Case names clearly highlighted – Easy-to-spot bold text makes those all important case names stand out from the rest of the answer, ensuring they are much easier to remember in revision and an exam.

[3] These two sentences succinctly summarise the development of common law. They immediately demonstrate that you are very familiar with this area of law and make your answer stand out from the start.

litigation. This complex area of case law has recently been clarified by the Privy Council in **Re Brumark** and the House of Lords in **Re Spectrum Plus Ltd**. Earlier authorities such as **Siebe Gorman & Co Ltd** (1979) and **Re New Bullas Trading Ltd** (1993) were overruled.[5]

A fixed charge is created over a specific asset of a company, for example, its land and buildings and fixed plant. The charge restricts the company's ability to deal with the asset. By contrast, a floating charge is not attached to any particular assets identified when the charge is created; the company is free to deal with the charged assets in the ordinary course of business without the need to obtain the consent of the chargee: **Re Yorkshire Woolcombers Association** [1903] 2 Ch 284.

[4] Although *Siebe Gorman & Co Ltd* has been overruled, a

Make your answer stand out – Really impress your examiners by going the extra mile and including these additional points and further reading to illustrate your deeper knowledge of the subject, fully maximising your marks.

 Make your answer stand out

■ Discuss the rules in relation to the issue of shares. Shares may not be allotted at a discount (s. 580).

■ Examine the payment of shares for non-cash consideration. If shares are issued for a non-cash consideration in a public company, the assets must be valued before allotment (s. 593).

■ Further reading on the doctrine of capital maintenance: Armour, J. (2000) Share capital and creditor protection: efficient rules for a modern company law. 63 *Modern Law Review* 355; Milman, D. (2007) Share capital maintenance: current developments and future horizons. *Company Law Newsletter* 1.

Don't be tempted to – Points out common mistakes ensuring you avoid losing easy marks by understanding where students most often trip up in exams.

Don't be tempted to . . .

■ Treat private companies and public companies in the same way. You should be aware that different rules may apply to these two types of companies.

■ Only focus on the reduction of share capital. Your answer should include other main aspects of the doctrine of capital maintenance, including making distributions to shareholders and purchasing its own shares by a company.

■ Provide an answer without reference to the relevant statutory provisions. Although the common law rules are still important, they have been modified by the statutory provisions in the Companies Act 2006.

Bibliography – Use this list of further reading to really delve into the subject and explore areas in more depth, enabling you to excel in exams.

Bibliography

Abarca, M.L. de E. (2004) The need for substantive regulation on investor protection and corporate governance in Europe: does Europe need a Sarbanes–Oxley? *Journal of International Banking Law and Regulation* 419.

Almadani, M. (2009) Derivative actions: does the Companies Act 2006 offer a way forward? 30 *Company Lawyer* 131.

Guided tour of the companion website

 Book resources are available to download. Print your own **Before you begin** and **Diagram plans** to pin to your wall or add to your own revision notes.

 Additional Essay and Problem questions with **Diagram plans** arranged by topic for each chapter give you more opportunity to practise and hone your exam skills. Print and email your answers.

 You be the marker gives you a chance to evaluate sample exam answers for different question types for each topic and understand how and why an examiner awards marks. Use the accompanying guidance to get the most out of every question and recognise what makes a good answer.

All of this and more can be found when you visit
www.pearsoned.co.uk/lawexpressqa

Table of cases and statutes

◼ Cases

TABLE OF CASES AND STATUTES

▮ Statutes

Statutory Instruments

European Union

United States

Incorporation

1

How this topic may come up in exams

Standard exam questions may ask you to discuss the following issues: the advantages and disadvantages of incorporation compared with partnerships and sole traders, the procedures for setting up a company and the considerations in choosing a company name. A clear understanding of the distinction between private companies and public companies is essential, as well as the change of company status from private to public companies and *vice versa*. The duties of promoters and the pre-incorporation contracts are also popular topics for examination. You should pay special attention to the personal liabilities of promoters with regard to these contracts.

■ Before you begin

It's a good idea to consider the following key themes of incorporation before tackling a question on this topic.

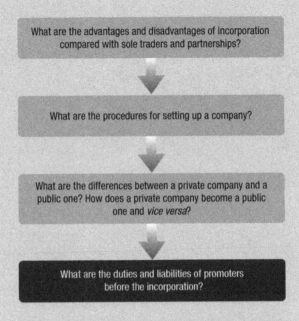

What are the advantages and disadvantages of incorporation compared with sole traders and partnerships?

What are the procedures for setting up a company?

What are the differences between a private company and a public one? How does a private company become a public one and *vice versa*?

What are the duties and liabilities of promoters before the incorporation?

A printable version of this diagram is available from **www.pearsoned.co.uk/lawexpressqa**

🖋 Question 1

Discuss the advantages and disadvantages of companies compared with other types of business organisations such as sole traders and partnerships.

Answer plan

→ Explain the features of sole traders.

→ Examine the nature of partnerships, including ordinary partnerships, limited partnerships and limited liability partnerships.

→ Analyse the special features of companies and focus on the principles of separate legal personality and of limited liability.

Diagram plan

	Sole traders	Ordinary partnerships	Limited partnerships	Limited liability partnerships	Companies
Key legislation	General law of contract	Partnership Act 1890	Limited Partnerships Act 1907	Limited Liability Partnerships Act 2000	Companies Act 2006
Individual's (partner or member) liabilities in respect of business debts	Unlimited	Each partner is jointly and severally liable	Limited liability for limited partners and unlimited liability for general partners	Limited to the amount as they have agreed	Depending on the type of companies
Separate legal personality?	No	No	No	Yes	Yes

A printable version of this diagram plan is available from **www.pearsoned.co.uk/lawexpressqa**

Answer

[1] This sentence sets out the general outline of your answer.

[2] This comment is useful because it compares a sole trader and a company in relation to the filing and registration requirements.

Companies are popular forms of business organisations, alongside sole traders and partnerships. Each has its own distinct features and is suitable for a particular type of business.[1]

A sole trader is a one-person business where an individual makes a contract in his own name. There are no legal filing requirements and therefore it has the advantage of privacy.[2] The individual who acts

3

[3] This phrase is important here because it shows a sharp contrast between a sole trader and a company limited by shares.

[4] Use this sentence to show the examiners where you are going with your answer. This is a broad essay question on various types of business organisation. To gain a higher mark for this type of standard question, you need to show a clear understanding of different types of partnership, in particular, the limited partnership and LLP.

[5] This is the main difference between a partnership and a company and therefore it should be included in a good answer.

[6] This shows that you understand the nature of a partnership and the use of this type of business in practice.

[7] The discussion of limited partnerships is essential here because it demonstrates your sound knowledge of the different types of partnerships. This is often missing in a good exam answer.

[8] Pay attention to the requirement of the general partner without limited liability in addition to the partners with limited liability. This is the basic feature of a limited partnership.

[9] It is very easy to get confused with an LLP because it has the features of both an ordinary partnership and a limited company. An accurate discussion of the features of LLPs makes your answer stand out.

as a sole trader has unlimited liability[3] in respect of the business debts. It is suitable for a one-person business with capital but not for large-scale investment.

There are three main types of partnerships: ordinary partnerships, limited partnerships and limited liability partnerships.[4] Ordinary partnerships are governed by the Partnership Act 1890 unless excluded by the partnership agreement. An ordinary partnership is defined in section 1 as 'the relationship which subsists between persons carrying on a business in common with a view of profit'. In this type of partnership, there must be at least two partners, each of whom becomes an agent of the other (s. 5). A partnership does not have a separate legal personality and its assets are owned directly by the partners. Partners personally are parties to the partnership contracts and do not have limited liability in respect of the partnership's debts. Each partner is jointly and severally liable for the debts and obligations of the partnership incurred while he is a partner.[5] The business affairs of a partnership are entirely private and no legal formality or public registration is required. It is therefore suitable for an association of a small number of persons having trust and confidence in each other.[6]

Limited partnerships are governed by the Limited Partnerships Act 1907.[7] In a limited partnership, there are limited partners with limited liability who are excluded from all management functions. Their liabilities for the partnership's debts are limited to the amount of their contribution to it. There must be at least one general partner with unlimited liability[8] who is liable for debts and obligations of the partnership (s. 4). Considering these requirements, limited partnerships are relatively rare.

Limited liability partnerships (LLPs), which are a hybrid of partnerships and companies, are governed by the Limited Liability Partnerships Act 2000. An LLP has a separate legal personality from its members. The liability of individual members is limited to such amount as they have agreed internally to contribute to the debts of the LLP.[9] It must be registered at Companies House and file annual reports and accounts. It is much closer to a company than to a partnership except in two aspects. First, the members in an LLP are taxed as if they were partners; secondly, there is no division between members and directors inside an LLP, and its members have the same freedom as in an ordinary partnership to decide on their internal decision-making structures.

Companies are governed by the Companies Act 2006 (CA 2006). A company can be limited or unlimited, limited by shares or by guarantee.[10] The most common type of registered company is the company limited by shares where the company's capital is divided into shares and the members' liability is limited to the amount, if any, unpaid on the shares held by them (s. 3(2)). In a company limited by guarantee,[11] the liability of its members is limited to such amount as the members undertake to contribute to the assets of the company in the event of its being wound up (s. 3(3)). The guarantee companies are widely used by charitable and quasi-charitable organisations such as schools, colleges, museums and galleries. In an unlimited company there is no limit on the liability of its members provided by shares or guarantee (s. 3(4)) and therefore it is not usually used for investment purposes.

On incorporation, following a prescribed registration process, a company becomes a separate legal entity, which is distinct and separate from its shareholders. This principle was established by the House of Lords in **Salomon v Salomon & Co Ltd** [1897] AC 22. Lord MacNaghten held that: 'The company is at law a different person altogether from the subscribers to the memorandum; ... the company is not in law the agent of the subscribers or trustee for them.'[12] The company conducts business in its own name, enters into contracts and incurs debts. The assets are in the name of the company, not in the name of its majority shareholder: **Macaura v Northern Assurance Co** [1925] AC 619. The company can sue and be sued: **Williams v Natural Life Health Foods** [1998] 1 BCLC 689. It can employ people including its majority shareholders: **Lee v Lee's Air Farming Ltd** [1961] AC 12. The company has the feature of perpetual succession in the sense that the existence of the company remains even if original members sell their shares. The corporate form may also facilitate borrowing as the lender can obtain an effective security of a floating charge on all the undertaking and assets of the company both present and future or together with a fixed charge on its land. As the use of such form of security is restricted to bodies corporate in practice, a business may be converted to a company solely to raise further capital by borrowing.

[10] This shows that you are aware of the different types of registered company.

[11] This type of company is not as common as companies limited by shares. Some students may fail to include it in their answers.

[12] This is the key case law authority on the principle of separate legal personality. The name of the leading judge and the important judgment are worth learning by heart because they show your specific knowledge of this case.

[13] This is another main advantage of incorporation in addition to the separate legal personality of a company. Clearly outlining this shows your sound knowledge.

[14] A discussion of the problems presents an analytical approach and a balanced view of incorporation. It will help you gain more marks.

In a company limited by shares, the principle of limited liability protects shareholders from personal insolvency.[13] Liability of the members for the company's debts is limited to the amount of their respective shareholdings. This makes it easier for the company to raise capital, as individuals may feel more secure in investing in the company. Another advantage for incorporation is that the word 'Ltd' or 'plc' confers 'prestige, legitimacy and credibility' on the business (Freedman, 1994). The corporate form, however, has some problems associated with it.[14] As Freedman (1994) suggests, the corporate form and its regulatory requirements are burdensome and costly as professional advice is needed to deal with these requirements. The function of limited liability may also be negated by the banks' requiring shareholders to provide personal guarantees for bank loans. In this way shareholders' personal assets could be used to repay any debts owed to the banks or other creditors.

Companies have to be registered with Companies House and their accounts are available for public inspection. Compared with sole traders and partnerships, there is less flexibility, less privacy and more formality after incorporation. Various administrative costs such as filing fees may also be incurred. Despite all these disadvantages, companies have become very popular forms of business. The choice of running a business as a sole trader, partnership or company varies, nevertheless, depending on a number of factors such as the scale of the business, its need for capital, the liability of its members, the internal organisation, privacy and taxation.[15]

[15] This sentence concludes your answer by referring back to the essay question and summarising the issues that need to be considered in choosing a particular type of business organisation.

 Make your answer stand out

- Point out that LLPs are the preferred business formats for solicitors and accountants as they combine the features of corporate personality with partnership structures.
- Briefly discuss the exceptions to the separate legal personality, for example, where an agency relationship exists between a company and its shareholders (*Smith, Stone & Knight Ltd* v *Birmingham Corp* [1939] 4 All ER 116).
- Consider the lifting of the corporate veil where the corporate structure is a mere façade (*Woolfson* v *Strathclyde Regional Council* (1979) 38 P & CR 521).

! Don't be tempted to . . .

- Forget to discuss the key principles of limited liability and separate legal personality.
- Misunderstand the principle of limited liability in relation to companies limited by shares. It refers to the liability of the members rather than that of the company.
- Get confused with limited partnerships and limited liability partnerships. These are two different types of partnerships and their distinction should be clearly examined.
- Only refer to companies limited by shares. You should also show a good understanding of companies limited by guarantee.

? Question 2

John and Peter are in a partnership running a furniture removal business. They have heard of the advantages of forming a company limited by shares and decided to incorporate their business. Please advise them on the following matters.

1   The differences between a private company limited by shares and a public one.
2   The procedures for setting up a private company limited by shares.
3   The procedures required for a private company to become a public one.
4   The restrictions on choosing a name for their company.

Answer plan

→ Compare a private company limited by shares with a public one.
→ Discuss the procedures for incorporation.
→ Consider the requirements for altering the status of a private company.
→ Examine the rules on choosing a company name.

Diagram plan

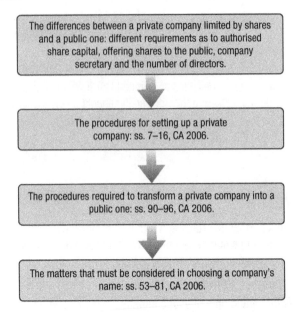

The differences between a private company limited by shares and a public one: different requirements as to authorised share capital, offering shares to the public, company secretary and the number of directors.

↓

The procedures for setting up a private company: ss. 7–16, CA 2006.

↓

The procedures required to transform a private company into a public one: ss. 90–96, CA 2006.

↓

The matters that must be considered in choosing a company's name: ss. 53–81, CA 2006.

A printable version of this diagram plan is available from **www.pearsoned.co.uk/lawexpressqa**

Answer

[1] State the main legal issues that will be addressed in your answer.

This question requires a comparison of a private company limited by shares and a public one, a discussion of the legal requirements for setting up a private company, a consideration of the change of the status of a private company and the matters that need to be taken into account when choosing a company name.[1]

1. Private and public companies[2]

[2] Try to adopt a clear structure by using headings which correspond with the legal issues raised in the question.

[3] Explore the common features of both types of companies before discussing their differences. Some students may only focus on their differences. A consideration of their common features shows your sound understanding of the nature of these companies.

Private and public companies limited by shares are two main types of companies. The liabilities of shareholders in both types of companies are limited to the amount, if any, unpaid on the shares held by them: section 3(2) of the Companies Act 2006 (CA 2006).[3] The vast majority of companies are private companies limited by shares, which are defined in section 4(1) which simply states that they are not public companies. A private company can have just one member and there is no minimum capital requirement. It must have the word 'limited' or 'Ltd' at the end of its name (s. 59) and cannot offer shares publicly (s. 755) or float its shares on the stock market. There is no requirement for annual general meetings; written resolutions can be used in a private company (s. 281).

[4] The statutory definition of a public company is an essential part of your answer because it is the basis of your discussion.

As 'a company whose certificate of incorporation states that it is a public company and the requirements of the Act as to registration as a public company have been complied with',[4] it is subject to more onerous regulations than a private company. There must be at least two directors (s. 154) and a company secretary in a public company (s. 271). It must have the words 'public limited company' or 'plc' at the end of its name (s. 58). A public company must have at least £50,000 of authorised share capital (s. 763) and it cannot start trading without a trading certificate[5] issued by the registrar of companies (s. 761). A public company has an unrestricted right to offer shares to the public and these shares may be floated on the stock market. It must hold an annual general meeting (s. 336); written resolutions cannot be used in a public company.

[5] Note that a trading certificate is required in addition to a certificate of incorporation. Some students may not notice this requirement.

2. The procedures for setting up a private company

Section 7 of the CA 2006 states that one or more persons can incorporate, provided it is for a lawful purpose. The following documents must be sent to Companies House: a memorandum of association, the articles of association signed by the subscriber(s), a statement naming the company's first director and company secretary, and a formal declaration that the terms of the statute have been complied with.

[6] Although a company's memorandum is no longer part of its constitution, it is still required for the registration with Companies House.

A memorandum[6] is a short piece of document which simply records the identity of the original founders of the company and indicates how many shares they took on formation (s. 8). The articles of association provide the rules for a company's internal management such as the appointment of directors, transfers of shares and voting rights. Every company must have a set of articles (s. 18). The CA 2006 seeks to achieve greater flexibility by providing different forms of model articles so that the terms found within are more applicable to each type of company.[7] The model articles for private companies are very useful, particularly for small businesses who wish to incorporate quickly without going through the time and expense of drafting their own set of articles. John and Peter are therefore advised to adopt most or all of the model articles when drafting their own.[8]

[7] This sentence shows your good understanding of the model articles and the reasons for drafting them. The latter will gain you more marks.

[8] Tie your answer back to the problem question when possible.

1 INCORPORATION

The registrar at Companies House can refuse to register a company if the terms of the Act have not been met, or the company is being established for an illegal purpose, or when the objectives of a company are contrary to public policy.[9] Once all the required documents are submitted, together with the registration fee, a certificate of incorporation will be issued by the registrar, which is conclusive evidence that there has been compliance with the requirements of the CA 2006 in respect of registration (s. 15).

3. From a private company to a public one

John and Peter are advised to initially form a private company limited by shares, taking into account the scale of their business and the relatively less regulation compared to a public company. It can be changed into a public company if they need to raise further share capital by offering shares to the public or simply wish to secure a more prestigious status of being a public company.[10] In order to achieve the change of status, the company must be re-registered and a new certificate of registration must be issued which states whether the company is private or public. It must also meet the requirement for the minimum authorised share capital of £50,000. A special resolution is required for the change of the company's status and the registrar of companies must be notified (ss. 90–96).

4. Choosing a company name

The key terms for naming a company are found within sections 53–81 of the CA 2006. A company may not use the name of another existing company (s. 66), use offensive language (s. 53) or give the impression that it is connected to the Government (s. 54). Within 12 months of registration the Secretary of State can order a company to change its name if it is too similar to that of another company (ss. 66–67). This time limit can be extended by the Secretary of State if the company name is misleading. In ***Association of Certified Public Accountants of Britain v Secretary of State for Trade and Industry*** [1997] 2 BCLC 307, Jacob J held that: ' ... what the court has to do is to decide on the evidence whether the name of the company gives so misleading an indication of the nature of its activities as to be likely to cause harm to the public. It is not sufficient to show that a name is misleading; a likelihood of harm must be shown too.'[11]

A person may object to a registered name on the ground that it is the same as a name associated with the applicant in which he has goodwill or that it is sufficiently similar to such a name that its use in the United Kingdom would be likely to mislead by suggesting a connection between the company and the applicant (s. 69). A company may change its name by a special resolution or by any other means provided by the company's articles (s. 77); in any case, a notice must be given to the registrar (s. 78). John and Peter would need to take into account the costs involved in relation to financial terms and the goodwill of customers if they decide to change their company's name.[12]

[12] This sentence shows the examiner that you are engaging with the question.

✓ Make your answer stand out

- Discuss the principles of separate legal personality and limited liability by reference to *Salomon* v *Salomon & Co Ltd* [1897] AC 22.
- In relation to company names, consider the ways of avoiding the use of an already existing name by checking the registrar's index of company names (ss. 1099 and 1100, CA 2006) and the WebCHeck facility on the Companies House website.
- Outline that the application for registration must state the company's proposed name, its registered office, whether the liability of the members of the company is to be limited, and if so whether it is to be limited by shares or by guarantee, and whether the company is to be a private or a public company (s. 9, CA 2006).

! Don't be tempted to . . .

- Discuss the choice of a company name without explaining certain names which cannot be used, such as the name of another existing company or a name containing offensive language: section 66, CA 2006.
- Include a detailed comparison between companies and partnerships. Although this is important in showing your good understanding of the nature of companies, it should not be discussed in detail here.
- Provide an answer without reference to the statutory provisions in the Companies Act 2006.
- Make generalised statements that may not affect the clients in particular. You should give specific advice which is tailored to the clients' needs.

❓ Question 3

Kate and Steve owned a local bakery and decided to incorporate their business as Organic Bakery Ltd. Steve purchased a warehouse next to the bakery store for £50,000 in May 2009. He then sold it to the company for £80,000 through an estate agent without disclosing his interest in the contract. Kate later discovered that Steve made a secret profit.

Kate and Steve ordered a high-technology oven from Professional Oven Ltd for £20,000. Upon the advice of their solicitors, they signed the agreement 'For and on behalf of Organic Bakery Ltd, as agents only, Kate and Steve'. Kate also signed a document which stated: 'It is hereby agreed that all expenses incurred by Kate in the formation of Organic Bakery Ltd shall be repaid from company funds within six months of the date of incorporation.'

Organic Bakery Ltd was incorporated in October 2009 but shortly went into insolvency. Kate incurred an expense of £10,000 in preparing the formation of the company. The oven was delivered and used but was not paid for.

Discuss:

1   Whether Steve should be held accountable to return the profit made from the sale of the warehouse.

2   Whether Kate should be reimbursed for the expense of £10,000 in the formation of the company.

3   Whether Kate and Steve will be held personally liable for the price of the oven.

Answer plan

→ Identify whether Kate and Steve are considered as promoters of the company.

→ Discuss the fiduciary duties of promoters.

→ Consider whether Steve should be held accountable to return the secret profit made from the sale of the warehouse.

→ Examine whether Kate can claim her expense back from the company.

→ Analyse whether Kate and Steve will be held personally liable for the pre-incorporation contract with regard to the oven purchase agreement.

Diagram plan

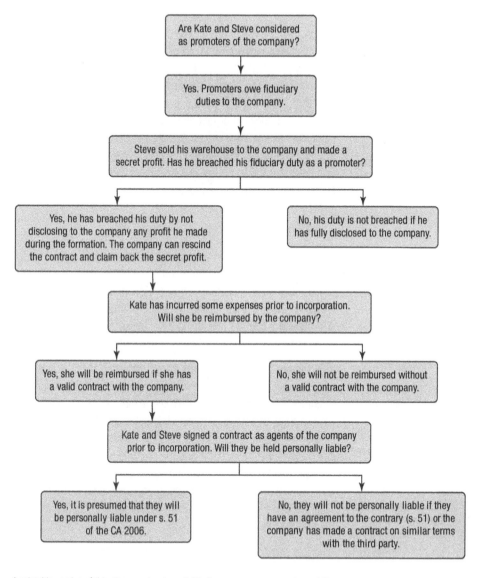

Are Kate and Steve considered as promoters of the company?

Yes. Promoters owe fiduciary duties to the company.

Steve sold his warehouse to the company and made a secret profit. Has he breached his fiduciary duty as a promoter?

Yes, he has breached his duty by not disclosing to the company any profit he made during the formation. The company can rescind the contract and claim back the secret profit.

No, his duty is not breached if he has fully disclosed to the company.

Kate has incurred some expenses prior to incorporation. Will she be reimbursed by the company?

Yes, she will be reimbursed if she has a valid contract with the company.

No, she will not be reimbursed without a valid contract with the company.

Kate and Steve signed a contract as agents of the company prior to incorporation. Will they be held personally liable?

Yes, it is presumed that they will be personally liable under s. 51 of the CA 2006.

No, they will not be personally liable if they have an agreement to the contrary (s. 51) or the company has made a contract on similar terms with the third party.

A printable version of this diagram plan is available from **www.pearsoned.co.uk/lawexpressqa**

Answer

This question raises the issues in relation to the duties of promoters and the legal implications of pre-incorporation contracts. As Kate and Steve have decided to promote a business project through the medium of a company, they are considered as promoters of Organic Bakery Ltd: *Emma Silver Mining Co* v *Lewis* (1879) LR 4 CPD 396.[1] The word 'promoter' is not defined judicially or in legislation; it is a question of fact as to who constitutes a promoter in a particular case. In *Twycross* v *Grant* (1877) 2 CPD 469 a promoter is defined as 'one who undertakes to form a company with reference to a given project and to set it going, and who takes the necessary steps to accomplish that purpose'.[2]

[1] Identify who are promoters at the beginning of your answer.

[2] This quotation shows your specific knowledge of the definition of a promoter.

1. Steve's secret profit

A promoter is in a fiduciary relationship with the company at common law. He must not make any secret profit out of the promotion without disclosing it to the company. Any profit which he makes on the promotion and fails to disclose must be returned to the company: *Gluckstein* v *Barnes* [1900] AC 240. The difficulty lies in deciding whether and how the duty of disclosure is satisfied.[3]

[3] This sentence demonstrates that you appreciate the difficulties in relation to the duties of promoters. It also leads to the discussion in the next two paragraphs.

In *Erlanger* v *New Sombrero Phosphate Co* (1878) 3 App Cas 1218, a syndicate purchased a mine for £55,000 and formed a company. The syndicate sold the mine to the company for £100,000 without disclosing their interest in the contract. The sale was successfully rescinded by the new board of directors of the company.[4] It was held that it was the promoter's duty to ensure that the company had an independent board of directors and to make full disclosure to it. Failure to disclose all material facts surrounding a contract to the independent board renders the contract voidable at the option of the company.

[4] You should be able to identify that the problem question is similar to the facts in *Erlanger*. The brief summary of the facts shows your good knowledge of this leading case and of its relevance to this question. The detailed facts of this case, however, are not necessary because they will add little to your answer. Many students spend too much time describing the facts of the case and not enough on the application of the relevant legal principles to the problem question.

This rule was considered too strict because an entirely independent board would be impossible in most private companies. In *Salomon* v *Salomon & Co Ltd* [1897] AC 22 it was accepted that, in the absence of an independent board of directors, a full disclosure to the original shareholders would be equally effective. The House of Lords in *Gluckstein* v *Barnes* (above), however, held that such disclosure would not be sufficient if the original shareholders were not truly

⁵ This paragraph demonstrates how the rule of disclosure was developed at common law since *Erlanger*. The discussion of case law is essential for a sound answer.

⁶ After analysing the relevant law, you should apply it to the problem question. The last sentence gives advice on the remedies available to the company. It goes beyond the issue of Steve's breach of duties.

⁷ Use a sentence like this to signpost your answer. It makes it easier for the examiners to follow.

independent and the scheme as a whole was designed to defraud the investing public.⁵

The current law appears to require that disclosure be made to an entirely independent board or to the existing and potential members as a whole. As Steve made a secret profit without disclosing to either an independent board or any existing member of the company, he has breached his fiduciary duty as a promoter. Organic Bakery Ltd can rescind the contract with Steve and recover the secret profit.⁶

2. The expense of £10,000 in promoting the company

The next issue concerns whether Kate can recover the expenses in promoting the company.⁷ Kate, as a promoter, is not entitled to recover any remuneration from Organic Bakery Ltd for her services unless there is a valid contract in this matter between her and the company. Without such a contract she is not even entitled to recover preliminary expenses or the registration fees: **Re English and Colonial Produce Co** [1906] 2 Ch 435. Although the document signed by Kate purports to bind the company to reimburse her, it has been long established that a company cannot be bound by, or ratify, a contract entered into prior to its incorporation, as the company did not exist at the time of the contract: **Kelner v Baxter** (1866) LR 2 CP 174. Kate therefore cannot recover her expenses as no valid contract exists in this matter between her and the company; however, she could do so if the company, after incorporation, entered into a new contract with her on similar terms.

3. The price of the oven

Prior to incorporation, Kate and Steve signed an agreement for the purchase of an oven as 'For and on behalf of Organic Bakery Ltd, as agents only'. The company is now insolvent and unable to pay for the oven. The issue arises as to whether Kate and Steve are personally liable for the purchase price. At common law the legal position of the promoter and the other party seems to depend on the terminology used. If the contract was entered into by the promoter and signed 'for and on behalf of X Co Ltd' the promoter would be personally liable: **Kelner v Baxter** (above). If, however, the promoter signed the proposed name of the company and added his own signature

[8] Although the distinction is no longer significant in the light of the Companies Act 2006, a discussion of *Kelner* (1886) and *Newborne* (1954) is crucial in showing your sound understanding of the historical development of the promoter's personal liabilities in a pre-incorporation contract.

to authenticate it (e.g., X Co Ltd, Y Director), there was no contract at all and the promoter would not be personally liable: **Newborne v Sensolid (GB) Ltd** [1954] 1 QB 45.[8] As they signed the contract 'as agents', Kate and Steve would be held personally liable at common law.

This narrow distinction was criticised in **Phonogram Ltd v Lane** [1982] QB 938 by Oliver LJ, who held that the whole of the contract should be looked at rather than just the formula used beneath the signature, in order to determine whether the contract purports to be one directly between the supposed principal and the other party or to be one between the agent himself and the other party. If it is the latter, the promoter would be personally liable at common law, no matter how he signed the document.

[9] This is a very important statutory provision that you should learn during your revision on the topics of promoters' duties and pre-incorporation contracts.

[10] This sentence examines the reasons for the introduction of section 51 in the Companies Act 2006. It will gain you more marks because it goes beyond a simple description of the statutory provision.

Following the implementation of Article 7 of the First Company Law Directive by section 36(3) of the Companies Act 1985 and now in section 51 of the Companies Act 2006, the subtle distinction made by **Kelner** and **Newborne** appears to be removed. Section 51(1) of the CA 2006 states that: 'A contract that purports to be made by or on behalf of a company at a time when the company has not been formed has effect, subject to any agreement to the contrary, as one made with the person purporting to act for the company or as agent for it, and he is personally liable on the contract accordingly.'[9] This provision seeks to protect the third party by making promoters personally liable when the company, after incorporation, fails to enter into a new contract on similar terms.[10] Thus, if a person does not contract as an agent or assume personal liability but his signature is appended to that of the company's name to authenticate it as in **Newborne**, he will still be personally liable. In accordance with section 51, Kate and Steve are personally liable to pay for the oven unless there is any agreement to the contrary.[11]

[11] This phrase shows that you fully understand section 51 and its legal implications. Although it is presumed under section 51 that promoters are personally liable, you should pay particular attention to 'any agreement to the contrary'.

✓ **Make your answer stand out**

■ Examine whether the solicitors are considered as promoters. If solicitors and accountants merely act in a professional capacity and undertake their normal professional duties, they are not considered as promoters: *Re Great Wheal Polgooth Co Ltd* (1883) 53 LJ Ch 42.

▶

- Discuss the circumstances where Kate and Steve would not be personally liable for the purchase contract. In *Natal Land Co & Colonization Ltd* v *Pauline Colliery and Development Syndicate Ltd* [1904] AC 120, it was held that a promoter will avoid personal liability if the company, after incorporation, and the other party substitute the original pre-incorporation contract with a new contract on similar terms.
- Make reference to *Whaley Bridge Printing Co* v *Green* (1880) LR 5 QBD 109 in relation to the meaning of a promoter.

! Don't be tempted to . . .

- Focus only on section 51 of the Companies Act 2006. You should also discuss the relevant common law and show a good understanding of how the law has developed in relation to the personal liabilities of promoters under pre-incorporation contracts.
- Forget to discuss the company's remedies against a promoter's breach of fiduciary duties. They should be applied to the problem question with reference to case law such as *Erlanger* v *New Sombrero Phosphate Co* (1878) 3 App Cas 1218.

⚔ Question 4

'A promoter of a company cannot avoid personal liabilities under a pre-incorporation contract which he has entered into on behalf of the company.'

Critically analyse the above statement in relation to the fiduciary duties of a promoter and his personal liabilities in a pre-incorporation contract.

Answer plan

→ Analyse the fiduciary duties of a promoter.

→ Discuss the remedies for breach of these duties.

→ Examine the common law in relation to the personal liabilities of a promoter in a pre-incorporation contract.

→ Consider the statutory provisions in relation to a promoter's liabilities in a pre-incorporation contract.

Diagram plan

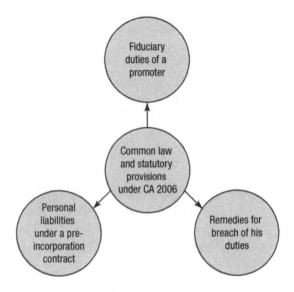

A printable version of this diagram plan is available from **www.pearsoned.co.uk/lawexpressqa**

Answer

[1] Try to engage with the question in your introduction.

A promoter of a company owes fiduciary duties to the company; however, he can, in certain circumstances, avoid personal liabilities under a pre-incorporation contract which he has entered into on behalf of the company.[1]

[2] This sentence shows your good understanding of the meaning of a promoter. The reference to case law will earn you more marks.

A promoter is not defined judicially or in legislation; it is a question of fact as to who constitutes a promoter in a particular case. In **Twycross v Grant** (1877) 2 CPD 469 a promoter is defined as one who undertakes to form a company and set it going.[2] He is not the agent of the company because it has no legal existence before the incorporation: **Kelner v Baxter** (1866) LR 2 CP 174. A promoter is in a fiduciary relationship with the company; he must not make any profit out of the promotion without disclosing it to the company. Thus, there is no absolute prohibition on making a profit – it is the making of secret profit that is forbidden: **Omnium Electric Palaces v Baines** [1914] 1 Ch 332. Any profit which he makes on the promotion and fails to disclose must be returned to the company: **Gluckstein v Barnes** [1900] AC 240. The difficulty lies in deciding how this duty of disclosure can be satisfied.

[3] Pay attention to this phrase and the different requirements in the subsequent cases because they demonstrate how the duty of disclosure evolves at common law.

In *Erlanger* v *New Sombrero Phosphate Co* (1878) 3 App Cas.1218, it was held that a promoter must make full disclosure to *an independent board of directors*.[3] Failure to do so renders the contract voidable at the option of the company. This requirement was considered as being too strict and impractical because an entirely independent board would be impossible in most companies.[4]

[4] You can further discuss why the requirement of an independent board is impractical in most companies. It will add more credit to your answer.

Subsequently in *Salomon* v *Salomon & Co Ltd* [1897] AC 22, it was accepted that in the absence of an independent board of directors a full disclosure to *the original shareholders* would be equally effective. The House of Lords, however, in *Gluckstein* v *Barnes* (1900) held that such disclosure will not be sufficient if the original shareholders are not truly independent and the scheme as a whole is designed to defraud the investing public.[5] It appears that the disclosure must be made to an entirely independent board or to the existing and potential members as a whole. The disclosure must also be explicit; a partial or incomplete disclosure is insufficient.

[5] This is a House of Lords judgment on the promoter's duty of disclosure and therefore it should be included in your answer.

[6] Explain what a pre-incorporation contract is before exploring further issues. It shows your sound understanding of the basic concept.

A pre-incorporation contract is one which a promoter enters into with a third party before the company is incorporated.[6] At common law, a company cannot be bound by a pre-incorporation contract, neither can it ratify the contract after incorporation. The legal position of the promoter depended on the terminology used.[7] If the contract was entered into by the promoter and signed for and on behalf of the company, the promoter would be personally liable. In *Kelner* v *Baxter* (1866), Kelner sold wine to Baxter who was acting 'on behalf of the proposed company'. The wine was delivered and used but the company went into liquidation before payment. Kelner successfully sued Baxter for the payment. It was held that where a contract was signed by those acting 'as agents' but who had no principal existing at the time, the contract would not be binding and the agents would be held personally liable. If, however, the promoter signed the proposed name of the company and added his own to authenticate it, there was no contract at all. In *Newborne* v *Sensolid (GB) Ltd* [1954] 1 QB 45, the contract was signed in the name of the company 'Leopold Newborne (London) Ltd' and also signed by the promoter Mr Newborne. It was held that neither the unincorporated company nor Mr Newborne could sue or be sued on the contract which was a complete nullity.[8]

[7] This sentence summarises the common law with regard to the liabilities of promoters in a pre-incorporation contract. It also shows where your answer is heading.

[8] You should demonstrate good understanding of both the facts and judgments in *Kelner* (1866) and *Newborne* [1954], which provide excellent illustrations of the common law.

[9] This case is important here because it adopts a different approach to the liabilities of a promoter.

Such narrow distinction was criticised in *Phonogram Ltd* v *Lane* [1982] 1 QB 938.[9] Mr Lane, the promoter of FM Ltd, accepted a cheque from Phonogram Ltd for £6,000 and signed his name 'for and on behalf of FM Ltd'. The money was to be used to finance the production of an LP; it was repayable if this was not achieved. When the LP was not produced, Phonogram Ltd sought to recover the money from Mr Lane on the ground that the company did not exist at the time of the contract.[10] Oliver L.J held that the whole contract should be looked at rather than just the formula used beneath the signature, in order to determine whether the contract purports to be one directly between the supposed principal and the other party or to be one between the agent himself and the other party. If it is the latter, the promoter would be personally liable at common law, no matter how he signed the document.

In order to address the confusing distinction at common law, the Jenkins Report (1962, Para. 44) recommended that the agent who acted for the unformed company should be personally liable on the contract.[11] Once incorporated the company should be able to adopt the contract unilaterally. These proposals were not adopted in the following pieces of legislation and as a consequence a company is still unable to ratify or adopt the contract unilaterally.

Following the implementation of Article 7 of the First Company Law Directive by the section 36 of the Companies Act 1985 which is now in section 51 of the Companies Act 2006, the subtle distinction between **Kelner** and **Newborne** appears to be removed. Section 51(1) of the Companies Act 2006 provides that 'A contract that purports to be made by or on behalf of a company at a time when the company has not been formed has effect, subject to any agreement to the contrary, as one made with the person purporting to act for the company or as agent for it, and he is personally liable on the contract accordingly'. This provision aims to provide third parties with more security of transactions through an enforceable contract against the promoters rather than the subsequently formed company.

Lord Denning in **Phonogram Ltd v Lane** (1982) interpreted the phrase 'subject to any agreement to the contrary' as that, in order for a promoter to avoid personal liability, the contract must expressly provide for the exclusion of his liabilities.[12] Thus, it can be concluded that a promoter may avoid personal liabilities on a pre-incorporation contract if they are expressly excluded in the contract;[13] or if the

[14] Some students may forget to discuss this circumstance where a promoter can avoid his personal liabilities under a pre-incorporation contract. The reference to case law strengthens your answer.

company, after incorporation, and the other party substitute the original pre-incorporation contract with a new one on similar terms: ***Natal Land Co & Colonization Ltd v Pauline Colliery and Development Syndicate Ltd*** [1904] AC 120.[14]

 Make your answer stand out

- Point out that the problems in relation to the pre-incorporation contracts are less acute in practice because the majority of companies are bought off the shelf from company incorporation agents.
- Discuss whether a person acting as an agent of an unformed company could enforce a pre-incorporation contract according to section 51 of the CA 2006, in other words, whether a promoter can sue as well as being sued under a pre-incorporation contract: *Cotronic (UK) Ltd v Dezonie* [1991] BCLC 721; *Braymist Ltd v Wise Finance Co Ltd* [2002] 1 BCLC 415.
- Refer to academic debates on the personal liabilities of a promoter, such as:
  - Griffiths, A. (1993) Agents without principals: pre-incorporation contracts and section 36 C of the Companies Act 1985. *LS* 241.
  - Gross, J. (1971) Pre-incorporation Contracts. *LQR* 367.
  - Savirimuthu, J. (2003) Pre-incorporation of contracts and the problem of corporate fundamentalism: are promoters proverbially profuse? *Company Lawyer* 196.

! **Don't be tempted to . . .**

- Discuss the duties of a promoter without explaining the meaning of a promoter.
- Only focus on the common law. You should also discuss section 51 of the Companies Act 2006 with regard to a promoter's liabilities under a pre-incorporation contract.
- Support your answer with little or no case law. The understanding of the development of case law in relation to a promoter's personal liabilities is essential for a good answer.

www.pearsoned.co.uk/lawexpressqa

 Go online to access more revision support including additional essay and problem questions with diagram plans, You be the marker questions, and download all diagrams from the book.

The *Salomon* principles and lifting the corporate veil

2

How this topic may come up in exams

The principles established in *Salomon* v *Salomon & Co Ltd* [1897] AC 22 are fundamental to English company law. A standard essay or problem question may expect you to comment on the advantages and limitations of these principles. The circumstances where the corporate veil is lifted are often examined in relation to fraud, sham and façade, agency, single economic unit as well as some statutory provisions. Recent cases on lifting the corporate veil should be considered in your answer, in particular, *Chandler* v *Cape plc* [2012] 3 All ER 640; *VTB Capital plc* v *Nutritek International Corp and others Ltd* [2013] 2 WLR 398; and *Prest* v *Petrodel Resources Limited* [2013] UKSC 34. You need to appreciate the uncertainties of this area of law and consider proposals for future reforms. The criminal and tortious liabilities of a company may also be subject to examination.

■ Before you begin

It's a good idea to consider the following key themes of the *Salomon* principles and lifting the corporate veil before tackling a question on this topic.

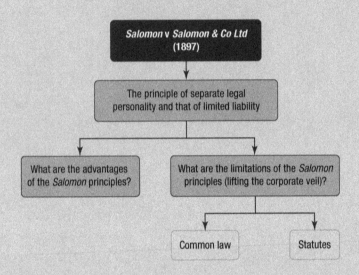

A printable version of this diagram is available from **www.pearsoned.co.uk/lawexpressqa**

🖎 Question 1

Limited liability, allowing people to 'trade without committing their personal fortune to a venture, requires a fine legislative balance. The limited company is in danger of being too wide a protection for free enterprise, and of providing a veil for the unscrupulous' (*The Times*, what a way to run the DTI, 1 November 1994).

Undertake a critical evaluation of the above statement.

Answer plan

→ Examine the case of *Salomon* v *Salomon & Co Ltd* [1897] AC 22.

→ Discuss the principles of separate legal personality and limited liability.

→ Evaluate how these principles have been upheld by the courts.

→ Consider the criticisms against these principles.

Diagram plan

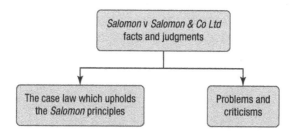

Salomon v *Salomon & Co Ltd* facts and judgments

The case law which upholds the *Salomon* principles

Problems and criticisms

A printable version of this diagram plan is available from **www.pearsoned.co.uk/lawexpressqa**

Answer

[1] This shows that you are engaging with the question at the beginning of your answer.

[2] Clearly state your argument in the introduction so that the examiner knows where you are going with your answer.

This question requires an analysis of the principle of separate legal personality of a company and the limited liability of its shareholders. It is commonly accepted that the limited liability is a very important invention in modern times as it allows people to 'trade without committing their personal fortune to a venture'.[1] It can be argued, however, that these principles have caused some problems and are in danger of exploitation.[2]

In **Salomon v Salomon & Co Ltd** [1897] AC 22 Salomon incorporated his business as a limited company with his wife and their

25

[3] Some students may deliberately ignore this aspect of the case, mostly because of a lack of understanding of debentures. A debenture is a document which acknowledges a loan to a company and gives the lender security over the assets of the company. On insolvency the lender can take the assets and recover payment ahead of the unsecured creditors.

[4] It is important to set out the liquidator's allegations against Salomon because they show your detailed knowledge of this case.

[5] Many students go straight to the House of Lords' judgment. You should discuss the decisions of the court at first instance and the Court of Appeal although they were overruled by the House of Lords. They demonstrate that you fully understand the rationale of the House of Lords' judgment.

[6] Try to learn the name of the leading judge and to quote the key judgment. You can also paraphrase it by saying that the company is at law a different person from the subscribers.

five children under the Companies Act 1862. Salomon received fully paid-up shares and debentures of the value of £10,000 for the sale of his business and he subsequently assigned the debentures to another party.[3] After a year the company became insolvent and was unable to meet the full claims of the unsecured creditors. These creditors argued that the company was merely an agent of Salomon. The liquidator attempted to hold Salomon liable for the debts of the company on the following grounds. First, the whole transaction was a fraud on the company's creditors and therefore Salomon should not be allowed to benefit. Secondly, the company was simply his agent and Salomon should reimburse the unsecured creditors with regard to the debts incurred by the company.[4]

The court at first instance held that the company was merely an agent of Salomon and therefore Salomon, as a principal, was liable for its debts. The Court of Appeal rejected Salomon's appeal and held that Salomon used the company as a device to carry on business in order to defraud creditors.[5] The House of Lords, however, reversed the decisions of the lower courts and held that the company had been fully formed and registered and was not the mere agent for Salomon. He was not liable to indemnify the company against the creditors' claims. It was held that a company is at law a distinct and separate person from the people who set it up. Any fully paid-up shareholder should not be required to pay anymore. Lord MacNaughten stated that: 'The company attains maturity on its birth ... The company is at law a different person altogether from the subscribers to the memorandum ... the company is not in law the agent of the subscribers or trustee for them. Nor are the subscribers as members liable, in any shape or form, except to the extent and in the manner provided by the Act.'[6] The House of Lords' decision affirms that a company is not the agent of its shareholders, even if it is a one-man company and the control is concentrated in only one shareholder.

The decision in **Salomon** is of vital importance as it encourages individuals to provide money for businesses without the threat of liability if the company becomes insolvent. The courts have confirmed that the company is a separate legal person in various different contexts. It is held, for instance, that property within a company belongs to the company in **Macaura v Northern Assurance** [1925] AC 619. Macaura incorporated a timber company and took out insurance on the timber in his own name instead of that of the company. After the timber was destroyed by fire he tried to rely on his insurance policy. The court held that the only person with an insurable interest in the timber was the company, which was a separate legal entity. The insurance company successfully resisted his claim on the policy. A company can also sue for defamation: *South Hetton Coal Co Ltd v North-Eastern News Association Ltd* [1894] 1 QB 133, employ members and outside individuals: *Lee v Lee's Air Farming* [1961] AC 12; sue directors who steal from them: *A-G's Reference (No. 2 of 1982)* [1984] 2 All ER 216; and continue without its original shareholders or directors: *Re Noel Tedman Holdings Pty Ltd* [1967] Qd R 561.[7]

[7] The reference to the case law authorities is essential to illustrate the courts' support of the *Salomon* principles.

The original purpose behind the ruling of *Salomon* was to encourage investors to provide money to a business without attracting further risk; however, the *Salomon* principles have been subject to criticisms mainly because they do not provide sufficient protection to creditors. Kahn-Freund (1944)[8] criticises that the *Salomon* decision is calamitous as the courts have rigidly applied the concept of separate corporate entity and it has become very easy to form a company. He incisively argues that the company has often been a means of evading liabilities and of concealing the real interests behind the business.

[8] You should include academic opinions in your answer to show your wider understanding. Kahn-Freund's criticisms are useful to demonstrate the problems caused by the *Salomon* principles.

Moreover, it can be argued that the principle of limited liability does not play a significant role in under-capitalised small private companies. The protection of limited liability is lost when the company wishes to borrow beyond its capacity. Banks and other creditors generally require that directors or shareholders provide a personal guarantee[9] so that they will be personally liable for the company's debts if it becomes insolvent. In this sense, the advantages of limited liability are restricted.

[9] The requirement of a personal guarantee may defeat the purpose of limited liability. This is a main restriction on the role of the principle of limited liability and therefore it should be discussed in your answer.

Problems also arise when people forming the companies are trying to abuse the principle of limited liability.[10] The *Salomon* decision creates a veil in front of the shareholders, which is a metaphor used to describe the effect of the legal principles of separate legal personality and limited liability. The veil may be lifted by the courts at common law or by statute in some circumstances. For instance, an individual shareholder or a director will be held liable for the company's debts when the corporate structure is a mere sham or

[10] This sentence suggests that this paragraph addresses the issues in relation to 'too wide a protection for free enterprise' and 'a veil for the unscrupulous'.

[11] This sentence shows your understanding of the circumstances when the courts would lift the corporate veil. The discussion here focuses on the most common example of 'fraud, sham or façade' because of time constraint in an exam.

[12] This sentence lists a few examples of statutory provisions whereby the corporate veil will be lifted.

[13] The conclusion shows your analytical skills by expressing your views on the issues raised in the question.

façade concealing the true facts as reaffirmed in **Prest v Petrodel Resources Ltd** [2013] UKSC 34.[11] In **Gilford Motor Co v Horne** [1933] Ch 935, the veil was lifted because the company was formed by the defendant as a device to avoid liabilities in breach of his pre-existing legal duty. The statutory provisions, such as section 213 and section 214 of the Insolvency Act 1986 with regard to the fraudulent and wrongful trading,[12] can deter dishonest or incompetent directors from abusing the **Salomon** principles. Despite the occasions where the veil has been lifted, the courts have gone to great lengths to protect the **Salomon** principles.

In conclusion, the principles of separate legal personality and limited liability play significant roles in promoting company prosperity and economic growth. A fine legislative balance, nevertheless, is required so that they are not abused by the unscrupulous.[13]

Make your answer stand out

- Include more academic opinions in your answer in relation to the criticisms of the *Salomon* principle, such as: Scanlan, G. (2004) The Salomon principle. 25 *Company Lawyer* 196; Ottolenghi, S. (1990) From peeping behind the corporate veil to ignoring it completely. 53 *Modern Law Review* 338; Hicks, A. (1997) Corporate form: questioning the unsung hero. *JBL* 306 (on whether it was appropriate that incorporation with limited liability should have become so freely available to small businesses following the *Salomon* decision).

- Make reference to more recent cases on lifting the corporate veil such as: *Chandler v Cape plc* [2012] 3 All ER 640; *VTB Capital plc v Nutritek International Corp and others* [2013] 2 WLR 398; and *Prest v Petrodel Resources Ltd* [2013] UKSC 34.

! Don't be tempted to . . .

- Spell *Salomon v Salomon & Co Ltd* incorrectly. Some students write '*Salmon v Salmon*'. Make sure you get the name of the leading case right.

- Only address part of the question. Students are generally more familiar with the importance of the *Salomon* principles and the cases which support them. In answering this question, you should pay special attention to the problems that the *Salomon* principles have caused and the criticisms against them.

📝 Question 2

'The Supreme Court's judgment in *Prest* v *Petrodel Resources Ltd* [2013] UKSC 34 has added clarity to the situations in which the corporate veil will be lifted.'

Critically evaluate the above statement in relation to the law on lifting the corporate veil.

Answer plan

→ Outline the Supreme Court's key judgment in *Prest* v *Petrodel Resources Ltd* in relation to the law on lifting the corporate veil.

→ Consider the circumstances where the corporate veil could be lifted before the judgment was made in *Prest* v *Petrodel Resources Ltd*.

→ Evaluate whether the Supreme Court's judgment has clarified the law on lifting the corporate veil or added confusion to this area of law.

Diagram plan

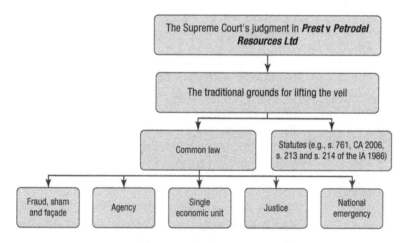

A printable version of this diagram plan is available from **www.pearsoned.co.uk/lawexpressqa**

Answer

[1] Explain the *Salomon* principles and the meaning of corporate veil at the beginning of your answer. It shows the examiner that you have identified the topic area of this question.

The courts are very protective of the ***Salomon*** principles[1] and only lift the corporate veil in a small number of exceptional cases at common law and by statute; however, there are no clear rules or guidelines for lifting the corporate veil and this area of law is vague

[2] These sentences directly address the question. The phrase 'correctly argued' shows that you are critically analysing the statement in the question rather than providing a narrative account.

[3] A brief summary of the facts shows your good knowledge of this important case.

[4] This sentence shows your excellent knowledge of the judgment in this case, which was ultimately not decided on grounds of piercing the veil.

[5] Lord Sumption's judgment in relation to lifting the corporate veil is essential for addressing this essay question.

[6] This is the key authority on the lifting of corporate veil. You should be familiar with the facts and judgment of this case.

[7] You can structure your answer according to the judgment of this case.

and confusing.[2] It is argued that the recent Supreme Court's judgment in **Prest v Petrodel Resources Ltd** [2013] UKSC 34 added some clarity and certainty to the law on lifting the corporate veil.

In **Prest v Petrodel Resources Ltd**, the Supreme Court unanimously allowed an appeal by a wife concerning properties vested in several companies belonging to the Petrodel Group which were wholly owned and controlled by the husband. The question on this appeal is whether the court has power to order the transfer of these properties to the wife given that they legally belong not to the husband but to his companies. It was held that the disputed properties vested in the companies are held on trust for the husband.[3] The trust approach was taken instead of directly piercing the corporate veil.[4] Lord Sumption held that the concept of piercing the veil was limited to when there is a deliberate evasion of an existing legal obligation or restriction and there is no other conventional remedy available so as to not be disarmed in the face of fraud. These considerations reflect the broader principle that the corporate veil may be pierced only to prevent the abuse of corporate legal personality.[5]

It appears that the Supreme Court's judgments in **Prest** reaffirm the judgment in **Adams v Cape Industries plc** [1990] BCLC 479 which has significantly narrowed the ability of the courts to lift the veil.[6] In this case, subsidiary companies were incorporated in the United States so that the parent company in the United Kingdom could avoid future asbestosis claims in the United States. The Court of Appeal reviewed this complex area of law and concluded that the veil could only be lifted in three circumstances.[7]

First, the veil may be lifted when the corporate structure is a mere sham or façade concealing the true facts. It is difficult to clearly define mere façade or decide whether the arrangements of a corporate group involve a façade. In **Adams v Cape**, the Court of Appeal held that the company structure was a façade when it had been used by a defendant to evade limitations imposed on his conduct by law or when it had been used to evade rights which third parties already possessed against him. In **Gilford Motor Co v Horne** [1933] Ch 935, the defendant formed the company as a device to avoid liabilities in breach of his pre-existing legal duty and the veil was lifted. In **Jones v Lipman** [1962] 1 WLR 832 the veil was lifted when the company was set up by the defendant to avoid specific performance in relation to a transfer of land. The court described the company as 'a device, a sham, a mask which he holds before his face in an attempt to avoid recognition by the eye of equity'.[8]

Secondly, the court may lift the veil if an express[9] agency relationship exists between a company and its shareholders, or between a parent and subsidiary company in a group structure. Although a company is a separate legal entity instead of an agent of its shareholders, it is possible that there is evidence of day-to-day control and that an agency relationship can be established on particular facts. It is, however, difficult to prove an agency relationship without an express agreement. Some guidance is provided in **Smith, Stone & Knight Ltd v Birmingham Corp** [1939] 4 All ER 116. In order to maximise the amount of compensation, the parent company argued that the subsidiary carried on the business as its agent. It was held that whether there was an agency relationship was a question of fact in each case, such as who was really carrying on the business, who received the profits, who was actually conducting the business, and who was in effective and constant control of the business. As the subsidiary was operating on behalf of the parent company, the court lifted the veil on the basis of the existence of an agency relationship. It can be argued that this is not a true exception to the **Salomon** principles; it is merely an instance where the normal agency principle applies.[10]

Thirdly, in relation to the debate on single economic unit, Lord Denning in **DHN Food Distributors Ltd v Tower Hamlets LBC** [1976] 3 All ER 462 argued that a group of companies was in reality a single economic entity *and* should be treated as one. This view was disapproved by the House of Lords in **Woolfson v Strathclyde Regional Council** (1979) 38 P& CR 521 which held that the veil would be upheld unless it was a façade.[11] Slade J in **Adams v Cape** held that: 'whether or not this is desirable, the right to use a corporate structure in this manner is inherent in our corporate law ... The fundamental principle is that each company in a group of companies is a separate legal entity possessed of separate legal rights and liabilities.' The court, however, will ignore the distinction between them and treat them as one on the interpretation of particular statutory or contractual provisions, the meaning of which is disappointingly unclear.[12]

[8] The short quotation of judgment shows your precise knowledge of this case.

[9] Pay particular attention to the requirement of an 'express' agency relationship as opposed to an 'implied' one. Some students may not appreciate the differences between these two.

[10] This comment shows that your answer has adopted an analytical approach.

[11] This is an important House of Lords' case in relation to the single economic unit argument. It should be included in a sound answer.

[12] This sentence focuses on the difficulties in applying the judgment in *Adams* v *Cape*; for instance, the meaning of the interpretation of a statute or document is vague and not defined in this case.

There is controversy as to whether the veil can be lifted in the interests of justice. This idea of lifting the corporate veil in pursuit of justice was championed by Lord Denning in **Wallesteiner v Moir** [1974] 3 All ER 217. It is held in **Adams v Cape** that the veil cannot be lifted *merely* in pursuit of justice.[13] Another ground for lifting the veil is where the country is at war and it is in the country's interests to do so: **Daimler v CTR** [1916] 2 AC 307. The application of this category is limited and it is more about politics than law.

[13] Some students are aware of the argument that the veil could be lifted in the interest of justice but they may fail to appreciate that it has been rejected in *Adams* v *Cape*.

In addition to the examples at common law, the courts may lift the veil and hold individual shareholders or directors liable for the company's liabilities according to statutory provisions such as section 761 of the Companies Act 2006, sections 213 and 214 of the Insolvency Act 1986.[14] Lord Diplock in **Dimbleby v National Union of Journalists** [1984] 1 WLR 427 states that the statutory provisions must be in 'clear and unequivocal language'.

[14] This sentence demonstrates that your discussion has progressed from common law to the statutory provisions.

The judgments in **Prest v Petrodel Resources Ltd** have, to some extent, added clarity to this area of law; however, the circumstances where the court can lift the corporate veil are still unclear and more precise guidance is required. The courts appear to proceed on a case-by-case basis in deciding whether the corporate veil will be lifted.[15]

[15] This paragraph summarises your main arguments and ties your discussion back to the statement in the essay question.

 Make your answer stand out

- Consider in more depth the Supreme Court's judgment in *Prest* v *Petrodel Resources Ltd* in relation to lifting the corporate veil.
- Refer to academic opinions on lifting the corporate veil, such as Bailey, P. (2013) Lifting the veil becomes a remedy of last resort after *Petrodel* v *Prest* in Supreme Court. *Company Law Newsletter* 1. Moore, M. (2006) A temple built on faulty foundations: piercing the corporate veil and the legacy of *Salomon v Salomon*. *Journal of Business Law* 180.
- Undertake a critical approach towards the uncertainties of this area of law.
- Discuss the statutory provisions in more depth with regard to section 761 of the Companies Act 2006, sections 213 and 214 of the Insolvency Act 1986.
- Discuss recent cases in relation to lifting the corporate veil, including *Chandler* v *Cape plc* [2012] 3 All ER 640; *VTB Capital plc* v *Nutritek International Corp and others* [2013] 2 WLR 398.

! Don't be tempted to . . .

- Forget to discuss *Adams* v *Cape Industries* (1990). This is a very important case in relation to the grounds upon which the veil can be lifted and therefore a detailed discussion of this case should be included in your answer.
- Provide detailed account of the facts in *Prest* v *Petrodel Resources Ltd.*
- Focus too much on the judgment in *Prest* in relation to family law or trust. Although it is a family law case and the court ruled on the basis of trust, your discussion should focus on the judgment in relation to lifting the corporate veil in this question.
- Fail to understand that the single economic unit argument is no longer valid after *Adams* v *Cape Industries.*
- Provide a purely descriptive account of the law on lifting the corporate veil by giving examples under different headings or categories. You should undertake a critical approach towards the uncertainties of this area of law.

? Question 3

Adrian was a director of Easyclean Ltd. He diverted the company's business opportunities to Pureclean Ltd, which is wholly owned and controlled by him. All the profits made were paid directly to Pureclean Ltd.

Adrian had an agreement with Easyclean Ltd that he would not compete against it within ten miles of the store premises. One week after his service contract ended, Adrian relocated Pureclean Ltd just one mile away from Easyclean Ltd. When challenged by the board of Easyclean Ltd, Adrian argued that he personally did not receive any profits or compete against the company.

Advise the board of Easyclean Ltd:

1 Whether Adrian will be personally liable for the return of the secret profits which he made while serving as a director; and

2 Whether Adrian will be held liable for the breach of his agreement with Easyclean Ltd.

Answer plan

→ Identify the legal issues in this question: whether the corporate veil in Pureclean Ltd should be lifted.

→ Examine whether and on what grounds Adrian will be personally liable for the return of the secret profits.

→ Discuss whether and on what grounds Adrian will be personally liable for breach of the agreement with Easyclean Ltd.

Diagram plan

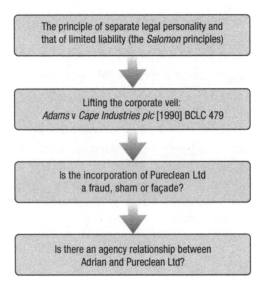

The principle of separate legal personality and that of limited liability (the *Salomon* principles)

⬇

Lifting the corporate veil:
Adams v *Cape Industries plc* [1990] BCLC 479

⬇

Is the incorporation of Pureclean Ltd a fraud, sham or façade?

⬇

Is there an agency relationship between Adrian and Pureclean Ltd?

A printable version of this diagram plan is available from **www.pearsoned.co.uk/lawexpressqa**

Answer

In order to advise the board of directors in Easyclean Ltd as to whether Adrian will be held personally liable for the return of profits and for the breach of the agreement with the company, it is necessary to examine whether and on what basis the corporate veil can be lifted in relation to Pureclean Ltd.[1]

[1] Clearly state the key legal issues that you are going to address in your answer.

[2] Some students go straight into examining the law on lifting the corporate veil without explaining the *Salomon* principles. You will lose some marks if the case of *Salomon* is not discussed.

The corporate veil is a metaphor to describe the principle of separate legal personality, as established in **Salomon v Salomon & Co Ltd** [1897] AC 22.[2] A company, once incorporated, is an independent legal entity separate from those who set it up. It can own property (**Macaura v Northern Assurance Co** [1925] AC 619), sue for defamation (**South Hetton Coal Co Ltd v North-Eastern News Association Ltd** [1894] 1 QB 133), employ members *and* outside individuals (**Lee v Lee's Air Farming** [1961] AC 12) and sue directors who steal from them (**A-G's Reference (No. 2 of 1982)** [1984] 2 All ER 216). Shareholders are protected by the principle of limited liability and are not personally liable for the company's actions or liabilities. The courts are very protective of the *Salomon* principles and only lift the corporate veil in exceptional circumstances.[3]

At common law, the veil may be lifted when the corporate structure is a mere sham or façade concealing the true facts. In **Prest v Petrodel Resources Ltd** [2013] UKSC 34, Lord Sumption held that the concept of piercing the veil was limited to when there is a deliberate evasion of an existing legal obligation or restriction and there is no other conventional remedy available so as to not be disarmed in the face of fraud.[4] In **Adams v Cape Industries plc** [1990] BCLC 479, the Court of Appeal held that the company was a façade where it has been used by a defendant to evade limitations imposed on his conduct by law or when the company structure was used to evade rights which third parties already possessed against him.[5] As a director of Easyclean Ltd, Adrian secretly set up Pureclean Ltd and used it to steal the former's business opportunities. Although Adrian argues that Pureclean Ltd, instead of himself, should be liable to return the profits, it is very likely that the court will hold both Adrian and Pureclean Ltd liable because the corporate structure is used as a sham or façade.[6] In **Jones v Lipman** [1962] 1 WLR 832, a vendor had agreed to sell a piece of land but subsequently changed his mind. He transferred the land to a company which he controlled. It was held that the company was set up by the defendant to avoid specific performance in relation to the transfer of land. Russell J held that the company was 'a device, a sham, a mask which he holds before his face in an attempt to avoid recognition by the eye of equity'. The veil was lifted and specific performance was ordered against both the vendor and the company.

Similarly, in **Gencor ACP Ltd v Dalby** [2000] 2 BCLC 734,[7] a director diverted to himself business opportunities which belonged to the company. The proceeds were paid directly to an offshore company which was wholly owned by him. The company had no staff or business and its only function was to receive profits. It was held that the company was no more than the director's offshore bank account; both the company and the director were held accountable for the profits. In **Trustor AB v Smallbone**

[2001] 2 BCLC 436 the defendant was the former managing director of Trustor AB, where a large amount of money was missing. Some of it ended up in another company which was effectively controlled by the defendant. It was held that the defendant used the other company as a device or façade for the receipt of the money and therefore the corporate veil was lifted. Applying the above case law, it is highly likely[8] that the court will lift the corporate veil on the basis of fraud, sham or façade, so that both Adrian and Pureclean Ltd should be liable to return the secret profits.

[8] The phrase 'highly likely' shows that you appreciate the uncertainties of this area of law. It demonstrates better analytical skills than simply concluding that the court will definitely lift the corporate veil.

In relation to Adrian's agreement with the company, it can be argued that Adrian used the corporate form to avoid his contractual liabilities and therefore the veil should be lifted.[9] In *Gilford Motor Co v Horne* [1933] Ch 935, an employee entered into an agreement not to compete with his former employer after ceasing employment. In order to avoid this restriction he set up a company and acted through it. It was held that the company was formed as a device to mask the carrying on of business by the defendant in breach of his pre-existing legal duty. The corporate veil was therefore lifted and an injunction was issued against the company and the defendant.

[9] You should adopt a clear structure. This sentence demonstrates that your discussion has moved on to the second legal issues in relation to Adrian's agreement with the company.

In addition to the façade argument, it can also be argued that there is an agency relationship between Adrian and Pureclean Ltd.[10] If it can be proved that Adrian used Pureclean Ltd as his agent, Adrian as the principal should be liable for the company's debts according to the law of agency. There is no presumption of such an agency relationship between a company and its share-holders. In the absence of an express agency agreement it is very difficult to establish one. In *Smith, Stone & Knight Ltd v Birmingham Corp* [1939] 4 All ER 116,[11] the parent company held almost all of the shares in the subsidiary and the profits of the subsidiary were treated as the profits of the parent company. The parent company was in effective control of the business and appointed the personnel who conducted the business. The veil was lifted on the ground of agency and it was held that whether there was an agency relationship was a question of fact in each case, such as who was really carrying on the business, who received the profits and who was in effective and constant control of the business. Following the above guidance, it appears

[10] An agency relationship may be another valid ground for lifting the corporate veil. A consideration of whether an agency relationship exists between Adrian and Pureclean Ltd shows your sound understanding of this area of law.

[11] This case provides some guidance on how an agency relationship can be established. It is also one of the very few cases where the veil was successfully lifted on the basis of an agency relationship. A clear discussion of this case makes your answer stand out.

[12] The judgments in *Salomon* v *Salomon* are very persuasive arguments against lifting the veil on the basis of an agency relationship. They are used here to illustrate the difficulties in establishing an agency relationship between a company and its shareholders.

[13] This phrase shows that you understand that this area of law is uncertain and lacks clear guidance.

[14] Your conclusion should directly refer back to the issues raised in the question and provide specific advice to the board of directors in Easyclean Ltd.

that Adrian used Pureclean Ltd as his agent to receive the secret profits and to compete with Easyclean Ltd because he held all the shares in the company and was in effective control of the business. On the other hand, the court may be reluctant to lift the veil on this ground. In **Salomon v Salomon & Co Ltd**, both the court at first instance and the Court of Appeal held that Salomon used the company as his agent and therefore he should be liable for the company's debts. This argument, however, was rejected by the House of Lords.[12] An express agency relationship, such as a written agreement, is required for lifting the corporate veil on this ground.

It is concluded that the court is most likely[13] to lift the corporate veil on the basis of fraud, sham or façade. Adrian will most probably be liable for the return of profits to Easyclean Ltd and be liable for damages for breach of his agreement with the company.[14]

 Make your answer stand out

■ Discuss whether Adrian has breached his fiduciary duties as a director of Easyclean Ltd, such as the duty to exercise his power for proper purposes (s. 171), to act *bona fide* for the benefits of the company (s. 172) and to avoid conflicts of interests (s. 175).

■ Consider whether the corporate veil could be lifted in the interest of justice by reference to *Wallesteiner* v *Moir* [1974] 3 All ER 217 and *Adams* v *Cape Industries plc* [1990] BCLC 479.

❗ Don't be tempted to . . .

■ Focus your answer solely on directors' duties. Although Adrian's breach of directors' duties is a relevant issue, your answer should focus on the law in relation to the lifting of corporate veil, which is the main issue in this question.

■ Ignore the agency argument. Some students do not apply the agency argument to the question or do not have a good understanding of the requirement of an *express* agency relationship.

■ Overlook the Supreme Court's judgment in *Prest* v *Petrodel Resources Ltd* [2013] UKSC 34. This is the most recent and authoritative judgment on lifting the corporate veil and therefore it should not be omitted in a good answer.

❓ Question 4

Babycare Ltd is registered in England and has three wholly owned subsidiary companies in India: A Ltd, B Ltd and C Ltd. A Ltd purchases cotton from local stores, B Ltd manufactures baby clothes and C Ltd markets and sells them. All the profits flow back to Babycare Ltd.

A large number of babies in India recently suffered from severe skin infections because of the poor quality of the dyeing product which is used in the manufacturing process in B Ltd. The estimated amount of compensation is £20 million. B Ltd has a liability insurance cover of up to £5 million but has no other assets apart from its factories.

Discuss whether Babycare Ltd will be held liable for the claims against B Ltd.

Answer plan

→ Identify the key legal issues: lifting the corporate veil in a group structure.

→ Discuss whether the corporate veil can be lifted on the ground of mere façade so that the parent company Babycare Ltd will be held liable for the actions of its subsidiary B Ltd.

→ Examine whether the corporate veil can be lifted on the ground of an agency relationship between Babycare Ltd and B Ltd.

→ Evaluate whether the corporate veil can be lifted based on the single economic unit argument.

Diagram plan

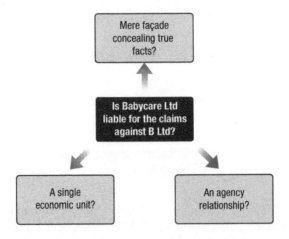

A printable version of this diagram plan is available from **www.pearsoned.co.uk/lawexpressqa**

Answer

[1] Rephrasing the question in your own words shows that you have understood the key legal issues raised.

This question requires an analysis of whether the parent company Babycare Ltd will be held liable for the claims against its subsidiary B Ltd; in other words, whether the corporate veil can be lifted in this group structure.[1] Both the parent company and its subsidiaries are incorporations which have been legally formed. A company, once incorporated, is a separate and distinct legal entity from the people who set it up: *Salomon v Salomon & Co Ltd* [1897] AC 22. In a company limited by shares, a shareholder is not liable for the company's debts. As Babycare Ltd holds shares in B Ltd, it enjoys the protection of limited liability in respect of debts of B Ltd. If the corporate veil could be lifted and the separate legal personality of B Ltd be ignored, Babycare Ltd would be liable for the claims against B Ltd.

[2] This is the leading case on lifting the corporate veil. You should show a good understanding of the judgments and summarise the facts of this case.

The court may lift the corporate veil if the corporate group structure is used as a mere façade concealing the true facts: *Prest v Petrodel Resources Ltd* [2013] UKSC 34. In *Adams v Cape Industries plc* [1990] Ch 433[2] Cape Industries plc ('Cape') was an English mining company and its products were marketed through its subsidiary companies in the United States. A large number of factory workers who had suffered from inhaling asbestos dust obtained judgment in a Texas court against Cape. They argued unsuccessfully that Cape had been present in the United States and should be liable for the obligations of the subsidiary towards the tort victims. In particular, they contended that the use of the subsidiaries was a device or sham or cloak for grave impropriety on the part of the parent company, by removing their assets from the United States to avoid liability for asbestos claims.

[3] A quotation of the important judgment demonstrates your detailed knowledge of this case and will add more credit to your answer.

The court considered whether the arrangements regarding the subsidiaries by the parent company constituted a façade so that the lifting of the corporate veil could be justified. It was held that: 'Whether or not this is desirable, the right to use a corporate structure in this manner is inherent in our corporate law ... Cape was in law entitled to organise the group's affairs in that manner and to expect that the court would apply the principle of *Salomon v Salomon & Co Ltd* [1897] AC 22 in the ordinary way.'[3] The company structure is a façade only when it has been used by a defendant to evade limitations imposed on his conduct by law

(*Jones* v *Lipman* [1962] 1 WLR 832; *Gilford Motor Co Ltd* v *Horne* [1933] Ch 935) or when it is used to evade rights which third parties already possess against him (*Trustor AB* v *Smallbone* [2001] 2 BCLC 436). The Court of Appeal in **Adams** (above) held that each company was a separate legal entity from its shareholders and the presence of the US subsidiaries did not automatically amount to the presence of the English parent company. It can be argued, therefore, that the group structure of Babycare Ltd and its subsidiaries is legitimate and it is very unlikely that the court will hold the parent liable on the ground of fraud, sham or mere façade.[4]

[4] Apply the relevant law to the problem question whenever you can. It shows that you engage with the question throughout the answer.

The court may also consider whether there is an express agency relationship between Babycare Ltd and B Ltd.[5] If Babycare uses B Ltd as its agent, then Babycare as the principal should be liable for the claims against B Ltd. It was held in **Adams** (above) that there was no presumption that the subsidiary was acting as the agent of the parent company and the court refused to infer that there existed an agency agreement between them. A company was entitled to arrange the affairs of its group in such a way that the business carried on in a particular foreign country was the business of its subsidiary and not its own.

[5] This sentence indicates that your discussion has progressed to the agency argument which may be another valid ground for lifting the veil.

In the absence of an express agency agreement or the evidence of day-to-day control, it is very difficult to establish an agency relationship.[6] In **Smith, Stone & Knight Ltd** v **Birmingham Corp** [1939] 4 All ER 116 the parent company held almost all of the shares in the subsidiary and the profits of the subsidiary were treated as the profits of the parent. The parent was in effective control of the business and also appointed the personnel who conducted the business. It was held that whether there was an agency relationship was a question of fact in each case, such as who was really carrying on the business, who received the profits and who was in effective and constant control of the business. The veil was lifted in this case on the ground of an agency relationship. Although Babycare Ltd holds all the shares in its subsidiaries and all the profits flow back to it, there is no evidence of the day-to-day control or an express agency agreement. It is therefore unlikely that the court would consider B Ltd as the agent of Babycare Ltd.[7]

[6] This sentence demonstrates that you understand the difficulties in proving an agency relationship. It will add credit to your answer by going beyond a simple narrative account of the agency theory.

[7] These sentences show your ability to analyse the problem scenario and apply the relevant law.

It can also be argued that Babycare Ltd and its subsidiaries may be treated as one economic unit.[8] This theory was first put

[8] The single economic unit argument should be discussed despite the fact that it has been rejected in later cases such as *Adams* v *Cape Industries* (1990). It demonstrates your sound knowledge of its background and the development at common law.

[9] This case and the name of the leading judge are worth learning.

[10] If you fail to show an accurate knowledge in relation to the single economic unit, your mark will be adversely affected.

[11] The examiners may be impressed by your discussion of a fairly recent case which shows your up-to-date knowledge.

[12] A concise conclusion directly addresses the question. It also enhances your arguments by summarising the courts' general approach towards lifting the corporate veil.

forward by Lord Denning[9] in ***DHN Food Distributors Ltd* v *Tower Hamlets*** [1976] 3 All ER 462, who argued that a group of companies was in reality a single economic entity and should be treated as one; the court was entitled to look at the realities of the situation to pierce the corporate veil. Slade J in ***Adams*** (above) rejected this argument by stating that there was no general principle that all companies in a group of companies were to be regarded as one.[10] The fundamental principle is that each company in a group of companies is a separate legal entity with separate legal rights and liabilities. The disapproval of the single economic unit theory was confirmed in ***Ord* v *Belhaven Pubs Ltd*** [1998] BCC 607,[11] where the court did not allow a plaintiff with a claim against one subsidiary company to substitute the parent company as defendant merely because the group might be a single economic unit. Given the judicial reluctance to ignore the ***Salomon*** principles, it is highly unlikely that the court will hold Babycare Ltd liable for the claims against B Ltd on the basis that the group structure is a mere façade, or there is an express agency relationship between them or that they should be treated as one economic unit.[12]

 Make your answer stand out

- Examine whether the court should lift the corporate veil in the interest of justice.
- Refer to academic debates on lifting the corporate veil in a group of companies, for instance: Griffin, S. (1991) Holding companies and subsidiaries—the corporate veil. 12 *Company Lawyer* 16; and Rixon, F.G. (1986) Lifting the veil between holding and subsidiary companies. 102 *LQR* 415.
- Consider recent cases in relation to lifting the corporate veil, in particular, *Chandler* v *Cape* 3 All ER 640 where the Court of Appeal held that a parent company owed a direct duty of care to an employee of one of its subsidiaries. It stressed that the duty of care from a parent company to subsidiary employees did not exist automatically and only arose in particular circumstances. This case has significantly expanded the potential liabilities of parent companies for their subsidiaries.

❗ Don't be tempted to . . .

- Have a vague understanding of the judgments in *Adams* v *Cape Industries plc* (1990). You must show a clear and detailed knowledge of this case in relation to the judgments on the lifting of the corporate veil.
- Treat it as an essay question on lifting the corporate veil. You should analyse the scenario of a group structure and focus on the issues with regard to façade, the agency relationship and the single economic unit argument.

www.pearsoned.co.uk/lawexpressqa

 Go online to access more revision support including additional essay and problem questions with diagram plans, You be the marker questions, and download all diagrams from the book.

Company constitution

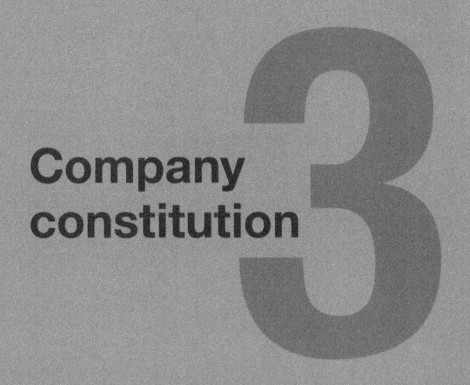

How this topic may come up in exams

A company's constitution creates a statutory contract which binds the company and its members as well as its members *inter se* (s. 33, Companies Act 2006). You are expected in an essay or problem question to show a good understanding of this statutory contract, in particular, with regard to its enforcement and the controversial principle established in *Hickman* v *Kent or Romney Marsh Sheepbreeders Association* [1915] 1 Ch 881. The alteration of a company's articles of association (s. 21) and the restrictions on the exercise of this power are often examined. Your knowledge of shareholders' agreements may also be tested in an exam question.

■ Before you begin

It's a good idea to consider the following key themes of company constitution before tackling a question on this topic.

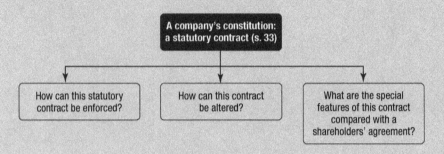

A printable version of this diagram is available from **www.pearsoned.co.uk/lawexpress**

🖋 Question 1

'The question as to the precise effect of [s. 33] has been the subject of considerable controversy in the past, and it may very well be that there will be considerable controversy about it in the future' (*Beattie* v *E and F Beattie* [1938] Ch. 708 CA at 721, per Lord Greene M.R.).

In light of the above statement, critically evaluate the enforcement of section 33 contract, in particular, whether rights contained within a company's constitution can be enforced.

Answer plan

→ Consider the special features of the statutory contract under section 33, CA 2006.

→ Discuss the differences between a statutory contract and an ordinary contract.

→ Examine the enforcement of a company's articles of association.

→ Evaluate the principles established in *Hickman* v *Kent or Romney Marsh Sheepbreeders Association* [1915] 1 Ch 881.

→ Analyse the controversy surrounding the section 33 contract.

Diagram plan

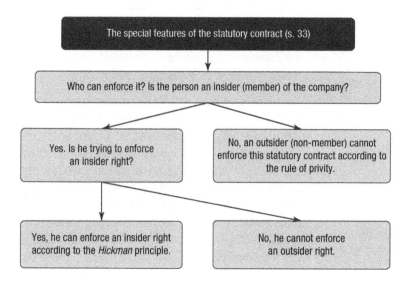

A printable version of this diagram plan is available from **www.pearsoned.co.uk/lawexpress**

Answer

Section 33 states that 'the provisions of a company's constitution bind the company and its members to the same extent as if there were covenants on the part of the company and of each member to observe those provisions'.[1] A company's articles of association therefore create a statutory contract between the company and its members, and between each individual member. There has been a lot of controversy surrounding the enforcement of this contract.[2]

[1] This is a key provision that you should learn.

[2] This sentence shows that you are engaging with the question instead of providing a generic answer.

The statutory contract has some features which are distinct from an ordinary contract, as the Court of Appeal explained in *Bratton Seymore Service Co Ltd* v *Oxborough* [1992] BCLC 693.[3] It originates from the statute instead of a bargain between parties; it will not be made invalid on the grounds of misrepresentation, mistake, undue influence or duress. This contract binds not only the present members but also future members who will join the company. Moreover, the contract can be amended by a special majority if three-quarters of the members vote in favour of the resolution (s. 21), compared to the need to obtain the consent of all parties in an ordinary contract. More significantly, unlike an ordinary contract where the parties can enforce the rights contained therein, not every member can enforce a right contained in the articles of association against the company. The enforcement of this statutory contract has been subject to contradictory case law and constant academic debates.[4]

[3] You should discuss the special features of the articles of association by reference to case law. You will lose some marks if you go straight into the enforcement of the statutory contract without considering its special features.

[4] This sentence shows that you are aware of the current complicated state of this area of law. It also leads to the discussion of the different judicial approach in the next paragraph.

The following two cases illustrate the complexities when a member tries to enforce a company's articles. In *Eley* v *Positive Life Association* [1876] 1 Ex D 88, the articles contained a clause which provided that a particular member would be appointed as a company's solicitor. He was not appointed as such and unsuccessfully sued the company for breach of that clause in the articles because there was no contractual relationship between a member as solicitor and the company. In some instances, however, the courts allowed a member to enforce a non-shareholder right conferred by the articles. In *Quin & Axtens Ltd* v *Salmon* [1909] AC 442[5] the company's articles contained a clause which stated that 'no resolution of directors on certain important matters would be valid if either of two named managing directors voted against the resolution'. The plaintiff, one of the managing directors, voted against such a resolution but the company tried to ratify it by a simple majority. The House of Lords enforced this clause and held

[5] You should demonstrate good knowledge of the judgment of this case, which was decided by the House of Lords.

the resolution invalid even though it indirectly enforced rights given to certain members in their capacity as directors.

There has been much discussion as to the capacity in which the articles are to be enforced and whether enforcement encompasses the entire articles or is limited to membership rights. Some guidance is provided in **Hickman v Kent or Romney Marsh Sheepbreeders Association** [1915] 1 Ch 881 in relation to which clauses can be enforced. In this case, the articles of association provided that disputes between the company and its members should be referred to arbitration. A member was in dispute with the company and commenced legal proceedings instead of arbitration. It was held that a company was entitled to enforce the articles against its own members; the member was bound by the articles and the dispute should be referred to arbitration. Astbury J held that: '... No article can constitute a contract between a company and a third person ... No right merely purporting to be given by an article to a person, whether a member or not, in a capacity other than as a member, as for instance, as solicitor, promoter, director, can be enforced against the company.'[6] Thus, a member can only enforce a membership right which is contained in the articles, such as the right to attend and vote at a general meeting (**Pender v Lushington** (1877) 6 Ch D 70) and the right to a declared dividend (**Wood v Odessa Waterworks Co** (1889) 42 Ch D 636). By contrast, a member cannot enforce his non-membership right (outsider right) such as the right to be the company's solicitor (**Eley** (above)) and the right to be a company director (**Beattie v E and F Beattie Ltd** [1938] Ch 708).[7]

The **Hickman** decision imposes *locus standi* restrictions on who can enforce the company's articles and prevents a floodgate of vexatious litigation against the company.[8] It reflects the courts' reluctance to get involved in the company's internal management according to the rule in **Foss v Harbottle** (1843) 67 ER 189.[9] This rule has two elements: first, the proper plaintiff in respect of an alleged wrong done to the company is *prima facie* the company; secondly, where the alleged wrong is a transaction which might be made binding on the company by a simple majority of the members, no individual member is allowed to bring a claim in respect of it. If a wrong is done to a member personally and it is an infringement of his personal rights, then the rule in **Foss v Harbottle** does not apply and he can proceed with his personal claim. A distinction is drawn by the courts

[6] It is worth stating the key judgment of this important case in relation to the enforcement of articles of association.

[7] Your discussion of the insider rights and outsider rights must be supported by the relevant case law authorities.

[8] The rationale behind the *Hickman* judgment demonstrates your sound understanding of this case and will gain you more marks.

[9] The reference to the rule in *Foss v Harbottle* will make your answer stand out because it shows your wider understanding of this area of law.

in order to reconcile the **Foss** rule and the enforcement of a section 33 statutory contract. A member can enforce provisions in the articles which create personal rights conferred on a member *qua* member. Breach of the provisions which relate to the matters of internal management of the company is a wrong done to the company, and therefore it cannot be challenged by individual shareholders. This distinction between membership rights and non-membership rights, however, is only an artificial line and is not clearly defined.[10]

[10] This sentence demonstrates that you are aware of the problems associated with the *Hickman* principle.

The **Hickman** decision appears to conflict with section 33.[11] The former states that only membership rights can be enforced whereas the latter does not make any distinction between membership and non-membership rights and simply states that 'those provisions' must be observed. The **Hickman** principle therefore has the effect of narrowing down the scope of rights which can be enforced under section 33. Moreover, it is difficult to reconcile the **Hickman** decision with an earlier and higher authority of the House of Lords in **Quin & Axtens Ltd v Salmon** (above). Wedderburn (1957) is of the opinion that every member has a personal right to see that the company is run according to the articles, except those already identified as concerning the internal procedures only. This view has been broadly shared by Gregory (1981), Goldberg (1985) and Drury (1986).[12] The current law on the enforcement of a company's articles is still complicated and confusing.[13] Further reforms are needed to clarify the distinction between insider and outsider rights and to achieve more consistency in this area of law.[14]

[11] This is one of the main reasons why the *Hickman* decision is often challenged.

[12] The discussion of the academic opinions shows your wider knowledge of the debates on this area of law. It will add more credit to your answer.

[13] Refer back to the question in your conclusion.

[14] This sentence, which expresses your opinion on the need for future reforms, will gain you more marks.

 Make your answer stand out

- Discuss the reform proposals put forward by the Company Law Review Steering Group, in particular, the catch-all solution whereby all the articles would be enforceable by the members against the company and each other unless the contrary was provided.

- Point out that it is preferable in practice to bring an unfair prejudice petition under section 994 of the Companies Act 2006 than to enforce a company's articles.

- Further reading on the enforcement of a company's articles of association: Drury, R. (1986) The relative nature of a shareholder's right to enforce the company contract. *Cambridge Law Journal* 219; Goldberg, R. (1985) The controversy on the section 20 contract revisited. 48 *Modern Law Review* 158; Gregory, R. (1981) The section 20 contract. 44 *Modern Law Review* 526; Sharazi, G. (2013) To what extent does the section 33 contract differ from an orthodox contract? 34 *Company Lawyer* 36.

> ## ! Don't be tempted to . . .
>
> ■ Answer the question without appreciating the controversial nature of section 33 contract.
>
> ■ Only focus on the case of *Hickman*. It is essential to discuss other cases which illustrate different judicial approach to the enforcement of a company's articles of association, for example, *Quin & Axtens* v *Salmon* (1909).
>
> ■ Discuss insider rights and outsider rights without reference to the relevant case law.

? Question 2

Tom, Jerry and Fiona incorporated Quality Tyres Ltd in 2009. The company's share capital is divided into 1,000 ordinary shares. All three are directors and shareholders who hold 250, 350 and 400 shares respectively.

The standard Model Articles of Association for private companies limited by shares are adopted with the additional clauses which state that: 'Fiona shall be the company director for life. On any resolution to remove her as a director she is entitled to two votes per share on a poll.'

Tom and Jerry recently are unhappy with Fiona's performance at board meetings and want to remove her from the board of directors.

Advise Tom and Jerry.

Answer plan

→ Discuss the statutory requirements for the removal of a director (s. 168, Companies Act 2006).

→ Consider how a member can enforce the company's articles of association.

→ Analyse whether Fiona can rely on the articles to remain as a director for life.

→ Examine whether Fiona can enforce the article in relation to two votes per share on any resolution to remove her.

→ Evaluate whether Tom and Jerry can alter the articles (s. 21, Companies Act 2006).

Diagram plan

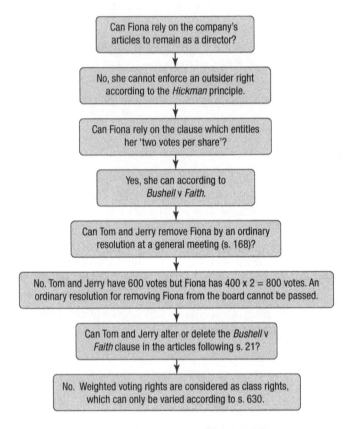

A printable version of this diagram plan is available from **www.pearsoned.co.uk/lawexpress**

Answer

[1] In your introduction, identify the key legal issues that need to be addressed.

In answering this question, it is necessary to examine how a director can be legally removed from the board and whether Fiona can remain as a company director by relying on the company's articles of association.[1] Section 168 states that: 'A company may by ordinary resolution at a meeting remove a director before the expiration of his period of office, notwithstanding anything in any agreement between it and him.' An ordinary resolution can be passed by a simple

[2] There are different ways of voting at a general meeting such as voting on a show of hands or on a poll; the methods of calculating the number of votes are different accordingly. On a show of hands, every member present in person has one vote. On a poll, every member has one vote in respect of each share. The poll vote is adopted in most companies and therefore used here as an example.

[3] The case of *Bushell* v *Faith* and the weighted voting right are often examined in a problem question with regard to the enforcement of a company's articles. Make sure you understand how the weighted voting right is applied.

[4] The name of the dissenting judge and the key judgment show your sound knowledge of this case.

[5] Remember to apply the case law to this problem scenario.

[6] Move on to the next legal issue after addressing the weighted voting rights in full. This sentence shows that your answer focuses on the question asked.

[7] You can discuss the special features of the statutory contract in detail here; for instance, it is binding on future shareholders and a special resolution is required for its alteration.

[8] It is worth learning this important judgment by Astbury J which distinguished between insider rights and outsider rights.

majority (s. 282). If a poll vote[2] is taken at a general meeting on a resolution to remove Fiona, every member has one vote in respect of each share (s. 284). As Tom and Jerry hold 600 shares in total whilst Fiona has 400 shares, *prima facie,* an ordinary resolution can be passed to remove Fiona. Fiona, however, is entitled by the articles to two votes per share on any resolution to remove her as a director.

The validity of the weighted voting right is recognised in *Bushell* v *Faith* [1970] AC 1099,[3] where two sisters and a brother were equal shareholders of the company with 100 shares each. The two sisters proposed to remove their brother as a director by an ordinary resolution. The brother challenged the removal on the grounds that the company's articles of association provided that on a resolution to remove a director from office 'any shares held by that director shall on a poll in respect of such resolution carry the right to three votes per share'. As the sisters had 200 votes whilst the brother had 300 votes, an ordinary resolution could not be achieved. The House of Lords by a majority approved the use of this clause despite Lord Morris, who gave the dissenting judgment, criticising that such device made a mockery of the law.[4] On the resolution to remove her from the board, Fiona would have 800 votes (400 × 2) whilst Tom and Jerry have 600 votes in total; therefore an ordinary resolution could not be passed for this purpose.[5]

Another issue is whether Fiona can rely on the articles to be a company director for life.[6] Articles of association, which are part of the company's constitution as defined in section 17, create a statutory contract between the members and the company (s. 33). The enforcement of this statutory contract is different from an ordinary contract.[7] It has been established that an outsider right which is contained in this contract cannot be enforced. In *Hickman* v *Kent or Romney Marsh Sheepbreeders Association* [1915] 1 Ch 881, Astbury J made a clear distinction between insider and outsider rights; he held that: 'No right merely purporting to be given by an article to a person, whether a member or not, in a capacity other than as a member, as for instance, as solicitor, promoter, director, can be enforced against the company.'[8] The right to be a company director is considered as an outsider right in *Beattie* v *E and F Beattie Ltd* [1938] Ch 708, where the articles of association provided that all disputes between the company and a member must be referred to arbitration. The defendant director who was also a member was sued for breach of duty and sought to rely on this clause. It was held that he could not rely on the article because it did not constitute a contract between the company and the defendant in the capacity as a director. Similarly, the right to be a company solicitor is an outsider right and cannot be enforced.[9] In *Eley* v *Positive Government Securities Life Assurance Co Ltd* (1876) 1 ExD 88, the articles of association provided that Eley shall be the solicitor of the company. When the company started to instruct another solicitor, Eley who was also a member of the company unsuccessfully brought an action for breach of contract. Applying the common law to the problem scenario, Fiona cannot rely on the articles to remain as a director for life.

[9] This is another example of an outsider right, which will gain you more marks.

Tom and Jerry may consider other options to remove Fiona, for instance, by removing the clause which gives Fiona the weighted voting right.[10] According to section 21, an alteration of articles requires a special resolution which must be passed by a majority of not less than 75 per cent (s. 283). The articles must also be altered in good faith for the benefits of the company as a whole: *Allen* v *Gold Reefs of West Africa Ltd* [1900] 1 Ch 656.[11] The judgment, however, offers little guidance as to the scope and substance of the subjective test. Evershed MR in *Greenhalgh* v *Arderne Cinemas Ltd* [1950] 2 All ER 1120 held that 'the company as a whole' meant the shareholders as a body. As Tom and Jerry hold 600 shares which account for 60 per cent of the company's share capital, a special resolution is unlikely to be passed for the alteration of articles.

[10] An examination of other options makes your answer stand out.

[11] Some students may forget to discuss the common law restrictions on the exercise of section 21.

Even if Tom and Jerry held more than 75 per cent of the company's shares, the weighted voting right clause would be unlikely to be amended or deleted by section 21.[12] In *Cumbrian Newspapers Group Ltd* v *Cumberland and Westmoreland Herald Newspaper and Printing Co Ltd* [1986] 2 All ER 816,[13] the articles entitled a member to appoint a director so long as he held 10 per cent of the shares. It was held that the rights or benefits that, although not attached to any particular shares, were conferred on the beneficiary in the capacity of member of the company and they created class rights. Scott J held that the articles which gave a director weighted voting rights as those in *Bushell* v *Faith* created class rights. Class rights can only be varied in accordance with the company's articles, or where the company's articles contain no such provision, the holders of three-quarter shares of that class must consent to the variation (s. 630). As Fiona is the only person in the class of shares with weighted voting right, the right cannot be varied without her consent and it is unlikely that she will agree to such variation.

[12] The analysis of class rights adds more credit to your answer. You will lose some marks if you fail to show a good understanding of the requirements in relation to the variation of class rights.

[13] This case is essential here because it establishes that weighted voting rights are class rights and therefore they attract the special protection under section 630.

[14] The discussion of the issue of shares will make your answer stand out. Some students may not be able to associate the topic of shares with the removal of directors.

[15] A service contract between a director and the company is quite common in practice. The implications of such a contract should be discussed when a director is removed from office. It adds extra credit to your answer.

Tom and Jerry may also consider issuing more shares to themselves or people outside the company (s. 551)[14] so that they can have sufficient votes to pass an ordinary resolution and remove Fiona. As directors of the company, they must exercise their power for proper purposes (s. 171) and comply with shareholders' pre-emption rights (s. 561). Fiona may bring an unfair prejudice petition against such issue of shares under section 994: *Re a Company (No 005134 of 1986), ex p Harries* [1989] BCLC 383. In addition, if Fiona has a separate service contract[15] with the company and she was removed in breach of the terms of this contract, the company may be liable for damages: *Southern Foundries (1926) Ltd v Shirlaw* [1940] 2 All ER 445.

✓ Make your answer stand out

- Discuss the possibility of increasing share capital in detail. According to section 551, directors may exercise the power to allot shares only if authorised to do so by the articles or by an ordinary resolution. As Tom and Jerry hold 60 per cent of the company's shares, Fiona's shareholding may be diluted by the allotment of more shares and her weighted voting right may not be able to prevent her from being removed.

- Consider that Tom and Jerry may breach their fiduciary duties in section 172 if the increase of share capital is designed to dilute Fiona's shareholding.

- Analyse the dissenting judgment of Lord Morris in *Bushell* v *Faith* (1970) in more detail by making reference to Ma, F., Removal of Directors: Lord Morris in *Bushell* v *Faith* [1970] AC 1099, in N. Geach and C. Monaghan (eds) (2011) *Dissenting Judgments*, with a Foreword by Lord Nicholls of Birkenhead (Wildy, Simmonds and Hill).

! Don't be tempted to . . .

- Give an incomplete answer by discussing only part of the additional clauses in the articles. You should analyse the clauses in relation to both Fiona's right to remain as a director and her weighted voting right.

- Forget to consider the class rights which are attached to the weighted voting rights. You should pay special attention to the requirements for a variation of class rights under section 630.

- Jump to the conclusion that Fiona cannot be removed from the board. You should analyse the legal issues one by one on the enforcement of the articles and consider other possible ways of removing Fiona.

 **Question 3**

'A company is free to alter its articles of association by a special resolution without any restriction.'

Evaluate the above statement.

Answer plan

➡ Discuss the statutory requirements for an alteration of a company's articles of association under section 21, CA 2006.

➡ Examine the common law restrictions on the company's power to alter its articles: *Allen* v *Gold Reefs of West Africa Ltd* [1900] 1 Ch 656.

➡ Evaluate the statutory limitations on section 21 including the provisions for entrenchment articles (s. 22), a variation of class rights (s. 630) and some specific requirements (s. 25).

Diagram plan

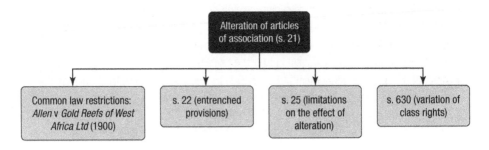

A printable version of this diagram plan is available from **www.pearsoned.co.uk/lawexpress**

Answer

The articles of association, as a part of a company's constitution, constitute a statutory contract between the company and its members and between its members *inter se* (s. 33, Companies Act 2006). Unlike an ordinary contract where the consent of all parties is required for its amendment, the articles may be altered by a special resolution (s. 21), which means a resolution passed by a majority of not less than 75 per cent (s. 283). It is argued that the power to alter the articles is not entirely unrestricted and some limitations are

[1] This sentence states your arguments and sets out a clear structure for your answer.

[2] This is the common law restriction on the alteration of a company's articles and therefore it is a key quote which should be learnt by heart.

[3] The reference to academic opinion enhances your critical analysis and adds more credit to your answer.

[4] This sentence includes the two key authorities on the interpretations of the common law test. It also leads to the discussion which follows in the next two paragraphs.

[5] This is an important judgment and should be stated accurately. Some students know about this case but cannot provide a precise summary of the judgment.

[6] Try to learn the name of the leading judge. It shows your specific knowledge of this case.

[7] The introduction of the objective test makes this case stand out.

imposed both at common law and by statutory provisions such as sections 22, 25 and 630.[1]

At common law, the power to alter the articles must be exercised *bona fide* for the benefit of the company as a whole: ***Allen v Gold Reefs of West Africa Ltd*** [1900] 1 Ch 656. Lindley MR held that the power 'must be exercised, not only in the manner required by law, but also *bona fide* for the benefit of the company as a whole'.[2] An alteration of articles therefore can be challenged for a lack of good faith or if it is not for the benefit of the company as a whole. This test of '*bona fide* for the benefit of the company as a whole' is criticised by Rixon (1986) as 'almost meaningless' when adjusting shareholders' conflicting interests.[3] The judgment in ***Allen*** (above) offers little guidance as to the meaning and scope of the test, which is still unclear despite the interpretations of the test by the Court of Appeal in ***Shuttleworth v Cox Bros & Co (Maidenhead) Ltd*** [1927] 2 KB 9 and ***Greenhalgh v Arderne Cinemas Ltd*** [1950] 2 All ER 1120.[4]

In ***Shuttleworth*** (above), the company's articles provided that the plaintiff and four other directors would hold office unless they were disqualified on one of six specified grounds. The plaintiff failed to account for company money and property. The articles were altered to add a further ground for disqualification that any director should resign if requested in writing by all his co-directors. After the alteration, the plaintiff was asked to resign and unsuccessfully challenged the validity of the alteration. It was held that it was for the shareholders, and not for the court, to decide whether an alteration of articles was for the benefit of the company, provided that it was not of such a character as that no reasonable men could so regard it.[5] Scrutton LJ[6] stated that: '... provided there are grounds on which reasonable men could come to the same decision, it does not matter whether the court would or would not come to the same decision or a different decision. It is not the business of the court to manage the affairs of the company.' Both the subjective and objective tests were adopted in this judgment. The subjective test of *bona fide* was followed where the court looked at whether the shareholders honestly believed that they were acting in the best interests of the company as a whole in altering the articles. The objective test of 'reasonable men' was also considered so that an alteration would not stand if no reasonable men could consider it to be for the benefit of the company.[7]

In **Greenhalgh** (above), the company's articles stated that any shareholder who wished to sell their shares should offer them first to existing shareholders. A special resolution was passed for the alteration of the articles so that the shares could be sold directly to an outsider with the approval of an ordinary resolution. A minority shareholder challenged the validity of this alteration. The Court of Appeal rejected his claim and held that a voting shareholder should 'proceed on what, in his honest opinion, is for the benefit of the company as a whole'.[8] The alteration was merely a relaxation of the stringent restrictions on the transfer of shares and therefore it was *bona fide* for the benefit of the company as a whole.

[8] Pay attention to this judgment because it confirms the subjective test of the common law restriction.

It should be noted that the courts are very reluctant to challenge a shareholder resolution for a lack of *bona fide* because the passing of a shareholder resolution is generally viewed as upholding the majority rule as established in **Foss v Harbottle** (1843) 2 Hare 461. In **Citco Banking Corp NV v Pusser's Ltd** [2007] 2 BCLC 483,[9] the company's articles were altered to give the chairman a voting control of the company. The Privy Council followed **Shuttleworth** (above) and held the alteration valid. Lord Hoffmann confirmed that the test was whether reasonable shareholders could consider the alteration to be for the benefit of the company.

[9] A more recent case shows your up-to-date knowledge. This case also reaffirms the objective test established in *Shuttleworth* (1927).

In addition to the common law restrictions, some limitations are imposed by the Companies Act 2006.[10] A company's articles may contain provisions for entrenchment so that the specified provisions of the articles may not be amended by a special majority; instead they can only be amended if conditions are met or procedures are complied with, by agreement of all the members of the company or by a court order (s. 22). Such provisions may only be made in the company's articles on formation or by an amendment of the company's articles agreed to by all the members of the company.

[10] This sentence indicates that your answer has moved on from a discussion of the common law to the statutory provisions.

Moreover, a member of a company is not bound by an alteration to its articles after the date on which he became a member in either of the following situations (s. 25):[11] first, if it requires him to take or subscribe for more shares than the number held by him at the date on which the alteration is made; secondly, if it increases his liability as at that date to contribute to the company's share capital or otherwise to pay money to the company. These provisions do not apply where the member agrees in writing to be bound by the alteration, either before or after the alteration is made.[12]

[11] An evaluation of the conditions in section 25 is often missing in the exam answers.

[12] Try to provide a sound discussion of section 25 by evaluating the situations where it does not apply.

Where the alteration of the articles constitutes a variation or abrogation of class rights, the procedure in section 630 must be followed.

Class rights, which are rights attached to a class of a company's shares, can be altered in accordance with the provision in the company's articles; or where the company's articles contain no such provision, the holders of at least three-quarter shares of that class consent to the variation in writing or by a special resolution at a separate class meeting (s. 630).

[13] Refer back to the question in your conclusion and briefly summarise your arguments. It shows that you are able to put forward a sound argument in a clear structure.

[14] This sentence shows your analysis of the common law and its need for reform. It will gain you more marks.

It is concluded that a company's articles of association can be altered subject to the common law test and the statutory provisions.[13] The interpretations of the common law test of '*bona fide* for the benefit of the company as a whole', however, need to be further clarified in order to provide more guidance and achieve more certainty in this area of law.[14]

✓ Make your answer stand out

- Explain what is meant by a variation of class rights. The courts have drawn an artificial distinction between matters affecting the rights attaching to each share and matters affecting the enjoyment of those rights. Only variation which affects the rights attached to each share attracts the protection of the procedure in section 630.
- In relation to the test of *bona fide* for the benefit of the company as a whole, discuss *Sidebottom* v *Kershaw, Leese & Co Ltd* [1920] 1 Ch 154 and *Dafen Tinplate Co Ltd* v *Llanelly Steel Co Ltd* [1920] 2 Ch 124.
- Examine the circumstance where a shareholder enters into a shareholder agreement, for example, a voting agreement (*Russell* v *Northern Bank Development Corp Ltd* [1992] BCLC 1016).

! Don't be tempted to . . .

- Consider the common law restrictions on the power to alter the articles without reference to the cases of *Shuttleworth* (1927) and *Greenhalgh* (1950).
- Only focus on the common law restrictions imposed by *Allen* v *Gold Reefs of West Africa Ltd* [1900] 1 Ch 656. The statutory provisions must also be discussed in your answer.

❓ Question 4

Chris, Peter and Simon are all directors of Prime Coffee Ltd; each holds 80 per cent, 15 per cent and 5 per cent of its issued shares. Its articles of association contain the following clauses: 'The company's director Peter shall be paid £50,000 per annum. As long as Peter holds 15 per cent of the company's shares, he is entitled to nominate a director.'

Peter has an agreement with the company that it will not alter its articles with regard to his right of nomination without his consent. He also has a service contract with the company which entitles him to £50,000 per annum as a director.

Chris recently finds out that Peter is secretly competing with Prime Coffee Ltd and he proposes to make the following changes to the articles:

1   All the directors should be appointed by the general meeting.

2   Peter's salary shall be reduced to £30,000 per annum.

3   A clause shall be added in the articles with the effect of allowing the directors to purchase any shareholder's shares at a fair price if that shareholder's conduct is detrimental to the company's interests.

Advise Peter.

Answer plan

→ Discuss whether Peter's right to nominate a director can be altered by a special resolution.

→ Examine whether Peter can enforce his right in the articles in relation to the annual salary of £50,000.

→ Evaluate whether the clause which has the effect of compulsory purchase of a shareholder's shares can be added to the articles.

Diagram plan

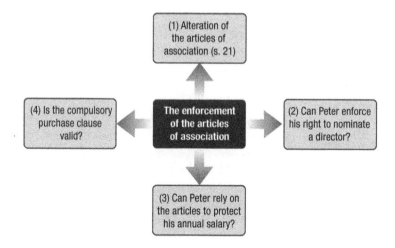

(1) Alteration of the articles of association (s. 21)

(4) Is the compulsory purchase clause valid?

The enforcement of the articles of association

(2) Can Peter enforce his right to nominate a director?

(3) Can Peter rely on the articles to protect his annual salary?

A printable version of this diagram plan is available from **www.pearsoned.co.uk/lawexpress**

Answer

Articles of association form part of a company's constitution which creates a statutory contract between the company and its members (s. 33, Companies Act 2006). A company's articles may be altered by a special resolution at general meeting (s. 21). As Chris holds more than 75 per cent of the company's shares, *prima facie*[1], the articles can be altered; however, the power to alter the articles is subject to various restrictions.

[1] The phrase '*prima facie*' shows that you understand the complicated legal issues arising from this question.

[2] Adopt a clear structure by using clear headings and address the legal issues one by one.

1. Peter's right to nominate a director[2]

Chris proposes to alter the articles so that all the directors should be appointed by the general meeting. This will have the effect of depriving Peter of his right to nominate a director as long as he holds 15 per cent of the company's shares. In **Cumbrian Newspaper Group Ltd v Cumberland & Westmoreland Herald Newspaper & Printing Co Ltd** [1986] 2 All ER 816, the claimant was given the right to nominate a director in the articles if he continued to hold a 10 per cent shareholding in the defendant company. It was held that such right constituted a class right. A class right may only be varied under section 630 in accordance with provision in the company's articles,

[3] Apply the relevant law to the problem question. It shows that you are engaging with the question rather than providing an essay-style answer.

[4] Set out Peter's arguments against the proposed alteration of the articles. It shows that you are engaging with the question by analysing the problem scenario.

[5] This is an important case on the enforcement of a company's articles of association because it provides some guidance on the distinction between insider and outsider rights.

[6] The reference to case law authorities here demonstrates your sound understanding of the distinction between insider and outsider rights.

[7] This case establishes that a director's entitlement to a certain salary in the articles is an outsider right. It should be discussed in detail in your answer because it is one of the main legal issues raised in the question.

[8] Do not forget to consider the service contract. The annual salary is not only stated in the articles of association but also the service contract. You need to examine whether the service contract can prevent the alteration of the articles in relation to the annual salary.

or if no such provision is contained in the articles, the holders of at least three-quarters in nominal value of the issued shares of that class must consent to the variation. As Peter is the only person in this class, his right of nomination cannot be varied without his consent.[3]

2. Peter's salary

Chris proposes to alter the articles and reduce Peter's annual salary from £50,000 to £30,000. Peter may try to prevent the company from doing so by relying on the articles and his service contract.[4] In ***Hickman v Kent or Romney Marsh Sheepbreeders Association*** [1915] 1 Ch 881,[5] it was held that members could only enforce membership rights contained in the articles; outsider rights could not be enforced. Membership rights include the right to attend and vote at shareholder meetings (***Pender v Lushington*** (1877) 6 Ch D 70) and to receive declared dividend (***Wood v Odessa Waterworks Co*** (1889) 42 Ch D 636). Outsider rights are non-membership rights, including the right to be a solicitor (***Eley v Positive Government Security Life Assurance Co*** (1876) 1 Ex D 88) and the right to be a director (***Beattie v E & F Beattie Ltd*** [1938] Ch 708).[6]

The key issue is whether the right to a certain amount of salary is an insider right or an outsider right. In ***Re New British Iron Co, ex p Beckwith*** [1898] 1 Ch 324,[7] the company's articles provided that the annual salary of the board of directors shall be £1,000. The directors sought unsuccessfully to claim the arrears of their salaries when the company was in liquidation. It was held that the articles did not constitute a contract between the company and the directors for the payment of directors' salary. Peter's right in relation to his salary as a director is therefore considered as an outsider right and cannot be enforced if it is contained in the articles.

Peter may argue that the company's right to alter its articles is restricted by the term of the service contract.[8] This argument is most likely to be invalid because it is established that the company's statutory power under section 21 to alter its articles cannot be restricted contractually. In ***Punt v Symons & Co Ltd*** [1903] 2 Ch 506, it was held that the company could not contract out of its statutory right to alter its articles either by way of a separate contract or by a provision in the articles. Chris therefore can alter the articles by a special resolution to reduce Peter's annual salary as long as the power is exercised *bona fide* for the benefit of the company as a whole: *Allen* v *Gold Reefs of West Africa Ltd* [1900] 1 Ch 656. Peter may, nevertheless, sue the company for damages if the alteration of the articles breaches his service contract: *Southern Foundries Ltd* v *Shirlaw* [1940] 2 All ER 445.[9]

[9] The reference to this case law authority strengthens your argument and will gain you more marks.

3. Compulsory transfer clause

Chris proposes to add a clause in the articles so that directors can purchase any shareholder's shares if that shareholder's conduct is detrimental to the company's interests. Peter may argue that the proposed alteration of the articles is not in good faith for the benefit of the company. In *Allen* (above), it was held that the court could set aside a proposed alteration of the articles which was not *bona fide* for the benefit of the company as a whole. The test for '*bona fide* for the benefit of the company as a whole', however, is not clear. In *Sidebottom* v *Kershaw, Leese & Co Ltd* [1920] 1 Ch 154, the defendant company altered its articles by allowing the directors to buy out shareholders at a fair price who competed with the company's business. The Court of Appeal held that the alteration was valid as the resolution had been passed *bona fide* for the benefit of the company as a whole.[10]

[10] The fact of *Sidebottom* is very similar to the problem question and therefore it should be included in a good answer.

By contrast, in *Dafen Tinplate Co Ltd* v *Llanelly Steel Co Ltd* [1920] 2 Ch 124,[11] the company was formed on the basis of an expectation that the shareholders would purchase supplies from the company. One shareholder began purchasing his supplies from another company in which he had an interest. The company altered the articles with the effect that the majority of shareholders could determine that the shares of any shareholders should be offered for sale by a director at a fair value to be fixed by the directors. The alteration was disallowed by the court, as it went beyond what was necessary to benefit the company. The alteration was for the benefit and advantage of the majority shareholders. Peterson J stated that: 'The question is whether in fact the alteration is genuinely for the benefit of the company.'[12]

[11] This case is used to compare with *Sidebottom* and it illustrates the circumstances where the alteration of articles is valid.

[12] A short quote like this is easy to remember and you may impress the examiners with your precise knowledge of this particular case.

As Peter is competing with Prime Coffee Ltd, it is very difficult for him to convince the court that this amendment of articles is not for the benefit of the company. The court is more likely to follow *Sidebottom* (1920) and allow the alteration when the shareholder's conduct is detrimental to the company's business.[13]

[13] In your conclusion clearly state your advice to Peter. The phrase 'more likely' demonstrates that you understand that this area of law is complicated and there may not be a simple black-and-white answer.

¹⁴ The discussion of the possibility of a successful unfair prejudice petition goes beyond the topic on the articles of association. It helps your answer stand out.

Peter may bring an unfair prejudice petition under section 994 to challenge the alteration of the articles, but it is unlikely to succeed because his own conduct may not render the alteration unfair.[14]

✓ **Make your answer stand out**

- Examine in detail the meaning of *bona fide* for the benefit of the company as a whole by reference to *Shuttleworth* v *Cox Bros & Co (Maidenhead) Ltd* [1927] 2 KB 9 and *Greenhalgh* v *Arderne Cinemas Ltd* [1950] 2 All ER 1120.
- Refer to the academic debates on the validity of a compulsory transfer clause in the articles such as: Hannigan, B. (2007) Altering the articles to allow for compulsory transfer – dragging minority shareholders to a reluctant exit. *JBL* 471.
- Consider whether Peter has breached his fiduciary duties in sections 172 and 175.

❗ **Don't be tempted to . . .**

- Get confused with the right to be a director and the right to nominate a director. Some students may come to the wrong conclusion that Peter's right to nominate a director is an outsider right and therefore cannot be enforced.
- Discuss the director's salary without reference to the case law authorities. Most students are able to recognise the outsider right but fail to analyse the relevant case law.
- Omit the leading authorities of *Sidebottom* (1920) and *Dafen Tinplate Co Ltd* (1920) with regard to the compulsory transfer clause.

Question 5

'Shareholders' agreements are often favoured as being more flexible than the articles of association, more appropriate for temporary and personal obligations, both easier and more difficult to change than the articles of association and less public. These advantages are thought to outweigh the disadvantage that new shareholders are not automatically bound by the contract ...' (Little, T.B. (1992) 'How far does shareholder's freedom of contract extend? – *Russell* v *Northern Bank Corporation Limited* and other recent cases. *ICCLR* 351 at 355). Undertake a critical evaluation of the above statement.

Answer plan

➡ Examine the advantages and disadvantages of shareholders' agreements compared with a company's articles of association.

➡ Discuss the distinctive features of the articles of association, in particular, the enforcement of a section 33 contract and the *Hickman* principle.

➡ Focus on the enforcement of a shareholder's agreement, in particular, when a company is a party to the agreement.

Diagram plan

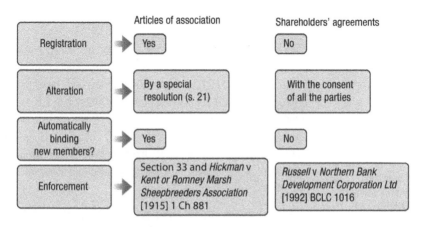

	Articles of association	Shareholders' agreements
Registration	Yes	No
Alteration	By a special resolution (s. 21)	With the consent of all the parties
Automatically binding new members?	Yes	No
Enforcement	Section 33 and *Hickman* v *Kent or Romney Marsh Sheepbreeders Association* [1915] 1 Ch 881	*Russell* v *Northern Bank Development Corporation Ltd* [1992] BCLC 1016

A printable version of this diagram plan is available from **www.pearsoned.co.uk/lawexpress**

Answer

[1] This sentence demonstrates that you have identified the main legal issues raised in the question.

[2] The explanations of the articles of association and shareholders' agreements should be the starting point of your answer.

This question requires a comparison of a shareholders' agreement and a company's articles of association.[1] The articles of association are internal rule books for the company and govern its internal running whilst a shareholders' agreement is a separate contract between some or all of the shareholders, or between the company and its shareholders.[2]

Articles of associations form a significant part of a company's constitution and must be filed with Companies House. By contrast, a shareholders' agreement is not normally treated as a company's constitution and usually addresses particular issues such as voting, the transfer of shares and the appointment of directors.

A shareholders' agreement exists outside and separate from the articles; it is a private document and registration with Companies House is not required. A shareholders' agreement therefore offers the advantages of privacy and is 'more flexible and less public'.[3]

The articles of association are binding not only on the present members but also future members of the company. By contrast, a shareholders' agreement is an ordinary contract in the way that it is binding on the parties and is subject to all the usual contractual remedies. A new member of the company will not be bound by the agreement unless the person assents to it: **Greenhalgh v Mallard** [1943] 2 All ER 234. A shareholders' agreement is therefore 'more appropriate for temporary and personal obligations'.

The articles of association may be amended by a special resolution at a general meeting if three-quarters of the members vote in favour of the resolution (s. 21). By contrast, a shareholders' agreement can only be altered with the consent of all the parties to it; it is therefore 'more difficult to change than the articles of association'. An alteration of the articles must be registered with Companies House whilst the registration is not required for the amendment of a shareholders' agreement. In this sense, it is correctly argued that the agreement is 'easier to change than the articles'.[4]

[4] These sentences address the seemingly contradictory statement in the question that shareholders' agreements are 'both easier and more difficult to change than the articles of association'. They demonstrate your good analytical skills.

The most significant differences between the articles and a shareholder agreement lie in their enforcement.[5] The articles constitute a statutory contract between the company and its members, and between members *inter se* (s. 33). The enforcement of this statutory contract is governed by the decision in **Hickman v Kent or Romney Marsh Sheepbreeders Association** [1915] 1 Ch 881, where the articles provided that disputes between the company and a member should be referred to arbitration. A member in dispute with the company commenced legal proceedings. It was concluded that the member was bound by the articles and the dispute should be referred to arbitration. Astbury J held that: 'No right merely purporting to be given by an article to a person, whether a member or not, in a capacity other than as a member, as for instance, as solicitor, promoter, director, can be enforced against the company.'[6] Thus, a member can only enforce a membership right which is contained in the articles, such as the right to attend and vote at a general meeting (**Pender v Lushington** (1877) 6 Ch D 70) and

[5] Point out the most important issue that you will discuss in detail. It also indicates where you are going with your answer.

[6] This is a very important judgment that you should learn. The name of the leading judge shows your specific knowledge of this case.

the right to a declared dividend (*Wood* v *Odessa Waterworks Co* (1889) 42 Ch D 636). Non-membership rights cannot be enforced, such as the right to be a company solicitor (*Eley* v *Positive Government Security Life Assurance Co Ltd* (1876) 1 Ex D 88) or a director (*Beattie* v *E and F Beattie Ltd* [1938] Ch 708).

By comparison, it is easier to enforce a shareholders' agreement in the sense that it is not governed by the *Hickman* principle. The courts are willing to enforce the agreement if it is merely between shareholders.[7] Shareholders, for instance, may enter into agreements to determine the way in which they exercise their voting rights. In *Puddephatt* v *Leith* [1916] 1 Ch 200 the court compelled a shareholder to vote as was agreed in the shareholders' agreement.

[7] You should discuss the enforcement of a shareholders' agreement in two aspects: first, when it is merely between shareholders; and, secondly, when it is between shareholders and the company. Many students do not differentiate between these two aspects.

In *Greenwell* v *Porter* [1902] 1 Ch 530 the defendant shareholders agreed to exercise their power to secure the election of two named persons as directors of a company and to vote for their re-election afterwards. When the defendants subsequently tried to oppose the re-election of one of the two named persons, the court granted an injunction restraining them from voting in any way inconsistent with the agreement.

If the company is a party to a shareholders' agreement which affects the statutory obligation of the company, it may not be enforceable. In *Punt* v *Symons & Co Ltd* [1903] 2 Ch 506 it was held that a company could not contract out of the right to alter its articles. The provision in the shareholders' agreement which binds the company not to alter its articles is therefore not enforceable. Similarly, in *Russell* v *Northern Bank Development Corporation Ltd* [1992] BCLC 1016,[8] an agreement was entered into between the company and its shareholders which provided, *inter alia,* that no further share capital would be created or issued without the consent of all the parties. The board of directors proposed to increase the company's share capital. One of the shareholders objected to this and was successful in obtaining a declaration that the agreement was binding on his fellow shareholders. The House of Lords held that the company's agreement not to increase its share capital was invalid because it was contrary to section 121 of the Companies Act 1985 which allowed a company to increase its share capital. This agreement was therefore not binding on the *company* itself; however, an agreement *outside*

[8] This is a House of Lords' authority on the validity of a shareholders' agreement. You should have a good understanding of the judgment of this case.

the articles between shareholders as to how they would exercise their voting rights on a particular resolution was valid. It emphasised that the shareholders' agreement was of a personal nature and was not embodied in the articles.

The case of **Russell** (above) confirms the principle that a company cannot contract out of its statutory power under section 21 to alter its articles by a shareholder agreement. A different judicial approach was taken when dealing with the issue as to whether the company can contract out of statutory provisions by its articles.[9] In **Bushell v Faith** [1970] AC 1099, a weighted voting right was included in the articles whereby in the event of a resolution to remove a director that director's shares would carry three votes per share. This has the effect of preventing that director from being removed by an ordinary resolution (now under s. 168, Companies Act 2006). The House of Lords held that the article in question was not inconsistent with the statutory power which was silent on the allocation of voting rights for an ordinary resolution.

In conclusion, shareholders' agreements are more flexible and private, more difficult to change and easier to enforce than the articles of association.[10]

[9] A consideration of the different judicial approach shows your sound knowledge of this legal issue and will gain you more marks.

[10] Your conclusion should echo the legal issues that arise in the question. A succinct conclusion will enhance your arguments and complete your answer.

 Make your answer stand out

- Point out that not all the clauses in the articles can be altered by a special resolution in accordance with section 21. You can discuss the common law restrictions and the different requirements for the variation of class rights (s. 630) and the entrenchment articles (s. 22).

- Refer to academic debates on the enforcement of a shareholders' agreement such as: Sealy, L. (1992) Shareholders' agreements – an endorsement and a warning from the House of Lords. *CLJ* 437; Davenport, B. J. (1993) What did *Russell* v *Northern Bank Development Corporation Ltd* decide? 109 *LQR* 553; Riley, C. A. (1993) Vetoes and voting agreements: some problems of consent and knowledge. 44 *NILQ* 34; Ferran, E. (1994) The decision of the House of Lords in *Russell* v *Northern Bank Development Corporation Ltd*. *CLJ* 343.

! Don't be tempted to . . .

- Provide an answer without detailed analysis of *Russell* v *Northern Bank Development Corporation Ltd* (1992). This is a very important case in relation to shareholders' agreements and must not be omitted in your answer.

- Give a narrative list of a comparison between the articles of association and shareholders' agreements. You should focus on the main differences which lie in their enforcement.

www.pearsoned.co.uk/lawexpressqa

Go online to access more revision support including additional essay and problem questions with diagram plans, You be the marker questions, and download all diagrams from the book.

Directors' duties

4

How this topic may come up in exams

Directors' general duties which existed in common law rules and in equitable principles are codified in the Companies Act 2006. The codified duties are very popular exam topics and therefore essential for your revision. Each of the general duties in sections 170–177 can be assessed in an essay or problem question, either on its own or with other duties. Section 172, in particular, has received considerable academic attention with regard to the enlightened shareholder value. You may also need to consider the law on shareholder remedies in problem questions in relation to directors' breach of duties.

◼ Before you begin

It's a good idea to consider the following key themes of directors' duties before tackling a question on this topic.

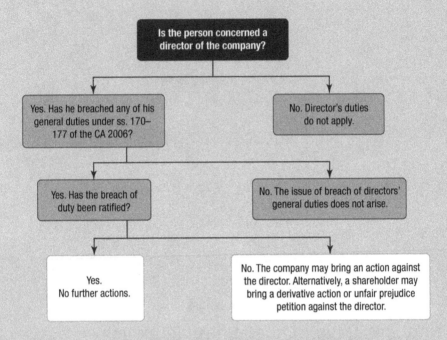

A printable version of this diagram is available from **www.pearsoned.co.uk/lawexpressqa**

🖋 Question 1

'The Company Law Review, in line with its objectives of maximising clarity and accessibility, recommended that the duties of directors should be codified by way of a statutory restatement ... [T]he issue of restating directors' duties in statutory form caused considerable controversy and generated widespread debate' (Dignam A. and Lowry, J. *Company Law,* 5th edn, (Oxford University Press 2009), p. 299).

Evaluate the above statements.

Answer plan

➡ Examine directors' general duties in sections 170–177 of the Companies Act 2006.

➡ Compare the codified duties with their equivalent common law duties.

➡ Discuss in detail the duty in section 172 which arguably has made one of the most significant changes in the CA 2006.

➡ Evaluate whether the codification of directors' duties has improved or clarified this area of law.

Diagram plan

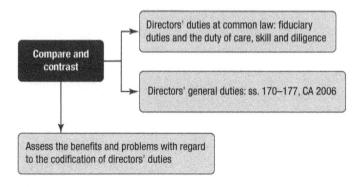

A printable version of this diagram plan is available from **www.pearsoned.co.uk/lawexpressqa**

Answer

[1] These opening sentences identify the key legal issues raised in the question and reassure the examiner that you clearly understand what is being asked in the question.

This question requires a discussion of the codification of directors' duties and an evaluation of whether it has clarified or improved this area of law. Although codification offers some advantages such as clarity and accessibility, it is argued that it has led to some uncertainties.[1]

A director is defined in section 250 as including 'any person occupying the position of a director, by whatever name called'. There are three categories of director: *de jure, de facto* and shadow directors (*Re Hydrodan (Corby) Ltd* [1994] BCC 161). All companies must have at least one director, and public companies must have at least two (s. 154). Directors owe their general duties to the company, not to its shareholders: section 170(1), *Percival* v *Wright* (1902) 2 Ch 421. They are considered as a company's trustees or agents and are in a fiduciary position in relation to the company: *Bristol and West Building Society* v *Mothew* [1998] Ch 1. Consequently, they must first and foremost act in good faith and in the best interests of the company. Directors also owe the duty of care and skill to the company at common law: *Re City Equitable Fire Insurance Co Ltd* [1925] Ch 407.[2]

² This shows your sound understanding of directors' fiduciary duties and common law duties prior to the CA 2006.

The Law Commission (Consultation Paper, 1998) considered that the complex law on directors' duties in equitable principles and at common law should be reformed and made simpler by a statutory form. It assessed the advantages of codification such as certainty and accessibility against its disadvantages such as loss of flexibility.[3] The duties are now codified in the CA 2006. Despite the codification, previous case law is still relevant to its application and interpretation because directors' general duties should be interpreted and applied in the same way as common law rules or equitable principles (s. 170). The general duties in sections 170–177 are assessed by comparison with their corresponding common law rules.[4]

³ The reference to the Law Commission Consultation Paper demonstrates your good understanding of the background of the codification of directors' duties. It will earn you more marks.

⁴ This sentence sets a clear structure for the discussion of directors' duties in your answer.

Section 171 states that directors must act in accordance with the company's constitution and that they should only exercise their powers for the purposes for which they have been conferred. It codifies the common law duty to act for proper purposes as established in *Hogg* v *Cramphorn* [1967] Ch 254 and *Howard Smith Ltd* v *Ampol Petroleum* [1974] AC 821. Section 171 has made the law more accessible whilst maintaining the clarity of the common law.[5]

⁵ This sentence goes beyond a descriptive account of section 171 and shows your critical analysis skills. It will add more credit to your answer.

Section 172 requires that a director act in the way he considers, in good faith, would be most likely to promote the success of the company for the benefit of its members as a whole. Directors must also have regard to the factors in the non-exhaustive list, such as the likely consequences of any decision in the long term, the interests of the company's employees, the company's business relationships with suppliers and customers, the impact on the community and environment, the reputation of the company and the need for the company to act fairly as between members. This duty is based on the common law duty to act *bona fide* in the interests of the company: *Re Smith & Fawcett* [1942] 1 All ER 542. It is subjective in nature in the sense that it is what a director considers, not what a court considers, would be most likely to promote the success of the company: *Bristol & West Building Society* v *Mothew* (above). Section 172 is much wider in scope than the previous case law; it introduces the enlightened shareholder value whereby the company should be run to generate maximum wealth for shareholders but also to take a properly balanced view of the wider implications of decisions over time.[6] Keay (2007) argues that section 172 is pivotal in providing guidance for directors in their activities and what a director should be aiming towards. The Law Society, however, criticises the fact that there is no indication in section 172 as to the meaning of the success of the company. This may lead to increased uncertainty because directors may have different interpretations. Moreover, the liabilities of directors seem to have been increased, which may deter people from taking up directorship.[7]

A director is required under section 173 to exercise independent judgement. It clearly restates the principle that a director should not fetter his discretion as established in *Fulham Football Club and Others* v *Cabra Estates plc* [1994] 1 BCLC 363. Section 174 states that a director has a duty to exercise reasonable care, skill and diligence. It replaces the previous common law duties as established in *Dorchester Finance Co Ltd* v *Stebbing* [1989] BCLC 498 *and Re Barings plc* [2002] 1 BCLC 401. The subjective and objective tests at common law are also adopted.[8]

Section 175 codifies the no-conflict and no secret profit rules at common law: *Cook* v *Deeks* [1916] 1 AC 554 and *Regal (Hastings) Ltd* v *Gulliver* [1942] 1 All ER 378. A director must avoid a situation in which he has, or can have, a direct or indirect interest that conflicts, or possibly may conflict, with the interests of the company. It applies in particular to the exploitation of any property, information or opportunity. This duty is not infringed if the matter has been effectively authorised by disinterested directors (s. 175(4)).[9] A director must not accept a benefit from a third party

[6] This sentence compares section 172 with the common law rules. A discussion of the enlightened shareholder value is essential for an excellent understanding of section 172.

[7] The discussion of the problems of section 172 by reference to academic opinions makes your answer stand out.

[8] If time permits, the dual tests for the levels of care, skill and diligence required in section 174 should be discussed in more detail.

[9] The authorisation is an essential part of section 175 and should not be omitted in your answer.

conferred by reason of him being a director (s. 176). He must also declare the nature and extent of any interest to other directors, if he is in any way interested in a proposed transaction or arrangement with the company (s. 177). It codifies the self-dealing rules as established in **Bentinck v Fenn** (1887) 12 App Cas 652 and **Aberdeen Railway Co Ltd v Blaikie Bros** (1854) 1 Macq 461.

The codification of directors' duties has clarified the complex rules at common law and made it easier for shareholders to detect and redress directors' breach of these duties. Significant problems, however, still exist. The duty to promote the success of the company, for example, is drafted in vague and ill-defined language. Moreover, a link to directors' duties at common law remains (s. 170(4)) and there is likely to be a period of uncertainty for the courts during which they will need to decide how to apply and interpret the new law. The Law Society has expressed concerns that it may result in new uncertainty, increased costs and legal bureaucracy. Despite all these initial concerns, it is argued that the codification, in overall terms, does not change the essential nature of directors' general duties and it is most likely to prove beneficial in the long run because of its improved clarity and accessibility.[10]

[10] The conclusion should directly address the question which requires a critical evaluation of a codification of directors' duties. It should also clearly summarise your main arguments on the concerns and benefits of the codification.

Make your answer stand out

■ Consider in more detail the changes introduced by section 172.

■ Discuss the duty in section 182 in respect of an existing transaction with the company.

■ Evaluate whether the duty of disclosure under section 177 is more onerous than before.

■ Discuss the rules in relation to ratification in section 239 and compare them with those at common law.

■ Further reading on the codification of directors' duties: Law Commission Consultation Paper (No. 153), *Company Directors: Regulating Conflicts of Interests and Formulating a Statement of Duties*; Attenborough, D. (2006) The Company Law Reform Bill: an analysis of directors' duties and the objective of the company. 27 *Company Lawyer* 162.

! Don't be tempted to . . .

■ Simply describe directors' duties at common law and then the codified duties. You should discuss each of the codified duties by comparing with its correspondence at common law.

■ Provide an answer without reference to case law. You should be aware that the case law is still relevant in the interpretation and application of the codified duties.

■ Simply describe the duties without any critical analysis. You must evaluate the strength of the codified duties and the problems of codification.

❓ Question 2

Ben, Harry and Samuel are all directors of Summer T-shirts Ltd, which designs and sells T-shirts. They hold 55, 15 and 30 per cent of the company's shares respectively. The company's share capital consists of 1,000 ordinary shares.

The articles of association, which otherwise follow the Model Articles for private companies limited by shares, contain the provision that: 'The directors have unrestricted power to allot shares.' Ben and Harry did not get along well with Samuel and they intended to dilute Samuel's shareholding so that Samuel would not have the power to block a special resolution at shareholder meetings. Ben and Harry only allotted to their friend Emily 500 ordinary shares, which Samuel was also interested in purchasing.

Ben and Harry recently have signed a contract with Hien Ltd, a Vietnamese company which supplies cotton T-shirts. They know that Hien Ltd has a reputation for poor industrial relations and suspect that the clothes are made of materials which are not environmentally friendly. Samuel is unhappy about this but Ben and Harry insist that the T-shirts are cheap and their only concern is to maximise the company's profits.

Advise Samuel as to whether Ben and Harry have breached any of their general duties as directors in the Companies Act 2006.

Answer plan

➡ Assess whether Ben and Harry breached their duties in section 171 in relation to the allotment of shares.

➡ Discuss whether Ben and Harry breached their duties in section 172 in relation to the contract with Hien Ltd.

Diagram plan

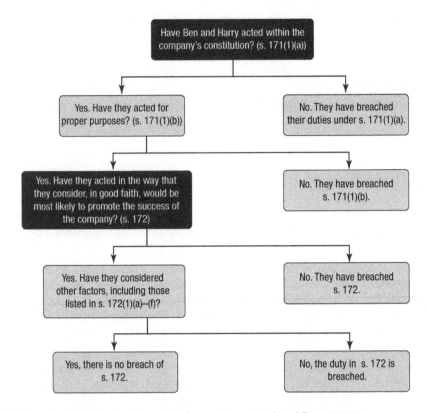

A printable version of this diagram plan is available from **www.pearsoned.co.uk/lawexpressqa**

Answer

[1] You should identify the key legal issues in the introduction so that your examiners know that you are able to understand the context of the subject and engage with the question.

The key legal issues here are whether Ben and Harry breached their general duties as directors of Summer T-shirts Ltd when they allotted shares only to Emily and when they signed the contract with Hien Ltd.[1] Directors' duties at common law and in equitable principles are now codified in sections 170–177, Companies Act 2006. Despite the codification, previous case law is still relevant to its application and interpretation (s. 170). Directors owe their general duties to the company, not to its shareholders: *Percival* v *Wright* [1902] 2 Ch 421.

Allotment of shares[2]

Where a private company has only one class of shares, the directors may exercise any power of the company to allot shares of that class (s. 550). Directors in a private company have authority to allot shares if they are authorised to do so by the articles of association or an ordinary resolution.[3] Summer T-shirts Ltd has only one class of shares and its articles grant directors unrestricted power to allot shares. As Ben and Harry hold 70 per cent of the company's shares, either a board decision which requires a majority voting or an ordinary resolution at a share-holder meeting which requires a simple majority (s. 282) can be passed.

It should be noted, however, that Samuel may have pre-emption rights. Unless such rights are excluded or dis-applied, the existing shareholders must be offered new shares before they are offered to people outside the company (s. 561). In this way, a shareholder can protect his proportion of the total equity of a company. If they are not excluded or dis-applied in the company's articles, Samuel's pre-emption rights have been infringed and he may bring an unfair prejudice petition under section 994 against the company's failure to allot shares on a rights basis: **Re a Company (No. 005134 of 1986), ex p Harries** [1989] BCLC 383.[4]

[4] This paragraph examines the pre-emption rights and the possible remedies for an infringement of such rights. It shows your wider understanding of company law beyond directors' duties and will impress your examiners.

It is essential to discuss whether Ben and Harry have breached their duties in relation to the allotment of shares. A director must act in accordance with the company's constitution and only exercise powers for the purposes for which they are conferred (s. 171). Section 171 restates the proper purposes rule at common law that directors should only exercise their powers for a proper purpose and not for any collateral purpose: **Hogg v Cramphorn** [1967] Ch 254.[5]

[5] The reference to previous case law is essential for the discussion of section 171 because it still applies in the interpretation and application of the codified duty.

Ben and Harry acted in accordance with the company's constitution in relation to the allotment of shares; however, it is important to examine whether they exercised this power for an improper purpose. In **Howard Smith Ltd v Ampol Petroleum** [1974] AC 821 directors abused their fiduciary powers by authorising the issue of shares for the purpose of altering the voting power in the company and such issue was held invalid. Lord Wilberforce established the four-step test in order to decide whether the actual exercise was proper. First, construe the article conferring the power in order to ascertain the nature of the power and its limits. Here it refers to the interpretation of the provision in the articles which grants directors unrestricted power to allot shares. Secondly, determine the substantial purpose(s) for which this power should be exercised. The substantial purpose for allotting shares in Summer T-Shirts Ltd should be to increase the company's share capital and promote the company's commercial interests. Thirdly, identify the substantial purpose(s) for which the power was actually excised. Ben and Harry exercised the power to manipulate share capital and dilute Samuel's shareholding. Finally, compare the actual purpose with the permissible purposes for the exercise of that power. By diluting Samuel's shareholding instead of promoting the company's interests, Ben and Harry did not exercise the power for proper purposes and therefore the allotment was invalid.[6] Samuel could also argue that Ben and Harry breached their duties in section 172 because they did not act in good faith or for the best interests of the company with regard to the allotment of shares.[7]

[6] The application of the four-step test demonstrates your ability to apply the relevant law to the problem question.

[7] The reference to section 172 will earn you more marks as it shows your excellent understanding of directors' duties.

The contract with Hien Ltd

Section 172 requires that a director act in the way he considers, in good faith, would be most likely to promote the success of the company for the benefit of its members as a whole. In doing so, directors must have regard to a number of factors, such as the likely consequences of any decision in the long term, the company's business relationships with suppliers and customers, the impact on the community and environment and the reputation of the company. This duty is based on the pre-existing duty to act *bona fide* in the interests of the company (**Re Smith & Fawcett** [1942] 1 All ER 542). It is very difficult to prove a breach of this duty because the test for this duty is subjective: **Regentcrest plc v Cohen** [2001] 2 BCLC 80. A director must act in the way he considers, not what a court may consider, would be most likely to promote the success of the company. This reflects the traditional concern that the courts must not get involved in reviewing the exercise of business judgement by directors: **Carlen v Drury** (1812) 1 Ves & B 154. Ben and Harry could argue that they acted in the way they believed would promote the success of the company by dealing with Hien Ltd. There are, however, some limits to this subjective test at common law. In **Charterbridge Corp Ltd v Lloyds Bank Ltd** [1970] Ch 62, an objective test was introduced where the court considered whether an intelligent and honest director could in the whole of the circumstances reasonably believe the transaction to be for the benefit of the

[8] This sentence shows that you are aware of the objective element at common law and, more importantly, the uncertainties in its application in section 172. The latter will gain you more marks.

company. This objective test is not codified in section 172 and it is unclear whether the courts, in interpreting section 172, will consider whether an intelligent and honest director would believe the transaction is for the benefit of the company.[8]

[9] This paragraph discusses the list of factors in section 172 and applies it to the problem question. Some students only focus on the requirements of 'good faith' and 'for the success of the company' in section 172. A consideration of the list of factors is often omitted.

Directors must also have regard to the non-exhaustive list of factors in section 172(1)(a)–(f), which reflects the enlightened shareholder value as opposed to the traditional theory of shareholder primacy. Although Ben and Harry may honestly believe that the contract is in the financial interests of the company, it appears that they have not considered the factors listed in section 172, in particular, the impact on the community and environment as well as the reputation of the company. It is therefore argued that they breached their duties in section 172, unless they can prove otherwise that they have considered these factors in reaching their decisions.[9]

 Make your answer stand out

■ Briefly discuss the controversial debates surrounding section 172 in relation to the enlightened shareholder value and those factors listed in section 172(1). As this is a problem question, a detailed discussion of these issues, however, is not appropriate.

■ Assess whether the breach of duties can be ratified at general meeting (s. 239).

■ Evaluate the legal actions which Samuel can bring against the breach of duties by Ben and Harry, such as the derivative action (ss. 260–264) and unfair prejudice petition (s. 994).

! Don't be tempted to . . .

■ Describe all of the directors' duties. You should only discuss those duties which are relevant to this problem question.

■ Ignore the common law on directors' duties. Despite codification, the common law is still relevant in the application and interpretation of the statutory duties.

■ Discuss section 172 without reference to *Charterbridge Corp Ltd* v *Lloyds Bank Ltd* [1970] Ch 62. This is an important case as it may place some restrictions on the subjective test in section 172.

■ Discuss section 171 without reference to the four-step test established in *Howard Smith Ltd* v *Ampol Petroleum* [1974] AC 821.

 **Question 3**

'Section 172 of the Companies Act 2006 has introduced into English company law the concept of enlightened shareholder value. It appears to be a dramatic shift from the common law position.'

Critically discuss the above statement. Has the English company law adopted the stakeholder theory?

Answer plan

→ Discuss directors' duty in section 172 by making a comparison with the previous common law duty.

→ Analyse the corporate governance issues, in particular, the shareholder primacy and stakeholder theories.

→ Evaluate the enlightened shareholder value which is introduced by section 172.

→ Conclude whether the stakeholder theory has been adopted in English company law.

Diagram plan

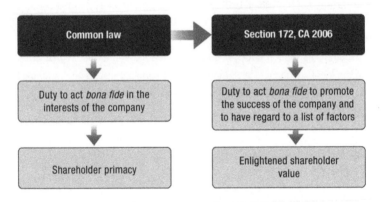

A printable version of this diagram plan is available from **www.pearsoned.co.uk/lawexpressqa**

Answer

A director must act in a way he considers, in good faith, would be most likely to promote the success of the company for the benefit of its members as a whole (s. 172). In doing so, he is obliged to have specific regard, among other matters, to the interests of company's employees, the impact of the company's operations on the community and the environment, and the need to act fairly between members of the company. Section 172 not only codifies the common law duty to act *bona fide* in what the director considers – not what a court may consider – is in the interests of the company (*Re Smith & Fawcett Ltd* [1942] 1 All ER 542) but also introduces the new concept of enlightened shareholder value. It is argued that the English company law has moved closer to, but has not firmly adopted, the stakeholder theory.[1]

[1] These two sentences outline the main arguments and reassure the examiner that you know exactly what the question is about in terms of its subject content.

The test in section 172 remains subjective because what constitutes the success of the company depends on the director's good faith judgement. It appears that there are no objective criteria in section 172 against which the actions of directors can be assessed and, therefore, it is very difficult to prove a breach of this duty. At common law, nevertheless, objective considerations were introduced by the courts to supplement the subjective test.[2] In *Charterbridge Corp Ltd v Lloyds Bank Ltd* [1970] Ch 62, the courts considered whether an intelligent and honest director could in the whole of the circumstances reasonably believe the transaction to be for the benefit of the company. Section 172 makes no reference to this objective consideration; however, given the significant role of common law rules in the interpretation and application of the codified duties (s. 170(3) and (4)), Keay (2007) incisively argues that it is most likely that the courts would consider the objective test in assessing directors' actions.[3]

[2] The objective test at common law is often ignored by students. A discussion of this test by reference to case law shows your sound understanding and will make your answer stand out.

[3] The reference to academic opinion on the uncertainties of the objective test will gain you more marks because it goes beyond a pure description of section 172 and the relevant case law.

There are many theories regarding in whose interests the company should be run. The traditional approach in the United Kingdom is the shareholder value principle (or shareholder primacy), whereby a company should be run for the wealth maximisation of its shareholders above those of other parties such as customers and suppliers. Directors are under a duty to act in the interests of the company (*Percival v Wright* [1902] 2 Ch 421), which are interpreted as the best interests of present and future shareholders (*Hutton v West Cork Railway Company* (1883) LR 23 Ch D 654). The shareholder value theory reflects the view that shareholders are the owners of the company and bear the residual risks.[4]

[4] The traditional shareholder value approach is an essential part of your answer because, without it, you cannot demonstrate how section 172 is different from the traditional approach.

The stakeholder theory (or the pluralist approach), by contrast, emphasises the interests of stakeholders, who can affect or be affected by a company's activities. It requires that directors manage the company for the benefit of all the stakeholders. The stakeholder theory was considered in the Company Law Review Steering Group (*The Strategic Framework*, 1999) but is not adopted in the CA 2006, mainly due to the difficulties faced by directors in balancing the interests of different groups and the concerns in enforcing these duties.[5]

The enlightened shareholder value is adopted as an alternative approach, as it is perceived to be able to better achieve wealth generation and competitiveness for the benefit of all. The non-exhaustive list in section 172(1) which a director has to consider in making decisions seeks to capture this new approach. A company should be run to generate maximum wealth for shareholders, and, at the same time, directors should take a properly balanced view of the implications of decisions over time and foster effective relation-

[6] You should explain clearly what is meant by the enlightened shareholder value approach.

ships with employees, customers and suppliers, and in the wider community.[6] Despite the introduction of the non-exhaustive list, it is clear that shareholder primacy is still dominant in the United Kingdom because a director must act to promote the success of the company for the interests of members as a whole. Kiarie (2006) is of the similar view that the enlightened shareholder value appears

[7] The differences between this new approach and the shareholder/stakeholder value are very important here because they directly address the issues raised in the essay question.

a compromise between the shareholder primacy and stakeholder theory by maintaining the primacy of shareholders' interests whilst considering other stakeholders' interests.[7]

Section 172 provides, for the first time, some guidance on directors' objectives in conducting the company's affairs. It is beneficial in the wider context and in the long term; however, there are two inherent problems. First, the long list of factors may extend the administrative process and lengthen the time the board takes to make decisions

[8] These sentences examine the ambiguities in the application of section 172 and the difficulties in balancing the various interests of stakeholders. They refer back to the question in relation to the enlightened shareholder value.

because directors must do all they reasonably can to have regard to these factors. It is unclear which criteria should be used to assess objectively whether the action of the directors has led to the success of the company.[8] Attenborough (2006) suggests that section 172 grants directors discretion to give their own interpretations of success. This may lead to increased uncertainty because directors may have different interpretations of the meaning of success. Moreover, the factors listed in section 172 are not exhaustive and other relevant factors should also be taken into account. It is unclear whether a director would be in breach of this duty if he considered all the factors, except the one relating to the environment. It is also problematic when there is a conflict between two or more of the factors, for example, if a decision benefits the employees but is detrimental to the community or the environment.

Secondly, while shareholders may bring a derivative action against directors for breach of duties (ss. 260–264), there is a lack of procedure for other stakeholders such as employees or the community to hold directors accountable if the directors fail to have regard to their interests set out in section 172(1).[9] As derivative actions are only available to *members* of the company (s. 260), it is most likely that directors will continue to exercise their power to promote the success of the company for the benefit of its members. As rightly observed in Boyle & Birds (2007, p. 618), the effect of section 172 is more likely to be 'educational rather than in any sense restrictive'.

[9] The lack of enforcement by stakeholders further strengthens the argument that the stakeholder theory is not adopted in English company law. This is often omitted in students' answers.

It can be concluded that section 172 aims to strike a delicate balance between the traditional shareholder value and the stakeholder approach. Although directors are required to consider various stakeholder interests in the light of enlightened shareholder value, it is argued that the stakeholder theory has not been adopted in English company law as shareholders' interests are still paramount in directors' decision-making.[10]

[10] The conclusion relates back to the question on the enlightened shareholder value and reinforces your argument that the stakeholder theory is not firmly adopted in the United Kingdom.

 Make your answer stand out

■ Point out that shareholders may challenge directors' breach of duties by bringing an unfair prejudice petition according to section 994, CA 2006.

■ In relation to the test for the duty to act in good faith in section 172, consider *Fulham Football Club* v *Cabra Estates plc* [1992] BCLC 863 and *Re Southern Counties Fresh Foods Ltd* EWHC 2810 (Ch).

■ Discuss the shareholder theory, stakeholder theory and enlightened shareholder value by reference to more academic opinions, in particular Keay, A. R. (2006) Enlightened shareholder value, the reform of the duties of company directors and the corporate objective. *LMCLQ* 335 and Yap, J. L. (2010) Considering the Enlightened Shareholder Value Principle. 31 *Company Lawyer* 35.

! Don't be tempted to . . .

- Give a narrative account of section 172 and the previous duty at common law. Although this shows some understanding of the relevant law, it is far from sufficient. You need to analyse the changes introduced in section 172 in relation to the enlightened shareholder value.

- Provide an answer without reference to academic opinions. As there is very little case law on section 172, it is essential to engage in a wide range of academic debates in your answer.

- Describe the seven main duties of directors in sections 170–177, CA 2006. This is greatly discouraged: your answer should focus on the key issues with regard to section 172 and the enlightened shareholder value.

Question 4

'Though the standard expected is now clearly identified [in s. 174, Companies Act 2006], the content of this duty [of care and skill] is still under development by the courts and it is not always easy to draw from the cases a comprehensive and coherent statement of what is required of directors' (Hannigan, B. (2009) *Company Law,* 2nd edn. Oxford: Oxford University Press, p. 224).

In the light of the above statement, analyse the development of director's duty of care, skill and diligence.

Answer plan

➜ Examine the development of the duty of care and skill at common law in three main aspects:
- – the required standards;
- – directors' continuous attention of the company's affairs; and
- – the delegation of power.
➜ Discuss the duty of care, skill and diligence in section 174 and the dual objective and subjective standards.
➜ Evaluate the problems associated with the duty in section 174.

Diagram plan

The common law duty of care, skill and diligence $\Rightarrow$ The codified duty in s. 174, CA 2006 $\Rightarrow$ The problems associated with s. 174 and its future reforms

A printable version of this diagram plan is available from **www.pearsoned.co.uk/lawexpressqa**

Answer

The duty of care, skill and diligence has evolved at common law over a long period of time and it is now stated in section 174, Companies Act 2006. Despite the codification, it is correctly argued that there is little guidance as to the content of this duty in terms of what is expected of a reasonably diligent director in his participation in the conduct of the company's affairs.[1]

[1] You should identify the key legal issues in the introduction so that the examiner knows where you are going with your answer.

Directors are often granted wide power to manage the company's business according to the general management clause[2] in the Model Articles of Association (Art. 3). Various duties are therefore imposed on directors to curb their potential abuse of power. Before the codification of directors' duties, directors owed to the company fiduciary duties and the duty of care and skill at common law: **Percival v Wright** [1902] 2 Ch 421. The distinction between these two types of duties is explained by Millett LJ in **Bristol & West Building Society v Mothew** [1996] 4 All ER 698. The essence of fiduciary duties is loyalty and a breach of them attracts equitable remedies; whilst the duty of care and skill is related to competence and the remedy is compensation to the company for the harm caused.[3]

[2] The general management clause in the Model Articles shows your good understanding of directors' wide-ranging power.

[3] These two sentences explore the differences between the two types of duties. They demonstrate your sound understanding of the wider context of directors' duties and will gain you more marks.

A director must exercise reasonable care, skill and diligence (s. 174). This means the care, skill and diligence that would be exercised by a reasonably diligent person with the general knowledge, skill and experience that may reasonably be expected of a person carrying out the functions carried out by the director in relation to the company (s. 174(2)(a)), and the general knowledge, skill and experience that the director has (s. 174(2)(b)).[4] Section 174(2)(a) sets an objective minimum standard of a reasonably diligent person who has taken on the office of director, taking into account the functions undertaken. Section 174(2)(b) sets a subjective standard

[4] If you cannot remember this long provision during an exam, try to summarise it, for example, by stating that 'the standards required are the general knowledge, skill and experience that may reasonably be expected of a person and that the director actually has'.

4 DIRECTORS' DUTIES

5 The reference to the
Insolvency Act 1986
demonstrates your good
knowledge of the duty of care,
skill and diligence. It will help
you gain more marks.

6 This sentence ties
your answer back to the
question with regard to the
development of the duty at
common law.

7 The reference to an early
case shows the low standard
required of directors and
forms the starting point
of your discussion of the
development of this duty.

8 This sentence sets a clear
structure for the analysis that
follows.

9 These sentences
demonstrate your analytical
skills by assessing the
subjective approach. It will
make your answer stand out.

in relation to the personal attributes of the director, which may raise the objective minimum standard. Section 174 is closely modelled on section 214(4) of the Insolvency Act 1986, which defines negligent conduct for the purposes of wrongful trading.[5] The current standards of care, skill and diligence adopted in section 174 are the results of its continual development at common law over 100 years.[6]

Some early decisions in the nineteenth century indicated that the courts generally had low expectations of the standard of care to be expected of directors. In *Re Cardiff Savings Bank, Marquis of Bute's case* [1892] 2 Ch 100, the director of a bank attended only one board meeting in 38 years. It was held that he did not share responsibility for the bank's heavy loss caused by the irregular conduct of its trustees and managers. Stirling J formulated the intermittent theory of directors' duties where a director must exercise care at the meetings at which he was actually present, but owed no duty to attend any specific meeting.[7]

In *Re City Equitable Fire Insurance Co Ltd* [1925] Ch 407 Romer J reviewed earlier authorities and summarised the principles for the director's duty of care in three aspects: the required standards, directors' continuous attention of the company's affairs and the delegation of power.[8] First, a director need not exhibit in the performance of his duties a greater degree of skill than might reasonably be expected of a person of his knowledge and experience. Second, a director was not bound to give continuous attention to the affairs of his company. His duties were of an intermittent nature and he was not bound to attend all meetings. Third, all duties, with regard to the exigencies of business and the articles of association, might properly be left to some other official. A director was, in the absence of grounds for suspicion, justified in trusting that official to perform such duties honestly. This judgment therefore set a pure subjective standard test and no minimal standard of competence was required. This highly subjective approach caused many problems because the law required very little from a director who had no experience or knew nothing. This judicial lenience might have contributed to the corporate governance scandals of the 1980s.[9]

The dual objective and subjective tests in section 214(4) of the Insolvency Act 1986 were accepted and applied in *Norman v Theodore Goddard* [1991] BCLC 1028 and *Re D'Jan of London Ltd*

[1994] 1 BCLC 561. In *Re D'Jan*, it was held that a director was negligent for signing an insurance proposal without checking it. The information provided in the form was incorrect and the insurance company refused to pay when the company's premises were burnt down. These tests are far more rigorous than the initial subjective test and they are effectively enacted in section 174.[10]

[10] This sentence goes beyond a description of cases by providing some critical analysis. It will gain you more marks.

With regard to director's continuous attention and the delegation of power, the modern authority has moved away from the judgments in *Re City Equitable Fire Insurance Co Ltd*. In *Re Barings plc (No. 5)* [2000] 1 BCLC 523 a number of senior directors failed to supervise a rogue trader within the bank, which resulted in a loss of £827 million and the collapse of the bank. The directors were found to be unfit and disqualified. It was held that directors, both collectively and individually, had a continuing duty to acquire and maintain a sufficient knowledge of the company's business to enable them to discharge their duties. Whilst directors, subject to the articles of association, are entitled to delegate particular functions to those below them in the management chain and to trust their competence and integrity to a reasonable extent, the delegation of power does not absolve a director from the duty to supervise the discharge of the delegated functions.[11]

[11] The judgment in *Re Barings plc* (2000) is essential for your answer as it has established the modern rules on the duty of care and skill.

Although little was expected of directors in terms of care and skill in the past, more recent cases suggest a movement towards an objective standard of care and the application of the tests in section 214 of the Insolvency Act 1986. Section 174 consolidates the previous development of this duty at common law and introduces an objective standard of care which could be enhanced by the actual knowledge, skill and experience of a particular director. As Gower and Davies (2008, p. 494) incisively argue, the move from a subjective to an objective test will give the courts a greater role in defining the functions of the board while trying to avoid the use of hindsight.[12] Further development of case law may help clarify the exact content of the duty of care, skill and diligence.[13]

[12] The reference to academic opinion shows your excellent knowledge and will add more credit to your answer.

[13] In your conclusion, refer your discussion back to the statement in the question.

Make your answer stand out

- Discuss the enforcement of a breach of duty of care and skill. The higher standard of the duty of care and the broader scope of derivative actions may open the litigation floodgates against directors.

- Consider the influence of sections 6–9 of the Company Directors Disqualification Act 1986 on the standards of directors' conduct by reference to *Bishopsgate Investment Management Ltd* v *Maxwell (No. 2)* [1994] 1 All ER 261.

- Evaluate the problems of the current standards required for directors in section 174 by reference to academic opinions, in particular: Finch, V. (1992) Company directors: who cares about skill and care? 55 *MLR* 179; and Riley, C. A. (1992) The company director's duty of care and skill: the case for an onerous but subjective standard. 62 *MLR* 697.

! **Don't be tempted to . . .**

- Get confused with the objective test and the subjective one in section 174(1). Make sure you clearly understand what each test means.

- List all directors' duties in sections 170–177 of the Companies Act 2006. Some students tend to have a slow and lengthy introduction by describing all the codified duties. Although they show your general knowledge of directors' duties, they add very little to your answer.

- Simply provide the names of particular cases without explaining the key legal principles. In order to show your accurate understanding, you must discuss the relevant judgments in detail.

- Rely solely or heavily on the old authority – *Re City Equitable Life Insurance Co Ltd* [1925] Ch 407 – which no longer represents good law. It is important to discuss the modern rules such as those laid down in *Re Barings plc (No. 5)* [2000] 1 BCLC 523.

▨ Question 5

Alice, Barry and Camilla are shareholders and directors of Summer Rose Ltd. Each of them holds 60, 30 and 10 per cent of the company's shares respectively. Alice is often away on holiday and she rarely attends the board of directors' meetings. In March 2014 Alice sold the company's product to her friend James at a price which is much lower than the market price and she secretly took £5,000 commission from James. Summer Rose Ltd has been negotiating with Autumn Daisy Ltd for purchasing autumn flowers but Summer Rose Ltd has decided not to go ahead due to insufficient funds. Alice then set up her own company which signed the same purchase contract with Autumn Daisy Ltd.

Barry and Camilla wish to sue Alice for her misconduct but Alice is planning to ratify her conduct at the next general meeting.

Advise Barry and Camilla in relation to Alice's breach of duty as a director of Summer Rose Ltd.

Answer plan

➜ Examine whether Alice has breached her director's duty in section 174 by not attending board meetings.

➜ Analyse whether Alice has breached her duty in section 176 by secretly taking the commission from James.

➜ Consider whether Alice has breached her duty in section 175 by taking up the contract with Autumn Daisy Ltd.

➜ Discuss whether Alice has breached her duty in section 172.

➜ Evaluate whether Alice's misconduct can be ratified according to section 239.

Diagram plan

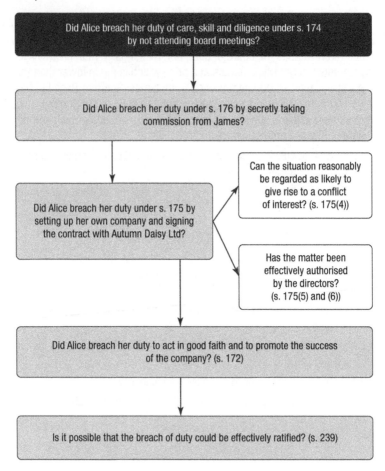

A printable version of this diagram plan is available from **www.pearsoned.co.uk/lawexpressqa**

Answer

[1] It is essential to identify the key legal issues in the introduction.

[2] This sentence highlights your clear knowledge of the codification of directors' duties and the relevance of previous case law.

The key legal issues here are whether Alice breached her director's duties by not attending board meetings, secretly taking the commission from James and taking up the contract with Autumn Daisy Ltd. The possibility of ratification of Alice's conduct will also be considered.[1] Directors' general duties are codified in sections 170–177 of the Companies Act 2006; nevertheless, the previous case law and equitable principles are still relevant in their application and interpretation (s. 170(4)).[2]

[3] The use of headings may
help you establish a good and
clear structure.

[4] You can state the statutory
provisions of section 174 here
if you can remember them.

1. Alice's absence from the board meetings[3]

Alice, as a director of Summer Rose Ltd, must exercise reasonable care, skill and diligence under section 174.[4] The standards required are the general knowledge, skill and experience that may reasonably be expected of a person and that the director actually has. Section 174(2)(a) sets an objective minimum standard of a reasonably diligent person who has taken on the office of director, taking into account the functions undertaken. Section 174(2)(b) sets a subjective standard in relation to the personal attributes of the director, which may raise the objective minimum standard. The dual objective and subjective tests were applied in **Norman v Theodore Goddard** [1991] BCLC 1028 and **Re D' Jan of London Ltd** [1994] 1 BCLC 561. In **Re Barings plc (No. 5)** [2000] 1 BCLC 523, it was held that directors, both collectively and individually, had a continuing duty to acquire and maintain a sufficient knowledge of the company's business to enable them to discharge their duties. Whilst directors, subject to the articles of association, are entitled to delegate particular functions to those below them in the management chain and to trust their competence and integrity to a reasonable extent, the delegation of power does not absolve a director from the duty to supervise the discharge of the delegated functions.[5] It can be argued that Alice breached her duty of care, skill and diligence under section 174 because she rarely attends board meetings.

[5] The judgment in Re Barings
plc (2000) is essential for your
answer as it has established
the modern rules on the duty
of care and skill.

2. The receipt of commission from James

Alice sold the company's product to her friend James at a price which is much lower than the market price and she secretly took £5,000 commission from James.[6] According to section 176, a director must not accept a benefit from a third party conferred by reason of him being a director. Alice, as a director of Summer Rose Ltd, accepted benefit from James; it is therefore concluded that Alice breached the duty in section 176.

[6] Try to refer back to the
problem scenario. It shows
that you are applying the legal
principles and engaging with
the question.

3. The purchase contract with Autumn Daisy Ltd

Alice set up her own company and took the business opportunity which belonged to Summer Rose Ltd. According to section 175, a director must 'avoid a situation in which he has, or can have, a direct or indirect interest that conflicts, or possibly may conflict with

4 DIRECTORS' DUTIES

[7] The case law here supports your discussion of the no-conflict rule at common law and will gain you more marks.

[8] This sentence refers back to the question and helps to move your answer to the next legal issue.

[9] This case adds more credit to your answer because it was decided by the House of Lords.

[10] This sentence links the discussion of these two cases together. The phrase 'strict approach' shows your analytical skills and gains you more marks.

[11] Students often forget to discuss this exception in section 175(4). Although it is straightforward and simple, you will lose some marks if it is not included in your answer.

the interests of the company'. Section 175 codifies the no-conflict rule and no secret profit rule at common law as established in *Aberdeen Railway Co v Blaikie Bros* (1854) 1 Macq 461 and *Cook v Deeks* [1916] 1 AC 554.[7] Alice might argue that Summer Rose Ltd had rejected the contract due to insufficient funds and therefore it had not lost out.[8] This would not relieve her from the breach of section 175 which applies to 'the exploitation of any property, information or opportunity' and 'it is immaterial whether the company could take advantage of the property, information or opportunity' (s. 175(2)). In *Regal (Hastings) ltd v Gulliver* [1942] 1 All ER 378,[9] the company could not finance the purchase of additional cinemas. Directors put up some capital for the purchase and later profited personally on the sale of the shares. The House of Lords held that these directors should return the profits to the company as they obtained their profits by reason and in the course of the execution of their office as directors. It made no difference whether the company could have taken up the opportunity or not. Similarly a strict approach was taken in *Industrial Development Consultants Ltd v Cooley* [1972] 2 All ER 162[10] where it was held that the defendant breached the no secret profit rule and was liable to account as information came to him while he was a managing director of the company. It is therefore reasonable to conclude that Alice should be held accountable for the profits she made by taking advantage of the information she obtained in the course of being a director of Summer Rose Ltd. The duty to avoid conflicts of interest is not infringed if the situation cannot reasonably be regarded as likely to give rise to a conflict of interest (s. 175(4)(a)) or if it has been effectively authorised by disinterested directors (s. 175(4)(b)).[11] In a private company, authorisation may be given by the directors if nothing in the company's constitution invalidates such authorisation (s. 175(5)). Authorisation is only effective when the following two conditions are met (s. 175(6)): firstly, the quorum requirement at the meeting is met without counting the director in question or any other interested director; secondly, the matter was agreed to without the votes of these directors or would have been agreed to if their votes had not been counted. It appears that Alice's conflict of interest was not authorised by the board.

Moreover, Barry and Camilla may claim that Alice breached her duty in section 172. A director must act in a way he considers, in good faith, would be most likely to promote the success of the company for the benefit of its members as a whole. In doing so, the director is obliged to have specific regard, among other matters, to the interests of company's employees, the impact of the company's operations on the community and the environment, and the need to act fairly between members of the company. Alice may argue that she acted in good faith and in the way she considered would be most likely to promote the success of the company for the benefit of its members as a whole. It is therefore very difficult for them to prove Alice's breach of section 172 because of the subjective nature of this duty: *Regentcrest plc* v *Cohen* [2001] 2BCLC 80.[12]

[12] The discussion of its subjective nature adds more credit to your answer because it extends beyond a descriptive account of the duty in section 172.

Alice is planning to ratify her misconduct at the general meeting. The resolution for ratification can only be passed if the necessary majority is obtained disregarding votes in favour of the resolution by the director and any member connected with him (s. 239). Although Alice holds 60 per cent of the company's shares, an effective resolution to ratify her misconduct is unlikely to pass, as her votes for the ratification would have been disregarded.[13] The consequences of breach of general duties are the same as would apply if the corresponding common law rule or equitable principle applied (s. 178). Since Alice has breached her duties as a director under sections 172, 174, 175 and 176, the chance of ratifying her misconduct appears very slim.[14]

[13] The evaluation of the possibility of ratification goes beyond a simple description of directors' duties. It will make your answer stand out.

[14] Your conclusion should provide specific advice to Barry and Camilla in relation to Alice's breach of duties and the possibility of ratification.

 Make your answer stand out

- Analyse the limits to the subjective nature of section 172. In *Charterbridge Corp Ltd* v *Lloyds Bank Ltd* [1970] Ch 62, an objective test was introduced where the court considered whether an intelligent and honest director could in the whole of the circumstances reasonably believe the transaction to be for the benefit of the company.

- Discuss other important cases on directors' duties in section 175, in particular, *Bhullar* v *Bhullar* [2003] 2 BCLC 241; *Item Software (UK) Ltd* v *Fassihi* [2005] 2 BCLC 91; *Gencor ACP Ltd* v *Dalby* [2000] 2 BCLC 734.

- Briefly consider the law on derivative claim (ss. 260–264) or unfair prejudice petition (s. 994). Barry and Camilla may be able to bring a derivative action or unfair prejudicial petition against Alice for her breach of directors' duties.

❗ Don't be tempted to . . .

■ Forget to discuss the law on ratification. Some students tend to focus solely on directors' duties and ignore the issue of ratification.

■ Describe all the duties of directors in sections 170–178 of the Companies Act 2006. You should only apply those duties which are relevant to the question.

■ Only apply the statutory provisions in relation to directors' duties. Since the common law and equitable rules are still relevant, your answer must be supported by the application of case law.

✒ Question 6

'Traditionally the courts have taken a strict approach to the no-conflict and no-profit rules at common law. These rules are relaxed in the Companies Act 2006 with respect to the authorisation and ratification of a director's conflicts of interest.'

Evaluate the above statements.

Answer plan

→ Analyse the no-conflict and no-profit rules at common law and the strict judicial approach.

→ Examine the duty to avoid conflicts of interest in section 175 and the requirements for authorisation.

→ Discuss the issue in relation to ratification of directors' breach of duties in section 239.

→ Conclude whether these duties have been relaxed and if so, what potential problems will arise.

Diagram plan

| The no-conflict and no-profit rules at common law | → | Section 175, Companies Act 2006 | → | Authorisation | → | Ratification |

A printable version of this diagram plan is available from **www.pearsoned.co.uk/lawexpressqa**

Answer

Directors were under the duties to avoid conflicts of interests (no-conflict rule) and not to make secret profits from their positions (no secret profit rule) at common law. The courts traditionally have taken a strict approach in applying these rules. In **Bray v Ford** [1896] AC 44, Lord Herschell held that 'a person in a fiduciary position ... is not ... entitled to make a profit; he is not allowed to put himself in a position where his interest and duty conflict'. This approach aims to prevent directors from pursuing their own interests at the expense of their company. It also helps reduce the company's agency costs in monitoring the conduct of its directors (Grantham, 2003). Business activities, however, may be stifled if onerous requirements are imposed on directors. A flexible approach needs to be developed to suit the needs of modern businesses.[1]

The no-conflict and no-profit rules are now codified in the Companies Act 2006. Section 175(1) provides that a director must 'avoid a situation in which he has, or can have, a direct or indirect interest that conflicts, or possibly may conflict with the interests of the company'. This provision replaced the no-conflict rule where a director is liable to account for any profits made personally if his interests conflict with those of the companies. Its scope is broad in the sense that it covers not only actual conflict but also the possibility of conflict between the interests of a director and the interests of the company: **Boardman v Phipps** [1966] 3 All ER 721.[2] Section 175 also applies to the exploitation of any property, information or opportunity and it is immaterial whether the company could take advantage of the property, information or opportunity. This reflects the no-profit rule and mirrors the House of Lords' judgment in **Regal (Hastings) Ltd v Gulliver** [1942] 1 All ER 378 that the directors should return the profits to the company because they had obtained their profits by reason and in the course of the execution of their office as directors.[3] It made no difference whether the company itself was incapable of taking up the opportunity.[4] Similarly, in **Cook v Deeks** [1916] 1 AC 554, a corporate opportunity was regarded as a company's asset which might not be misappropriated by the directors. This rule equally applies to the situations where a director came across an opportunity personally instead of in his capacity as director: **Industrial Development Consultants Ltd v Cooley** [1972] 2 All ER 162. This strict approach could deter directors from pursuing their own interests at the expense of the company; nevertheless, it has been strongly criticised by Lowry and Edmunds (2000) as being too harsh on directors and unduly curbing entrepreneurial freedom to compete with companies.[5]

A few court decisions have shown support for a flexible approach. In **Island Export Finance Ltd v Umunna** [1986] BCLC 460,

---

[1] These sentences outline the main arguments. They also demonstrate your critical analysis of the statement by exploring the reasons behind the different approaches.

[2] You are analysing the scope of section 175 here instead of merely describing it. It will gain you more marks.

[3] This House of Lords' case should be included in your answer because of its significance.

[4] Some students have the wrong understanding that the no-conflict rule does not apply if the company was unable to take up the opportunity.

[5] This sentence shows your wider understanding of the legal issue by engaging your discussion with academic literature. It will make your answer stand out.

Hutchinson J held that it was plainly in the public interest that directors should be free to exploit an opportunity in a new position. In **Balston Ltd v Headline Filters Ltd** [1990] FSR 385, it was held that a director did not breach his fiduciary duty by setting up a business in competition with his former company after his resignation, even where the intention to commence business was formed prior to the resignation. This more relaxed approach may promote the business activities, but, at the same time, there is a greater risk of the company being exploited by its own directors.[6]

[6] An analysis of the recent flexible approach goes beyond a description of case law. It also demonstrates your analytical skills and adds more credit to your answer.

The Company Law Review (*Modern Company Law for a Competitive Economy: Completing the Structure,* 2000) expressed concerns that the common law on the no-conflict rule might fetter entrepreneurial and business activities. It recommended that the statutory statement of duties should only prevent the exploitation of business opportunities where there was a clear case for doing so. These concerns were echoed by the Company Law Reform – White Paper (2005, Para. 3.26) which emphasised that directors' duties should not impose impractical and onerous requirements which would stifle entrepreneurial activities.[7] These recommendations were carried out in the CA 2006 and the common law rules have been significantly altered by section 175(4) and (5) with regard to the board authorisation.[8]

[7] The reference to the Company Law Review and the White Paper shows your excellent knowledge of this subject and will impress your examiners.

[8] This sentence ties your answer back to the question in relation to the issue of authorisation.

The duty to avoid conflicts of interest is not infringed if the matter has been authorised by disinterested directors (s. 175(4)). There is no need to gain shareholders' approval prior to entering into transactions with third parties where the interests of directors conflict with those of the company. This can be regarded as one step towards taking a more relaxed view of the no-conflict and no-profit rules. Authorisation is effective only if the following two conditions in section 175(6) are met. First, the director in question or any other interested director is not counted towards the quorum and any requirement as to the quorum at the meeting at which the matter is considered is met. Second, the matter was agreed to without counting the votes by the director in question or any other interested director.

[9] Try to use a new paragraph when you are moving on to the next issue. It makes it easier for your examiners to follow your answer and allocate marks.

A director, who breached his duty under section 175, will not be liable to return the profits if the breach has been ratified by a company's resolution (s. 239(2)).[9] Where the resolution is proposed at a meeting, it is passed only if the necessary majority is obtained disregarding votes in favour of the resolution by the director (if he is a member of the company) and any member connected with him (s. 239(4)). The director or any such member is not prevented from attending, being counted towards the quorum and taking part in the meeting where the decision is considered. This approach helps to clarify the question as to whether directors can use their own votes for ratification. Section 252 defines what is meant by a person being connected with a director such as a director's family. Despite the company law reform, some problems still exist; for instance, shareholders may not make the right choice in exercising their votes for ratification at general meetings because of a lack of crucial information. Moreover, the distinction between wrongs which can or cannot be ratified has not been clarified in the Companies Act 2006.[10]

[10] The analysis of the problems of the current law on ratification demonstrates your excellent understanding.

In conclusion, it appears that the courts still take a strict approach towards the no-conflict and no-profit rules; nevertheless, such a rigorous approach is moderated by the potential authorisation and ratification of a breach of such duties. It is essential to strike a fine balance between imposing strict duties on directors and allowing some degree of entrepreneurial freedom.[11]

[11] The conclusion refers back to the question and summarises your main arguments. A succinct conclusion helps complete and strengthen your answer and will gain you more marks.

✓ Make your answer stand out

- Discuss the duty not to accept benefits from third parties in section 176 which forms part of the wider no-conflict duty.

- Analyse the self-dealing rules in sections 177 and 182. A director who is interested in a proposed or existing transaction with the company is required to declare the nature and extent of that interest to the other directors.

- Examine the different requirements for private companies (s. 175(5)(a)) and public companies (s. 175(5)(b)) in relation to authorisation.

- Compare the strict English approach to the corporate opportunity doctrine with the more relaxed and flexible approach in other common law jurisdictions such as Canada and Australia. The courts would consider the line of business of the particular company and the good faith of the director in question when determining whether or not a director has misappropriated a corporate opportunity: *Peso Silver Mines* v *Cropper* (1966) 58 DLR (2d) 1 and *Queensland Mines Ltd* v *Hudson* (1978) 52 ALJR 399.

- Make reference to academic opinions on the strict approach of the common law, such as: Prentice, D. (1974) The corporate opportunity doctrine. *MLR* 464; Worthington, S. (2000) Corporate governance: remedying and ratifying directors' breaches. *LQR* 638; Prentice, D. and Payne, J. (2004) The Corporate Opportunity Doctrine. 120 *LQR* 198; Lowry, J. (2008) Judicial Pragmatism: Directors' Duties and Post-resignation Conflicts of Duty. *JBL* 83.

> **❗ Don't be tempted to . . .**
>
> ■ Examine other duties of directors. This is an essay question on the no-conflict and no-profit rules and therefore the discussion should focus on this area of law.
>
> ■ Forget to discuss the law on authorisation and ratification, which are important parts of this question.
>
> ■ Write everything you know about section 175 and the issue of ratification. You should refer your discussion to the question throughout your answer, in particular, with regard to the traditional strict judicial approach and the move towards a more flexible approach.

❓ Question 7

Ethan, Joshua and Daniel are all directors of Quality Sofa & Bed Ltd. The company desperately needed to purchase a warehouse. At a board meeting, Daniel successfully persuaded Ethan and Joshua that one particular warehouse was perfect for the company and that it was worth £140,000. Ethan and Joshua later discovered that Daniel was the owner of the warehouse and it was only worth £120,000.

Daniel, who is a chartered accountant, is in charge of insuring the company's warehouse against burglary and fire. He signed an insurance form without checking the content of the policy. The warehouse was burgled and the company suffered a loss of £30,000. The insurance company claimed that the insurance policy did not cover burglary and therefore refused to pay.

Ethan and Joshua recently found out that Daniel offered a cheaper price to a company's client, Paul Ltd, from which he obtained a personal benefit of £3,000.

Advise Ethan and Joshua as to whether Daniel breached any of his duties as a director of Quality Sofa & Bed Ltd.

Answer plan

→ Analyse whether Daniel breached the duties in sections 177 and 182 in relation to the warehouse transaction.

→ Discuss whether Daniel breached the duty of care, skill and diligence in section 174 in relation to the insurance policy.

→ Examine whether Daniel breached the duty not to accept a bribe from a third party in section 176 in relation to the personal benefit of £3,000.

Diagram plan

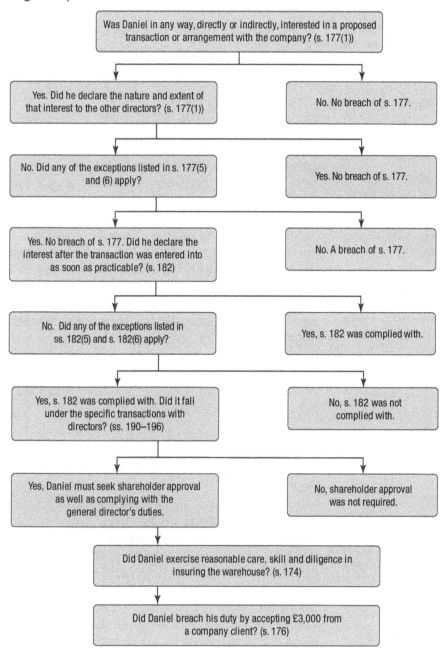

Was Daniel in any way, directly or indirectly, interested in a proposed transaction or arrangement with the company? (s. 177(1))

Yes. Did he declare the nature and extent of that interest to the other directors? (s. 177(1))

No. No breach of s. 177.

No. Did any of the exceptions listed in s. 177(5) and (6) apply?

Yes. No breach of s. 177.

Yes. No breach of s. 177. Did he declare the interest after the transaction was entered into as soon as practicable? (s. 182)

No. A breach of s. 177.

No. Did any of the exceptions listed in ss. 182(5) and s. 182(6) apply?

Yes, s. 182 was complied with.

Yes, s. 182 was complied with. Did it fall under the specific transactions with directors? (ss. 190–196)

No, s. 182 was not complied with.

Yes, Daniel must seek shareholder approval as well as complying with the general director's duties.

No, shareholder approval was not required.

Did Daniel exercise reasonable care, skill and diligence in insuring the warehouse? (s. 174)

Did Daniel breach his duty by accepting £3,000 from a company client? (s. 176)

A printable version of this diagram plan is available from **www.pearsoned.co.uk/lawexpressqa**

Answer

[1] Your introduction should identify the main legal issues that arise from the question. It should also show careful planning and a clear structure for the answer.

The legal issues here are whether Daniel, as a director, has breached any of his duties in the Companies Act 2006 in relation to the sale of warehouse, the insurance form and the acceptance of £3,000 from a company client.[1]

The warehouse transaction[2]

[2] The use of headings is useful in clearly distinguishing each part of the answer.

[3] Pay attention to the 'proposed' transaction. An existing transaction with the company is covered by section 182, instead of section 177.

[4] The reference to case law is essential as the general duties are interpreted and applied in the same way as common law rules (s. 170(4)).

If a director is in any way, directly or indirectly, interested in a *proposed* transaction[3] with the company, he must declare the nature and extent of that interest to the other directors before the transaction is entered into (s. 177). It reflects the self-dealing rules at common law. In **Aberdeen Railway Co v Blaikie Bros** (1854) 1 Macq 461, the chairman of its board of directors of the company entered into a contract for the purchase of equipment with a partnership of which he was also the managing partner. The company was entitled to set aside the contract and the director was held to account for any profit which he made on the conflicted transaction. In **Gwembe Valley Development Co Ltd v Koshy** [2004] 1 BCLC 131,[4] the company's managing director sold foreign currency to the company from another business which he controlled. There was a conflict between the director's personal interest and the interests of the company, as he acted on behalf of himself and the company at the same time in the transaction.

It appears that Daniel was directly interested in the transaction before it was entered into but he did not declare it to the other directors. He was therefore in breach of section 177 unless one of the following exceptions applied. First, a declaration is not needed if the director in question is not aware of the interest or where the director is not aware of the transaction in question (s. 177(5)). Secondly, a director need not declare an interest if it cannot reasonably be regarded as likely to give rise to a conflict of interest (s. 177(6)(a)), or the other directors are already aware of it (s. 177(6)(b)), or if it concerns terms of his service contract that have been or are to be considered by a meeting of the directors (s. 177(6)(c)).[5] It is evident that Daniel was aware of the warehouse transaction and the situation can reasonably be regarded as likely to give rise to a conflict of interest. Moreover, neither Ethan nor Joshua was aware of the conflict of interest at

[5] The discussion of the situations where a declaration is not required demonstrates your excellent understanding of section 177. It will make your answer stand out.

[6] It is important to apply the relevant law to the problem scenario because it shows that you have a good grasp of the previous case law which still applies now.

[7] The consequences for directors' breach of duties are often omitted in students' answers. You should point out that, despite the codification of directors' duties, the consequences for breach of duties are the same as the corresponding common law.

[8] Note that a brief declaration of an interest in the transaction is insufficient for the purpose of section 182. Both the nature and the extent of the interest must be declared.

[9] Section 182 is often ignored by students. Your sound knowledge of section 182 will impress your examiners.

[10] The discussion of the requirement of shareholder approval in the substantial property transactions will gain you more marks because it demonstrates your excellent understanding of directors' duties.

[11] The test for a substantial property transaction which is laid out in section 191 is often missing in students' answers.

the time of entering into the transaction; the transaction was not related to terms of Daniel's service contract. It is therefore argued that neither of the exceptions applied to this transaction and Daniel breached his duty in section 177.[6]

The consequences for non-disclosure under section 177 are the same as would apply if the corresponding common law rules applied (s. 178).[7] The contract with the company should be voidable and may be set aside by the company: *Movitex Ltd v Bulfield* [1988] BCLC 104. The company can hold the director to account for any profit which he has made from the transaction or to indemnify the company against any loss incurred.

Moreover, a director is also under the duty to disclose his interest in an existing transaction. Section 182 provides that a director, who is in any way, directly or indirectly, interested in a transaction that has been entered into by the company, must declare the nature and extent of that interest[8] to the other directors as soon as is reasonably practicable. After the transaction was entered into, Daniel did not disclose his interest in the transaction; thus, he breached his duty in section 182.[9]

It is argued that Daniel also breached the specific duties in relation to the substantial property transactions which are governed by sections 190–196.[10] A company may not enter into an arrangement to acquire a substantial non-cash asset from a director, unless it has been approved by a resolution of the members of the company (s. 190). The requirement of shareholder approval aims to provide shareholders with an opportunity to curb the potential abuse of power by directors. Shareholder approval is required only if, at the time the arrangement is entered into, the value of the asset exceeds 10 per cent of the company's asset value and is more than £5,000, or exceeds £100,000 (s. 191).[11] As the purchase price of the warehouse was £140,000, which exceeds £100,000, the warehouse transaction between Daniel and the company should be subject to shareholder approval. If shareholder approval was not obtained, the company should not be subject to any liability (s. 190(3)).

The insurance form

A director must exercise reasonable care, skill and diligence that would be exercised by a reasonably diligent person with (a) the general knowledge, skill and experience that may reasonably be expected of a person carrying out the functions in question and (b) the general knowledge, skill and experience that the director has (s. 174). The former sets an objective minimum standard whilst the latter raises the objective minimum standard in the light of the particular attributes of the director in question. In **Dorchester and Finance Co Ltd v Stebbing** [1989] BCLC 498, the non-executive directors, who were qualified accountants, had been negligent in signing blank cheques. Similarly, in **Re D'Jan of London Ltd** [1994] 1 BCLC 561, it was held that the director was negligent for signing an insurance proposal without checking its accuracy. The information provided in the form was incorrect and therefore the insurance company refused to pay when the company's premises burned down. Daniel, as an accountant with special knowledge in accounting, failed to exercise reasonable care, skill and diligence in checking the insurance policy carefully before signing; it can be argued therefore that he breached his duty in section 174.[12]

[12] This sentence refers back to the question in relation to the insurance form.

Acceptance of £3,000 from a third party

A director must not accept a benefit from a third party conferred by reason of his being a director or his doing anything as director (s. 176). This duty is not infringed if the acceptance of the benefit cannot reasonably be regarded as likely to give rise to a conflict of interest (s. 176(4)).[13] In the current scenario, Daniel accepted a bribe from a company's client, which could reasonably be regarded to give rise to a conflict of interest. He breached the duty in section 176 by accepting the benefit and exercising his powers in the interests of the third party rather than the company. It is concluded from the discussion of the above three circumstances that Daniel breached his duties under sections 177, 182, 190, 174 and 176 of the Companies Act 2006.[14]

[13] The discussion of section 176 is essential in your answer with regard to the acceptance of a bribe from a company client.

[14] The conclusion addresses the specific issues on directors' duties in relation to the warehouse transaction, the insurance form and the acceptance of a bribe.

✓ **Make your answer stand out**

■ Examine the consequences of the non-compliance with section 182. A director who has failed to comply with the statutory duty of disclosure under section 182 has committed an offence and, on conviction on indictment, is liable to a fine (s. 183). The company, however, does not have a separate claim for damages against this director for non-compliance with section 182: *Coleman Taymar Ltd* v *Oakes* [2001] 2 BCLC 749.

■ Discuss Daniel's breach of the duty to avoid conflicts of interest (s. 175) in relation to the acceptance of a bribe from a third party.

■ Consider Daniel's breach of duty in section 172 to promote the success of the company in relation to all of the three circumstances.

! **Don't be tempted to . . .**

■ Get confused with the duty to avoid conflicts of interest (s. 175) and the duty to declare interests with the transactions with the company (s. 177). They are separate duties in the Companies Act 2006. The distinct situation where a director is interested in a proposed transaction with the company is governed by section 177, not section 175.

■ Discuss all the legal issues at the same time. You should clearly structure your answer and address one legal issue in full before moving on to the next one.

Question 8

Steve and Mr and Mrs Walker were directors in London Hairdressing Ltd. In May 2009, the Walkers secretly sold two of the company's cars which were worth £50,000 to their son, Jason, for £6,000. The company went into insolvent liquidation in October 2010.

Advise Mr and Mrs Walker as to whether this transaction was valid and whether they breached any of their fiduciary duties.

Answer plan

→ Analyse whether the Walkers breached their fiduciary duties under sections 172, 177 and 182 of the CA 2006.

→ Discuss whether the sale of cars was considered as substantial property transaction: sections 190–196, CA 2006.

→ Examine whether the sale of cars to Jason was a transaction at an undervalue: section 238, IA 1986.

➡ Consider that the court may make an order in section 423 of the IA 1986 in relation to the transaction at an undervalue.

➡ Evaluate the summary remedy against delinquent directors according to section 212 of the IA 1986.

Diagram plan

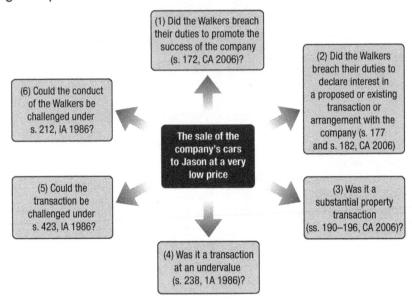

(1) Did the Walkers breach their duties to promote the success of the company (s. 172, CA 2006)?

(2) Did the Walkers breach their duties to declare interest in a proposed or existing transaction or arrangement with the company (s. 177 and s. 182, CA 2006)

The sale of the company's cars to Jason at a very low price

(6) Could the conduct of the Walkers be challenged under s. 212, IA 1986?

(5) Could the transaction be challenged under s. 423, IA 1986?

(3) Was it a substantial property transaction (ss. 190–196, CA 2006)?

(4) Was it a transaction at an undervalue (s. 238, 1A 1986)?

A printable version of this diagram plan is available from **www.pearsoned.co.uk/lawexpressqa**

Answer

[1] This sentence shows that you are engaging with the problem question.

[2] The subjective nature of this duty is the key feature of section 172 and therefore it should be discussed and applied to the problem scenario. You can also make reference to the objective test for the duty to act *bona fide* at common law: *Charterbridge Corp Ltd* v *Lloyds Bank Ltd* [1970] Ch 62.

In relation to the sale of the company's assets at an unreasonably low price, it can be argued that the Walkers, as directors of the company, breached their fiduciary duties in sections 172, 177 and 182 of the Companies Act 2006.[1] Section 172 requires that a director act in the way he considers, in good faith, would be most likely to promote the success of the company for the benefit of its members as a whole. In particular, a director is required to consider or act in the interests of creditors of the company in certain circumstances (s. 172(3)). It is very difficult, however, to prove that the Walkers breached this duty because of its subjective nature: *Regentcrest plc* v *Cohen* [2001] 2 BCLC 80).[2]

[3] You should distinguish between the duties under sections 177 and 182. Section 177 applies to the proposed transaction whilst section 182 applies to an existing transaction which has already been entered into by the company. Students are often not aware of this distinction.

[4] The reference to case law is essential as the general duties are interpreted and applied in the same way as the common law rules (s. 170(4)).

[5] You should clearly state the test for substantial property transaction, which is important for an application of section 190. You will lose some marks if this test is not included in your answer.

[6] It should be noted that this legal issue in relation to the transaction at an undervalue arises because London Hairdressing Ltd went into liquidation; otherwise, section 238 would not apply.

[7] This is one of the key requirements in section 238. If the transaction was entered into outside the two-year limit, it cannot be challenged as a transaction at undervalue under this section. You should also pay attention to the different time requirements for connected and unconnected persons.

Moreover, it can be argued that the Walkers breached their duties under sections 177 and 182 because of the failure to disclose their interest in the transaction to the other director, Steve. A director must declare the nature and extent of that interest to the other directors before the transaction is entered into, if he is in any way, directly or indirectly, interested in a *proposed* transaction[3] with the company (s. 177) or in an existing transaction with the company (s. 182). These duties reflect the self-dealing rules at common law. In **Aberdeen Rly Co v Blaikie Bros** (1854) 1 Macq 461,[4] the chairman of its board of directors of the company entered into a contract for the purchase of equipment with a partnership of which he was also the managing partner. The company was entitled to set aside the contract and the director was held to account for any profit which he made on the conflicted transaction.

A company may not enter into an arrangement under which a director of the company, or a person connected with him, acquires from the company (directly or indirectly) a substantial non-cash asset unless it has been approved by a resolution of the members of the company (s. 190, CA 2006). Shareholder approval is required only if, at the time the arrangement is entered into, the value of the asset exceeds 10 per cent of the company's asset value and is more than £5,000, or exceeds £100,000 (s. 191).[5] Jason was connected with the Walkers and the value of cars exceeded £5,000; the car transaction therefore should be subject to shareholder approval if the value was more than 10 per cent of the company's asset value in May 2009.

As the company went into insolvent liquidation, the transaction can be challenged by a liquidator if it was previously entered into by the company at an undervalue (s. 238, Insolvency Act 1986).[6] A transaction at an undervalue arises if the company enters into a transaction with that person on terms that provide no consideration for the company, or for a consideration which is significantly less than that provided by the company (s. 238(4), IA 1986). The court may make an order if the company has entered into a transaction with a connected person at an undervalue within two years (six months for unconnected persons) ending with the onset of insolvency.[7] Moreover, the transaction must have been entered into when the company was unable to pay its debts or it becomes unable to pay its debts in consequence of the transaction (s. 240(2), IA 1986). This requirement is presumed to be satisfied when the transaction was entered into by a company with a connected person such as family members of directors. The court shall make such order as it thinks fit for restoring the position to what it would have been if the company had not entered into that transaction (s. 238(3)). Such order shall not be made if the court is satisfied both that the company entered into the transaction in good faith and for the purpose of carrying on its business, and that there were reasonable grounds for believing that the transaction would benefit the company (s. 238(5)).[8]

[8] An analysis of the specific circumstances where a transaction is not caught by section 238 will gain you more marks.

The company's cars were sold to Jason, who was considered as a connected person, within two years ending with the onset of insolvency. It can be presumed, therefore, that the transaction was entered into when the company was unable to pay its debts or it became unable to pay its debts as a consequence of this transaction. Moreover, the transaction was made for a consideration which was significantly less than the value of the cars. It is unlikely that the directors could convince the court that the transaction was entered into in good faith or that the transaction would benefit the company. The court will order Jason to make payment to the liquidator in respect of benefits received by him from the company: *Re Paramount Airways Ltd* [1992] 3 All ER 1.[9]

[9] This sentence adds more credit to your answer because it applies the law to the question rather than simply stating the law.

[10] Some students are not aware of the provision in section 423. As the problem question is essentially concerned with a transaction at an undervalue, your mark will be adversely affected if the discussion of section 423 is omitted in your answer.

The court may also make an order under section 423, IA 1986 in relation to the transaction at an undervalue.[10] If the court is satisfied that the transaction was entered into with the purpose of putting assets beyond the reach of the creditors or of prejudicing the interests of the creditors, the court may make such order as it thinks fit for restoring the position to what it would have been if the transaction had not been entered into, and protecting the interests of persons who are victims of the transaction. Section 423 covers a broader range of circumstances than section 238: for instance, it applies even when the company is not in liquidation or administration; there is no time limit in relation to the transaction in section 423, unlike the two-year limit in section 238.[11]

[11] The comparison between sections 238 and 423 shows your excellent understanding with regard to transactions at an undervalue. It will make your answer stand out from those which only describe these two provisions.

[12] The misfeasance procedure in section 212 is another power that the liquidator may exercise against directors. It is another ground on which the conduct of the Walkers may be challenged and therefore it should be included in a sound answer.

The liquidator may also apply to the court according to section 212 of the IA 1986, which provides a summary remedy against delinquent directors.[12] The court may examine the conduct of the Walkers, if, in the course of the winding up of a company, it appears that they have misapplied or retained, or become accountable for, any money or other property of the company, or been guilty of any misfeasance or breach of any fiduciary or other duty in relation to the company. As such, the court may compel the Walkers to repay the money or restore property or to make contribution to the company's assets as the court thinks just.

 Make your answer stand out

- Discuss that the Walkers may be liable for fraudulent trading under section 213 of the IA 1986. If, in the course of the winding up of a company, it appears that the business of the company has been carried on with intent to defraud creditors or for any fraudulent purpose, the court may declare that any persons who were knowingly parties to the carrying on of the business are to be liable to make such contributions (if any) to the company's assets as the court thinks proper.

- Consider that the Walkers may be held liable for wrongful trading under section 214 of the IA 1986. If at some time before the company was wound up, they knew or ought to have concluded that there was no reasonable prospect that the company would avoid going into insolvent liquidation. The court, on the application of the liquidator, may declare that the directors are liable to make such contribution (if any) to the company's assets as the court thinks proper. It shall not make a declaration if it is satisfied that the director took every step to minimise the potential loss to the company's creditors as he ought to have taken (s. 214(3)): *Re Brian D Pierson Ltd* [2001] 1 BCLC 275.

- Point out that the Walkers may be disqualified under section 6 of the Company Directors Disqualification Act 1986 if the court is satisfied that their conduct as directors make them unfit to be concerned in the management of a company.

Don't be tempted to . . .

- Describe directors' general duties in sections 170–177 of the CA 2006. You should only discuss the duties which are relevant to this question.

- Forget to apply the provisions in relation to the transaction at an undervalue in section 238, IA 1986. You should show your understanding of the implications which arise from the winding up of London Hairdressing Ltd.

- Apply the director's duty to avoid conflicts of interest in section 175, CA 2006. You should understand that section 175 does not apply to a conflict of interest arising in relation to a transaction or arrangement with the company (s. 175(3)). Such transaction or arrangement is governed by sections 177 and 182.

www.pearsoned.co.uk/lawexpressqa

 Go online to access more revision support including additional essay and problem questions with diagram plans, You be the marker questions, and download all diagrams from the book.

Corporate
governance

How this topic may come up in exams

Corporate governance is mainly concerned with public companies and it is a popular topic, particularly in light of the recent financial crisis. Students often struggle with the breadth of information. You are expected to show a good knowledge of the basic corporate governance theories, such as the agency theory, shareholder primacy and stakeholder theory. The legal framework on corporate governance is frequently examined in relation to the board structure, non-executive directors, directors' remuneration and the increasingly important role of institutional shareholders. Your understanding of the UK Corporate Governance Code and its 'comply or explain' approach may also be tested. This topic overlaps with directors' duties and shareholders' remedies. As corporate governance is not covered in all company law courses, you are advised to check your syllabus before revising.

■ Before you begin

It's a good idea to consider the following key themes of corporate governance before tackling a question on this topic.

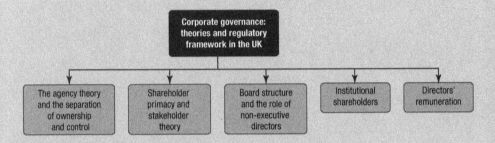

A printable version of this diagram is available from **www.pearsoned.co.uk/lawexpressqa**

 **Question 1**

'Shareholders are more likely to lose money because the relevant people in the firm are not up to the mark than merely because they are "agents" bent on pursuing their own interests at the expense of others' (Clarkham, J. and Simpson, A. (1999) *Fair Shares: The Future of Shareholder Power and Responsibility*. Oxford: Oxford University Press).

Undertake a critical discussion of the above statement in relation to the legal and regulatory framework in the United Kingdom in addressing the agency problems.

Answer plan

➔ Discuss the separation of ownership and control in large public companies.

➔ Explain the agency theory and agency costs.

➔ Analyse the statutory framework of directors' duties and their enforcement.

➔ Examine the self-regulatory code on corporate governance, in particular, the UK Corporate Governance Code ('The Code') and the 'comply or explain' approach.

Diagram plan

The separation of ownership and control ⟩ The agency problems and agency costs ⟩ The legal and regulatory framework: the Companies Act 2006 and the UK Corporate Governance Code

A printable version of this diagram plan is available from **www.pearsoned.co.uk/lawexpressqa**

Answer

[1] You should identify the key legal issues which arise in the question. It gives your examiners a good impression that you know where your answer is going.

[2] Make sure you know who are the agents and principals. Some students get confused and make the mistake of stating that shareholders are the agents.

This question requires a discussion of the agency problems in corporate governance and the legal and regulatory framework in addressing them.[1] Corporate governance is defined in the Cadbury Report 1992 as the system by which a company is directed and controlled. A balanced relationship between the board of directors and shareholders is essential for good corporate governance.

The agency theory identifies the agency relationship between directors and shareholders: directors are the agents and shareholders are the principals.[2] Problems may arise when the agents do not act in the best interests of the principals: for example, the agents may misuse their power or take inappropriate risks when pursuing the principals' interests. When the agents have access to more information than the principals, the latter may suffer from information asymmetry. These problems lead to the agency costs, which refer to the costs resulting from directors misusing their positions, as well as the costs of monitoring and disciplining them to ensure that they do not act in their own interests.

[3] The reference to Adam Smith and his work shows your sound knowledge. It is worth learning the title of his book.

The agency problems are more acute in large companies where there is a separation of ownership and control. Adam Smith in *The Wealth of Nations* (1776)[3] made for the first time the observation that the directors of joint stock companies 'being the managers rather of other people's money than of their own, it cannot well be expected that they should watch over it with the same anxious vigilance [as if it were their own]'.[4] In order to expand, companies need to gain capital by issuing more shares to a diverse number of shareholders. This leads to a dilution of shareholders' powers, and the controlling power is effectively vested in the majority shareholders. Later, Berle and Means, in *The Modern Corporation and Private Property* (1932),[5] identified the problem caused by the separation of ownership and control in US companies in the 1930s. They discovered that many of the large companies had such widely dispersed share ownership that no individual shareholder had an interest in controlling management. The board of directors, instead of shareholders, was therefore able to exert real control over the company. There was a great danger that directors would be free to run the company for their own benefit, rather than on behalf of the shareholders.

[4] If you cannot remember the exact quotation, try to paraphrase it by stating that 'as directors are managing other people's money, they may not watch over it vigilantly as if it were their own'.

[5] This is another classic work on the separation of ownership and control and the agency problems. The reference to Berle and Means will gain you more marks.

[6] This sentence demonstrates your sound knowledge of corporate governance. The majority of students have a general understanding of the separation of ownership and control, but may wrongly believe that it applies to all types of companies in every country.

It should be noted that the separation of ownership and control is mostly applicable to the companies in the United States and the United Kingdom but not to those in many other countries.[6] As highlighted by La Porta *et al.* (1999), the most common form of ownership around the globe is the family firm with controlling shareholders, rather than a broad and dispersed shareholding. In addition, institutional shareholders, such as pension funds and insurance companies, hold a large number of shares in recent years. As a consequence, shareholdings in some major companies are no longer widely dispersed and the rise of institutional shareholders may to some extent mitigate the agency costs.[7]

[7] The discussion of the influence of institutional shareholders will make your answer stand out because it shows your wider understanding of the corporate governance issues.

In order to address the agency problems and reduce agency costs, it is important to ensure that directors do not abuse their power.

[8] This sentence summarises
the recent reforms on
directors' duties and leads
to the detailed discussion of
directors' duties in the next
few paragraphs.

[9] Although the reference
to the section number is
not essential, it shows
your precise knowledge on
directors' duties and will add
more credit to your answer.

[10] The previous case law
on directors' duties is
still relevant despite the
codification in the Companies
Act 2006. A lack of reference
to case law will negatively
affect your marks.

[11] This is one of the key
aspects of section 172 and
it is also a significant theory
in corporate governance. You
will lose some marks if it is
not included in your answer.

Directors in both private and public companies are subject to various duties in the Companies Act 2006. Directors in listed companies must also state whether The Code is complied with as required by the Listing Rules.

A director owes fiduciary duties to the company. The duties at common law and in equitable rules are now codified in the Companies Act 2006 (ss. 170–177).[8] A director must act in accordance with the company's constitution and exercise his powers for proper purposes (s. 171)[9]: **Hogg v Cramphorn** [1967] Ch 254.[10] He must also act in the way he considers, in good faith, would be most likely to promote the success of the company for the benefit of its members as a whole (s. 172): **Re Smith & Fawcett** [1942] 1 All ER 542. In doing so, he must also have regard to other factors, such as the likely consequences of any decision in the long term, the interests of the company's employees, the impact on the community and environment, and the need for the company to act fairly as between members. Section 172 introduces the enlightened shareholder value,[11] whereby a company should be run not only to generate maximum wealth for shareholders but also to take a properly balanced view of the wider implications of decisions over time.

A director is required to exercise independent judgement (s. 173): **Fulham Football Club and Others v Cabra Estates plc** [1994] 1 BCLC 363. He must exercise reasonable care, skill and diligence in carrying out his functions (s. 174): **Dorchester Finance Co Ltd v Stebbing** [1989] BCLC 498. The subjective and objective tests at common law are also adopted. A director must avoid a situation in which he has a direct or indirect interest that conflicts with the interests of the company (s. 175): **Regal (Hastings) Ltd v Gulliver** [1942] 1 All ER 378. He is prohibited from accepting a benefit from a third party conferred by reason of him being a director (s. 176). If he is in any way interested in a proposed transaction or arrangement with the company, he must declare the nature and extent of any interest to other directors (s. 177): **Aberdeen Railway Ltd v Blaikie** (1854) 1 Macq 461.

If a director breaches any of these duties, the company is the proper claimant to sue him: **Foss v Harbottle** (1843) 67 ER 189. Shareholders may apply for the court's permission to bring a statutory derivative action and challenge directors' breach of duties (ss. 260–263). Shareholders may also bring an unfair prejudice

[12] This sentence briefly summarises the main principles which are set out in The Code. It shows your sound knowledge of The Code and will add more credit to your answer.

[13] This is the distinctive feature of the Combined Code compared to the corporate governance in other countries. An explanation of the 'comply or explain' approach must be included in a good answer.

[14] The reference to the current events and the suggestions for future reforms in your conclusion will earn you more marks.

petition if their interests have been unfairly prejudiced by the company's affairs (s. 994).

In addition to their statutory duties, directors in listed companies need to consider the UK Corporate Governance Code 2014 which consists of principles of good governance in relation to leadership, effectiveness, accountability, remuneration and relations with share-holders.[12] It adopts the 'comply or explain' principle,[13] whereby the board of a listed company is required by the Listing Rules to include a statement in its annual financial report of whether it has complied with The Code. If any provision of The Code has not been complied with, the reasons for non-compliance must be specified.

It can be argued that the company performance and shareholders' interests may be undermined if there is insufficient monitoring of directors' conduct. The recent financial crisis and corporate scandals indicate that the current legal and regulatory framework needs strengthening in order to sufficiently address the agency problems and ensure that directors act in the best interests of the company.[14]

 Make your answer stand out

- Assess the enlightened shareholder value in more detail.
- Evaluate in more detail the main principles in the UK Corporate Governance Code.
- Examine the corporate governance reports such as the Cadbury Report 1992, Greenbury Report 1995, Hampel Report 1998, Turnbull Report 1999, Myners Report 2001, Higgs Report 2003 and Smith Report 2003.
- Include more academic opinions in relation to the agency theory: Clark, T. (2004) *Theories of Corporate Governance*. Abingdon: Routledge: 55–78; Mallin, C. (2012) *Corporate Governance*, 4th edn. Oxford: Oxford University Press: 16–17.

Don't be tempted to . . .

- Ignore the enforcement of directors' duties by the company or shareholders. It is a powerful way to reduce the agency costs and therefore should be included in a good answer.
- Forget to discuss The UK Corporate Governance Code. It is a very influential corporate governance code for listed companies and therefore should not be omitted in your answer.

🔷 Question 2

'In light of the recent financial crisis, it is apparent that the UK Corporate Governance Code (The Code) is insufficient to promote good corporate governance in the United Kingdom. It is time to adopt a more robust approach similar to that in the United States.'

Critically analyse the above statement in relation to the development of The Code in the United Kingdom. Would the corporate governance in the United Kingdom be improved by following the approach of the Sarbanes–Oxley Act?

Answer plan

➡ Discuss the development of The Code by reference to the corporate governance reports, in particular, the Cadbury Report 1992, Greenbury Report 1995 and Hampel Report 1998.

➡ Evaluate the effect of the 'comply or explain' approach in The Code.

➡ Analyse the key provisions of the Sarbanes–Oxley Act.

➡ Examine the advantages and disadvantages of the mandatory approach in the United States.

Diagram plan

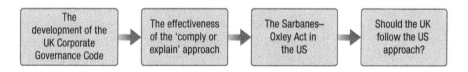

| The development of the UK Corporate Governance Code | ➡ | The effectiveness of the 'comply or explain' approach | ➡ | The Sarbanes–Oxley Act in the US | ➡ | Should the UK follow the US approach? |

A printable version of this diagram plan is available from **www.pearsoned.co.uk/lawexpressqa**

Answer

[1] A succinct introduction immediately gives examiners a good impression that your answer is well organised.

[2] A few examples of the corporate scandals show your detailed knowledge and will add more credit to your answer.

[3] This sentence justifies the discussion of the Cadbury Report and other corporate governance reports in your answer.

This question requires a critical evaluation of the historical development of The Code, the effectiveness of its 'comply or explain' approach and whether the mandatory approach to corporate governance in the United States should be adopted in the United Kingdom.[1]

In response to various corporate scandals such as Mirror Group Newspapers, Coloroll and Polly Peck,[2] the Cadbury Committee was set up to report into financial aspects of corporate governance. The Cadbury Report 1992 stresses the division of responsibilities of the board and the importance of non-executive directors. Its recommendations and those of subsequent reports form the framework for corporate governance in the United Kingdom.[3]

The first Combined Code 1998 drew upon the recommendations of the Cadbury, Greenbury and Hampel Reports. The Cadbury Report created The Code of Best Practice and introduced the philosophy of 'comply or explain'. It is adopted by the London Stock Exchange, which requires that the boards of all listed companies comply with The Code but, if they cannot comply with any particular aspect of it, they should explain their reasons for non-compliance. This approach is based on the assumption that the market will monitor compliance with The Code and will either penalise non-compliance through lowering share prices or accept that non-compliance is justified in the circumstances.[4] The disclosure provides investors with detailed information on a company's non-compliance and enables them to decide whether non-compliance is justified. It can be an influential factor in making their investment decisions. The Combined Code is a self-regulatory code and therefore no legal sanction will arise for non-compliance with it. Failure to include it in the company's annual report, however, leads to penalties for non-compliance with the Listing Rules.[5]

The Greenbury Report 1995 focuses on strengthening accountability and enhancing the performance of directors. It recommends setting up a remuneration committee comprising independent non-executive directors and linking rewards of directors to the performance of both the company and individual directors. The Hampel Report 1998 endorses the majority of the findings of both the Cadbury and the Greenbury Reports and goes further by considering the relationships of the company with stakeholder constituencies. It states that 'the directors as a board are responsible for relations with stakeholders; but they are accountable to the shareholders'.[6]

The application and interpretation of different aspects of the Combined Code are addressed in various reports.[7] The Turnbull Report 1999 is concerned with the implementation of the internal control requirements in The Code. It requires the board to periodically assess the control measures in place and report on them annually. The Myners Report 2001 promotes shareholder activism and encourages institutional investors to be more proactive. The Higgs Report 2003 focuses on the independence of the non-executive director whilst the Smith Report 2003 considers the functions of the audit committee.

The Combined Code has been constantly revised and the current version is the UK Corporate Governance Code 2014.[8] It sets out the

[4] This sentence explains the rationale of the 'comply or explain' approach. It will gain you more marks than simply explaining what the approach means.

[5] Although no penalties are imposed for non-compliance of The Code itself, you should understand that a failure to include a statement in the company's annual report breaches the Listing Rules. You may lose marks if this issue is not addressed.

[6] A short quotation like this is easy to remember. It may impress your examiners by showing such detailed knowledge of the Hampel Report.

[7] This sentence shows your good understanding of the relationship between the Combined Code and other corporate governance reports.

[8] The reference to the UK Corporate Governance Code 2010 demonstrates your up-to-date knowledge and will make your answer stand out.

[9] Although this sentence seems to repeat the previous explanation of the 'comply or explain' approach, it does reaffirm its application in the most recent Code and therefore emphasises the importance of this approach.

standards of good practice in relation to issues such as leadership, effectiveness, accountability, remuneration and relations with shareholders. It adopts the 'comply or explain' principle and requires listed companies, in their annual reports and accounts to report on how they apply the principles, and confirm that they comply with The Code's provisions or, where they do not, provide an explanation.[9] The effectiveness of The Code as a corporate governance control mechanism has been widely debated. It has been criticised as a purely cosmetic box-ticking exercise that companies adhere to only in name. Although the scale of compliance has increased over time, there remains a significant incidence of non-compliance. The disclosures of non-compliance made by companies are often extremely brief and uninformative; this may defeat the purpose of the 'comply or explain' approach. Moreover, the research by Dedman (2002) shows

[10] This sentence echoes the statement in the question and shows that you are engaging with the question.

that there is no clear link between compliance with The Code and superior performance of the company. It is argued, therefore, that corporate governance issues are too important to be left to The Code and the soft obligations should be replaced by statutes following the mandatory approach to corporate governance in the United States.[10]

[11] The Enron scandal should be referred to in your answer because it was so influential in leading to the passing of the Sarbanes–Oxley Act.

In response to major corporate and accounting scandals such as Enron[11] and Worldcom, the Sarbanes–Oxley Act was passed in 2002 in the United States in order to strengthen corporate governance and restore investor confidence. It establishes enhanced standards for boards and management of public companies. Compliance with the 2002 Act is mandatory.[12] Section 302 requires that the CEO and CFO of a company that files reports must certify in each annual and quarterly report. Section 906 requires that every periodic report containing financial statements must be accompanied by written statements by the company's CEO and CFO. The statements must certify that they have reviewed the report, the information contained in the report fairly presents the financial condition of the company, and the report does not contain any untrue statements or omissions of material facts. Failure to comply with these provisions is a criminal offence. Although the possibility of criminal sanctions for directors may deter their misuse of power, it is difficult to attract international companies to list in the United States. In fact, the extra costs for compliance with the Sarbanes–Oxley Act have led to some listed companies delisting in the United States.[13]

[12] This sentence demonstrates the sharp contrast between the approach in the United States and the voluntary approach of The Code in the United Kingdom.

[13] These sentences analyse the problems associated with implementing the Sarbanes–Oxley Act. It will add more credit to your answer than simply describing the main sections of this Act.

The legislative approach in the United States requires higher standards of transparency, direct accountability on the part of the CEO and a greater degree of independence in the boardroom. The rigidity of this legislative approach, however, is costly to implement and may not foster trust or improve corporate performance. By comparison, the 'comply or explain' approach in the United Kingdom has the advantage of flexibility and discretion. It can be more easily amended and less administratively burdensome than legislation. Moreover, it is impossible to adopt a 'one size fits all' approach to corporate governance codes, primarily because companies differ in terms of size and structure. The Company Law Review (*Completing the Structure*, 2000) considered the high level of compliance with The Code and found no support for putting it on a statutory basis. It concludes that The Code strengthens awareness of the importance of an effective board structure and creates a climate of openness and accountabilities. It is therefore preferable that The Code should remain on a non-statutory basis.

✓ Make your answer stand out

- Discuss in more detail the main principles in the UK Corporate Governance Code 2014.
- Evaluate in more detail the effect of the Sarbanes–Oxley Act in the United States.
- Make reference to more academic opinions on the effectiveness of The Code: Abarca, M.L. de E. (2004) The need for substantive regulation on investor protection and corporate governance in Europe: does Europe need a Sarbanes–Oxley? *Journal of International Banking Law and Regulation* 419; MacNeil, I. and Li, X. (2006) "Comply or explain", market discipline and non-compliance with the Combined. *Corporate Governance* 486.

! Don't be tempted to . . .

- Apply The Code to all types of companies. Although private companies are encouraged to follow its recommendations, The Code only applies to listed companies which are public companies listed on the London Stock Exchange.
- Only discuss the old versions of The Code. You should also make reference to the latest Code – the UK Corporate Governance Code 2014.
- Only focus on The Code. You should also discuss the corporate governance reports which are important for the development of The Code.
- Misunderstand the 'comply *or* explain' approach. Some students tend to make the mistake by writing 'comply *and* explain'.

📝 Question 3

'Effective and robust boards are an essential feature of successful companies. Within the unitary board, non-executive directors have a crucial part to play' (*Review of the role and effectiveness of non-executive directors* (Higgs Review 2003, Para. 1.1)).

Discuss the role and effectiveness of non-executive directors in corporate governance by reference to the Higgs Review 2003 and the UK Corporate Governance Code 2014 (The Code).

Answer plan

➡ Discuss the board structure and the role of the board.

➡ Consider the role of non-executive directors by reference to The Code and the Higgs Review.

➡ Examine the requirements for independent non-executive directors.

➡ Analyse the appointment procedure and the required number of non-executive directors.

➡ Evaluate whether the existence of non-executive directors is effective in promoting good corporate governance.

Diagram plan

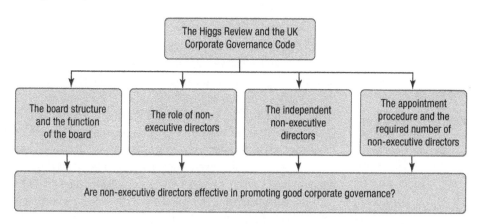

A printable version of this diagram plan is available from **www.pearsoned.co.uk/lawexpressqa**

[1] This sentence identifies the key issues. Try to interpret the question in your own words and avoid repeating the question. It shows that you understand what this question is about.

Answer

This question requires an evaluation of the role of non-executive directors, in particular, whether they are effective in promoting good corporate governance and preventing corporate scandals.[1]

² The reference to the current
version of The Code shows
your up-to-date knowledge
and will add more credit to
your answer.

³ The reference to the
general management clause
emphasises the important role
of the board of directors.

⁴ Some students have only a
vague understanding of the
functions of non-executive
directors. The explanation
of the differences between
executive and non-executive
directors is essential for a
good answer because it shows
that you understand what
non-executive directors do.

⁵ This sentence relates
the corporate governance
issues to directors' duties
in the Companies Act
2006. It shows your sound
understanding of the legal
framework that applies to
non-executive directors.

⁶ If you cannot remember
the exact numbering of
the paragraph, a general
reference to the Higgs Review
should suffice.

⁷ This sentence explains the
'comply or explain' approach,
which is the basis of The
Code. You will lose some
marks if it is omitted in your
answer.

The role of non-executive directors has been subject to detailed consideration in the UK Corporate Governance Code 2014[2] and the Higgs Review 2003.

The board of directors plays an extremely important role in good corporate governance because it is effectively in charge of the management of the company. The general management clause in the Model Articles (Art. 3) states that subject to the articles, the directors are responsible for the management of the company's business, for which purpose they may exercise all the powers of the company.[3] The board consists of executive and non-executive directors. Executive directors are concerned with the actual management of the company. Non-executive directors do not have executive management responsibilities but are concerned with general management policy and the monitoring of executive directors.[4] Both executive and non-executive directors are all required to act to promote the success of the company and owe the same duties to the company (ss. 170–177, Companies Act 2006).[5] Such a unitary board structure brings the benefit of the executive knowledge within the board and the wider experience brought by non-executive directors (Higgs Review, Para. 4.2[6]).

The Code sets out standards of good practice in relation to board leadership and effectiveness, remuneration, accountability and relations with shareholders. It is a voluntary code and adopts the 'comply or explain' approach. Listed companies are required to report on how they have applied the main principles of The Code, and either to confirm that they have complied with it or, if they have not complied, to provide an explanation.[7] The Code recommends that every company should be headed by an effective board which is collectively responsible for the long-term success of the company. The board should include an appropriate combination of executive and non-executive directors so that not any individual or small group of individuals dominates the board's decision taking. It should also have the appropriate balance of skills, experience, independence and knowledge of the company to enable them to discharge their respective duties and responsibilities effectively.

The Higgs Review 2003 emphasises the essential role of non-executive directors in monitoring executive activity and contributing to the development of strategy (Para. 6.1). It argues that the Combined Code 1998[8] offered little guidance on the role of non-executive directors and the lack of clarity affected their performance in corporate governance. It therefore suggests that the non-executive directors' powers and responsibilities for monitoring should be clarified. This recommendation is embodied in The Code: for instance, non-executive directors should constructively challenge and help develop proposals on company strategy as part of their role as members of a unitary board (The Code, A.4).[9] With respect to the appointment procedure, non-executives should be selected through a formal process and be appointed for specific terms. Any term beyond six years should be subject to particularly rigorous review and should take into account the need for progressive refreshing of the board (The Code, B.2.3).

Non-executive directors play a significant role in monitoring executive activity and contributing to the development of strategy (Higgs Review, Para. 6.1). They not only play a supervisory role in controlling conflicts of interest, but also provide a broader view and bring a fresh perspective to strategic matters. To ensure that they fulfil their roles, non-executive directors should be capable of providing an independent and impartial view of the board's considerations and challenging or questioning the executive decisions.[10] The presence of independent non-executive directors on the board may mitigate the agency costs through their mutual monitoring functions.

The Combined Code 1998 required the majority of non-executive directors to be independent of management; however, the board was left to determine whether a non-executive director was independent and there was little guidance to the companies as to what the independence should entail. In order to address this problem, the Higgs Review recommends that the independence should be clearly defined and it is desirable if a definition is provided in The Code to address relationships or circumstances that would affect the directors' independence. A checklist which identifies the level of independence was put forward in the Higgs Review and later incorporated into The Code.

The Code (B.1.2) recommends that at least half of the members of the board, excluding the chairman, should be independent non-executive directors.[11] A smaller company should have at least two independent non-executive directors. The board is now required to identify in the annual report each non-executive director it considers to be independent. It should determine whether the director is independent in character and judgement and whether there are relationships or circumstances which are likely to affect the director's judgement. Moreover, it should state its reasons if it determines that a director is independent notwithstanding the existence of relationships or circumstances which may appear relevant to its determination. For instance, if the director has been an employee of the company within the last five years; or has had, within the last three years, a material business relationship with the company; or has received or receives additional remuneration from the company apart from a director's fee; or has close family ties with any of the company's advisers, directors or senior employees; or holds cross-directorships or has significant links with other directors through involvement in other companies or bodies; represents a significant shareholder (The Code, B.1.1). Although it is imprac-

[12] This sentence demonstrates your analytical skills by examining the advantages of the checklist approach. It will make your answer stand out from those which only describe the checklist.

tical comprehensively to list all possible criteria in defining what independence really means, this checklist approach provides some guidance on developing best practice and increasing the accountability of the boards of listed companies.[12]

Independent non-executive directors are perceived to play a monitoring role on executive directors and enhance corporate governance; however, they have not effectively prevented corporate scandals, as revealed by the collapse of Enron in the United States and the scandals at Equitable Life and Maxwell Communications in the United Kingdom, all of which had independent non-executive directors.[13] It may be difficult to ensure complete independence of non-executive directors; nevertheless, it is essential that they follow the recommendations in The Code and have suitable skills, experience and knowledge in performing their functions.

[13] The reference to the specific examples of corporate scandals shows your excellent knowledge of corporate governance. It will gain you more marks.

Make your answer stand out

- Consider whether the dual board structure such as that in Germany, which consists of directors and supervisors, should be adopted in the United Kingdom.
- In your discussion of the appointment of non-executive directors, make reference to the Tyson Report on the Recruitment and Development of Non-Executive Directors.
- Explain the agency problems and agency costs in more detail.
- Further reading on the role of non-executive directors: Burke, P. (2003) The Higgs Review. 24 *Company Lawyer* 162; Griffin, S. (2003) Corporate collapse and the reform of boardroom structures – Lessons from America. 6 *Insolvency Law Journal* 214.

Don't be tempted to . . .

- Only discuss the recommendations in the UK Corporate Governance Code. You should also make reference to the Higgs Review 2003, as required by the question.
- Only focus on the role of non-executive directors. You should also discuss the role of the board and that of executive directors.

 # Question 4

'Institutional investors play an important monitoring role in corporate governance. There are, however, concerns over their reluctance to tackle corporate underperformance in the companies in which they invest.'

Critically analyse the above statements by reference to the Combined Code 2008 and the UK Stewardship Code 2010.

Answer plan

→ Discuss the important monitoring roles that institutional shareholders play in corporate governance.

→ Analyse the recommendations in the Combined Code 2008 in relation to institutional shareholders.

→ Examine the main principles in the UK Stewardship Code 2010.

→ Assess the advantages and disadvantages of institutional shareholders using 'voice' or 'exit'.

Diagram plan

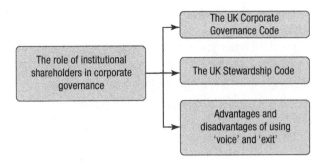

A printable version of this diagram plan is available from **www.pearsoned.co.uk/lawexpressqa**

Answer

¹ Although the Combined Code 2008 is not the latest version of the UK Corporate Governance Code, it contains detailed recommendations on the role of institutional shareholders. The latest version of the UK Corporate Governance Code 2012 contains very few principles in this respect because detailed recommendations are now contained in the UK Stewardship Code 2010.

² These sentences are helpful in showing the examiner that you are engaging with the question.

³ Many students understand that institutional shareholders can use their voice in voting at general meetings but may not appreciate that one-to-one meeting with the companies is another way of using their voice.

This question requires an examination of the role of institutional shareholders in corporate governance by reference to the recommendations in the Combined Code 2008[1] and the UK Stewardship Code 2010. The benefits and problems of institutional shareholders using the 'voice' or 'exit' are also analysed.[2]

The main types of institutional shareholders are insurance companies, pension funds, unit trusts and investment trusts. As the largest block of shareholders in listed companies in the United Kingdom, institutional shareholders are in a significant position to monitor company management and improve company performance. The forms of actions that institutional investors can take when faced with poor corporate governance are often referred to as the 'voice' and 'exit'. By using their voice, institutional shareholders remain with the company and use their influence to change corporate behaviours: for instance, they can vote on shareholder resolutions at companies' general meetings or engage with the company through one-to-one meetings with the company management.[3] By using the 'exit', institutional investors sell their shares and invest somewhere else.

Institutional shareholders are more sophisticated investors than individual shareholders. They are less likely to suffer from the problems of information asymmetry and therefore more likely to make informed choices about how they exercise their votes in

4 This phrase shows that you are aware that institutional investors may misuse their power. It will add more credit to your answer.

5 These sentences show your wider understanding of company law and will gain you more marks.

6 The reference to the agency problems shows your good knowledge of the corporate governance theories.

7 The discussion of the Cadbury Report will help your answer stand out because it is a very important corporate governance report.

8 This sentence leads on to your discussion of the Combined Code and the Stewardship Code in the next two paragraphs. It shows your ability to clearly signpost your answer.

general meetings. The block vote of an institutional investor, if used appropriately,[4] can enforce a significant change in company policy and make their involvement in monitoring meaningful and effective. Shareholders who own over 50 per cent of the company's shares can dismiss directors and appoint new management (s. 168, Companies Act 2006). Shareholders with 75 per cent of the shares can alter the company's articles of association (s. 21, CA 2006).[5] The active role of institutional shareholders in corporate governance can alleviate the agency problems by aligning the interests of management with those of the shareholders.[6] The use of voice by institutional shareholders has been highly recommended in the United Kingdom, although it does have its own drawbacks.

The role of institutional investors received significant attention in the Cadbury Report (1992).[7] It states that, given the weight of their votes, the way in which institutional shareholders use their power to influence the standards of corporate governance is of fundamental importance. They should act as responsible owners to use such power and bring about changes in companies rather than selling their shares. This emphasis on the active role of institutional shareholders is reflected in the Combined Code 2008 and the Stewardship Code 2010.[8]

The Combined Code 2008 encourages institutional investors to enter into a dialogue with companies based on the mutual understanding of objectives (E1). When evaluating companies' governance arrangements, particularly those relating to board structure and composition, institutional shareholders should give due weight to all relevant factors drawn to their attention (E2). They should consider carefully explanations given for departure from this Code and make reasoned judgements in each case. If they are not satisfied with the company's position, they should give an explanation to the company and be prepared to enter a dialogue. A box-ticking approach should be avoided when assessing a company's corporate governance. In relation to voting, institutional shareholders have a responsibility to make considered use of their votes (E 3). Major shareholders should attend AGMs where appropriate and practicable and should, on request, make available to their clients information on the proportion of resolutions on which votes were cast and non-discretionary proxies lodged.

The Stewardship Code 2010 aims to enhance the quality of engagement between institutional investors and companies and to

[9] The 'comply or explain' approach is the essence of the Combined Code. Your understanding of the voluntary basis will gain you more marks.

[10] This phrase demonstrates your knowledge of the inconclusive evidence that the active role of institutional shareholders will improve corporate performance. It may impress your examiners.

[11] An examination of the potential problems caused by the active role of institutional shareholders shows your excellent analytical skills. It will make your answer stand out from those narrative answers which focus only on the recommendations of the Combined Code and the Stewardship Code.

[12] This discussion of short-termism is often omitted in students' answers.

help improve long-term returns to shareholders and the efficient exercise of governance responsibilities. It adopts the principle of 'comply or explain' in the Combined Code.[9] It recommends that institutional investors should publicly disclose their policy on how they will discharge their stewardship responsibilities and have a robust policy on managing conflicts of interest in relation to stewardship. They should monitor their investee companies and establish clear guidelines on when and how they will escalate their activities as a method of protecting and enhancing shareholder value. Moreover, they should have a clear policy on voting and disclosure of voting activity and report periodically on their stewardship and voting activities.

There are perceived benefits[10] of shareholder activism that more efficient monitoring of company management aligns the interests of shareholder and those of directors and therefore helps to maximise shareholders' wealth. Although institutional shareholders are encouraged to take an active role, there are concerns that this approach is not necessarily beneficial to the company for a number of reasons.[11] First, institutional investors owe fiduciary duties to their own shareholders, not to the companies (investee companies) in which they invest. In some circumstances they may find that it is in the best interests of their own shareholders to exit the company. Secondly, institutional investors may only be interested in short-term maximisation of profits and therefore pressure the investee companies to focus on short-term rather than long-term profits.[12] This can be detrimental to the long-term survival of the investee companies because they need to invest in long-term projects in order to maintain a sustainable growth. Thirdly, the action by institutional shareholders may lead to adverse media publicity which results in a fall in share price of the investee companies and a reduction in the value of their investment. Moreover, it can be difficult for institutional shareholders to take legal actions such as the derivative claims (s. 260, CA 2006) and unfair prejudice petitions (s. 994, CA 2006). The litigation may be costly in terms of time and money. Fourthly, institutional shareholders may lack sufficient incentives to initiate proceedings due to the free-rider problems when other shareholders benefit from their monitoring roles. Finally, although institutional shareholders are more sophisticated than individual investors, the pension fund managers may not be professionally trained or qualified in corporate governance or financial management. If they become too involved in the affairs of the investee companies and receive price-sensitive information that has not been publicly disclosed, they may become insiders and be restricted from dealing with the company's shares according to the Financial Services and Market Act 2000.[13] In the light of the problems associated with using their voice, institutional investors may prefer the use of exit which clearly avoids the free-rider problems. The use of exit, however, may be expensive because institutional shareholders have to accept substantial discounts to liquidate their holdings. In conclusion, it is argued that institutional investors should take an active interest in their investment and act as responsible owners of the investee companies, which will in turn improve the corporate governance and enhance the financial performance of their investee companies.

[13] The discussion of insider dealing and market abuse shows your wider knowledge and will gain you more marks.

✓ Make your answer stand out

■ Consider the main guidelines on corporate governance and shareholder activism, such as *The Responsibilities of Institutional Shareholders and Agents – Statement of Principles* (Institutional Shareholders' Committee, 2007).

■ Provide examples of institutional shareholders using their voice by engaging in constructive dialogue with its investee companies. Kingfisher plc, for instance, changed some aspects of its directors' remuneration packages following criticisms from its institutional shareholders (see Mallin, C. (2012) *Corporate Governance*. Oxford: Oxford University Press: p. 105).

! Don't be tempted to . . .

■ Ignore the main principles in the Stewardship Code 2010. This is the most recent and important document on the role of institutional investors and it should not be omitted in your answer.

■ Overlook the recommendations in the Combined Code 2008. Although this is not the most recent version of the UK Corporate Governance Code, it contains detailed guidance on the role of institutional shareholders.

■ Only describe what is meant by the use of 'voice' or 'exit'. You should also analyse the advantages and disadvantages of both mechanisms.

❓ Question 5

Urban Bank plc is listed on the London Stock Exchange. Its recent annual report shows that it has suffered heavy losses. It reveals that each of its executive directors is paid an annual salary of £800,000 plus £1 million bonus; the chief executive director has been appointed as the chairman of the board. There are only two non-executive directors on the board; both are family members of the executive directors and both lack banking expertise and experience.

River Pension Ltd, who owns 30 per cent of the shares in Urban Bank plc, is unhappy with these business practices.

Advise River Pension Ltd as to whether Urban Bank plc has complied with the UK Corporate Governance Code 2014 (The Code) and what actions it should take to improve the corporate governance of Urban Bank plc.

Answer plan

→ Consider the main principles in The Code in relation to directors' remuneration.

→ Examine the board structure and whether the chief executive director and the chairman of the board can be the same person.

→ Discuss the requirements in The Code in relation to the independence and competence of non-executive directors as well as the number of non-executive directors on the board.

→ Evaluate the role of institutional shareholders which is recommended by The Code and the Stewardship Code.

→ Analyse whether River Pension Ltd should use its voice or exit Urban Bank plc.

Diagram plan

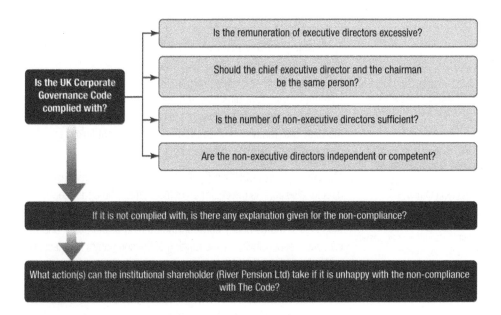

Is the UK Corporate Governance Code complied with?

- Is the remuneration of executive directors excessive?
- Should the chief executive director and the chairman be the same person?
- Is the number of non-executive directors sufficient?
- Are the non-executive directors independent or competent?

If it is not complied with, is there any explanation given for the non-compliance?

What action(s) can the institutional shareholder (River Pension Ltd) take if it is unhappy with the non-compliance with The Code?

A printable version of this diagram plan is available from **www.pearsoned.co.uk/lawexpressqa**

Answer

[1] You should point out in your introduction that River Pension Ltd is an institutional shareholder because it indicates that your answer is going in the right direction.

[2] This part of the sentence summarises the key legal issues that arise in the problem scenario. It will give your examiners a good impression that you know what this problem question is about.

[3] The reference to the problem scenario shows that you are engaging with the question.

[4] The precise section number shows your excellent knowledge of The Code and makes your answer stand out.

In order to advise River Pension Ltd, which is an institutional shareholder,[1] it is essential to examine whether Urban Bank plc has complied with the UK Corporate Governance Code 2014 (The Code) in relation to directors' remuneration, board structure and the role of non-executive directors.[2] It is also important to weigh the advantages and disadvantages of any action that River Pension Ltd may take to improve the corporate governance of Urban Bank plc.

Despite the failure in company performance, as indicated by the heavy losses, the executive directors of Urban Bank plc are paid generously in terms of base salary and bonus.[3] The Code (section D)[4] recommends that the remuneration committee should be set up to recommend and monitor the level and structure of remuneration for senior management. It should consist of at least three independent non-executive directors. There should be a formal and transparent procedure for fixing the remuneration packages of individual directors. In particular, the levels of remuneration should be sufficient to retain and motivate directors to run the company successfully. A company, however, should avoid paying more than is necessary for this purpose. A significant proportion of executive directors' remuneration should be structured so as to link rewards to corporate and individual performance.[5] This performance-related element of executive directors' remuneration should be designed to promote the long-term success of the company. It can be argued that the directors' remuneration in Urban Bank plc is not linked to either corporate or individual performance.

The annual report of Urban Bank plc reveals that its chief executive director also acts as the chairman of the board.[6] The Code (Section A) recommends that there should be a clear division of responsibilities at the head of the company between the running of the board and the executive responsibility for the running of the company's business. No one individual should have unfettered powers of decision. In particular, the roles of chairman and chief executive should not be exercised by the same individual. The division of responsibilities between the chairman and chief executive should be clearly established, set out in writing and agreed by the board. It is therefore argued that Urban Bank plc does not comply with The Code in this respect.

In relation to the number of non-executive directors, The Code (Section B) recommends that at least half the board, excluding the chairman,[7] should comprise independent non-executive directors. The board should have the appropriate balance of skills, experience, independence and knowledge of the company to enable them to discharge its duties and responsibilities effectively. The independence and competence of non-executive directors are essential for an effective board as illustrated by the Enron scandal.[8] The non-executive directors in Urban Bank plc are family members of the executive directors and lack finance or banking expertise. It is apparent that they lack independence and expertise.

Moreover, the board should identify in the annual report each non-executive director it considers to be independent (The Code, Section B). It should determine whether the director is independent in character and judgement and whether there are relationships or circumstances which are likely to affect the director's judgement.[9]

[5] This is the key recommendation in The Code in relation to directors' remuneration. You will lose marks if it is omitted in your answer.

[6] This sentence shows that you are moving on to the next issue. Try to use a new paragraph to address a different legal issue. The use of clear paragraphs helps examiners follow your answer and allocate marks.

[7] Pay attention to the recommended number of non-executive directors on the board. It is often missing in exam answers.

[8] The Enron scandal is the classic case to illustrate the importance of independent non-executive directors. The reference to Enron will gain you more marks.

[9] Note here that the independence of non-executive directors is decided by the board, instead of shareholders.

The board should state its reasons if it determines that a director is independent, notwithstanding the existence of relationships or circumstances which may appear relevant to its determination: for example, if the director has close family ties with any of the company's directors as is the case in Urban Bank plc. The board of Urban Bank plc should, in its annual report, justify the independence of these non-executive directors who are family members of executive directors.

[10] Some students may have the wrong understanding that the Combined Code applies to all types of companies.

Urban Bank plc is a listed company, to which The Code applies.[10] The Code adopts the principle of 'comply or explain'. It requires that the boards of all listed companies should comply with The Code but, if they cannot comply with any particular aspect of it, they should explain their reasons for non-compliance. It is a voluntary code and no legal sanction will arise for non-compliance with it. Failure to include it in the annual report, however, is a breach of the Listing Rules and penalties may be imposed for such non-compliance. As some aspects of The Code are not complied with, the board of Urban Bank plc should provide explanations for such non-compliance in its annual report.

Due to the large block of shares it holds, River Pension Ltd has the potential to influence the company management and monitor the board. It may use its voice by voting on shareholder resolutions at general meetings or engaging with the company through one-to-one meetings with the board. Alternatively, it may choose to exit by selling its shares in Urban Bank plc. The Combined Code 2008 (Section E)[11] recommends that institutional investors are encouraged to enter into a dialogue with companies. They should consider carefully explanations given for departure from this Code and make reasoned judgements in each case. If they are not satisfied with the company's position, they should give an explanation to the company and be prepared to enter a dialogue. In relation to voting, institutional shareholders have a responsibility to make considered use of their votes and should attend AGMs where appropriate and practicable.

[11] The Combined Code 2008 is discussed here instead of the latest Code 2014 because the former contains detailed recommendations on the role of institutional shareholders.

The Stewardship Code 2010 recommends that institutional investors should publicly disclose their policy on how they will discharge their stewardship responsibilities and have a robust policy on managing conflicts of interest in relation to stewardship[12]. They should monitor their investee companies and establish clear guidelines on when and how they will escalate their activities as a method of protecting and

[12] The reference to the Stewardship Code 2010 demonstrates your wider knowledge on this topic.

enhancing shareholder value. Moreover, they should have a clear policy on voting and disclosure of voting activity and report periodically on their stewardship and voting activities.

As River Pension Ltd is unhappy with the management arrangement in Urban Bank plc, it is encouraged by the UK Corporate Governance Code and the Stewardship Code to enter into dialogue with the board or vote at the company's general meeting. Any action, however, may lead to adverse media interests that result in a fall in share price and a reduction in the value of its investment.[13] River Pension Ltd may also consider the use of exit; however, it could be expensive because of the substantial discounts to liquidate its entire shareholdings. After balancing the advantages and disadvantages of both options, River Pension Ltd is advised to take an active role by entering into a dialogue with the board and, if it is not satisfied with the response, using their voting power at the general meeting of Urban Bank plc.[14]

[13] This sentence discusses the disadvantages of using voice. It will gain you more marks than only focusing on the perceived benefits of the active role of institutional shareholders.

[14] Clearly answer the question in your conclusion by stating your advice to River Pension Ltd.

✓ Make your answer stand out

■ Discuss the recommendations in the *Walker Review of Corporate Governance of UK Banking Industry* in relation to directors' remuneration, board structure and the role of institutional shareholders in corporate governance of banks.

■ Consider the legal actions that River Pension Ltd may take to challenge directors such as the derivative actions (ss. 260–264, Companies Act 2006).

■ Assess in more detail the benefits and problems with regard to the use of voice by River Pension Ltd.

! Don't be tempted to . . .

■ Treat the Combined Code or the UK Corporate Governance Code as law. You must understand that it is only a self-regulatory code and the compliance with it is not mandatory.

■ Make no reference to the Stewardship Code 2010 in your discussion of the role of institutional shareholders.

 Question 6

'Despite the collapse of banks and other large public companies, their directors still receive generous pay packages. It seems that remuneration committees have not made any significant changes in the amount of remuneration awarded.'

Analyse the above statements by reference to directors' remuneration and the role of remuneration committees in corporate governance.

Answer plan

➡ Consider the agency problems and directors' remuneration.

➡ Examine the role of remuneration committees in deciding directors' pay by reference to the Greenbury Report and the UK Corporate Governance Code 2014 (The Code).

➡ Discuss the recommended levels of remuneration for non-executive directors.

➡ Analyse the legal requirements for the disclosure of directors' remuneration in the Companies Act 2006.

Diagram plan

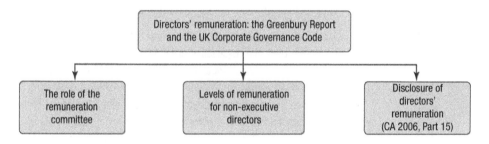

A printable version of this diagram plan is available from **www.pearsoned.co.uk/lawexpressqa**

Answer

Directors' remuneration has attracted considerable public attention and media publicity in light of the recent financial crisis and corporate scandals. One high-profile example is the controversy behind the pension entitlement of Sir Fred Goodwin, the former chief executive officer of the Royal Bank of Scotland.[1] He was awarded a very generous pension despite the failure in company performance. In order to align the interests of directors with those of shareholders, it is

[1] A specific example shows your good knowledge of the recent events from the national press. It makes your answer stand out from the start.

[2] This sentence identifies
the key legal issues that
arise in this essay question.
It demonstrates to the
examiners that you know
clearly what this question is
asking.

[3] The reference to the book by
Berle and Means shows your
excellent knowledge of the
agency problem. It will gain
you more marks than simply
explaining agency problems.

[4] This sentence leads
to the discussion of the
two important corporate
governance documents.
It also shows that you are
engaging with the question
by referring back to the core
issues raised in the question.

[5] Note the differences in the
recommended number of
non-executive directors in a
remuneration committee in
the Greenbury Report and
The Code.

[6] Your reference to the
exact section number of the
recommended principle in
an exam answer will impress
your examiners.

essential to assess the role of the remuneration committee in corporate governance and the appropriate levels of remuneration for directors.[2] It can be argued that the remuneration committee has a significant role to play in maintaining the appropriate levels of directors' remuneration.

Directors' remuneration mainly comprises base salary, bonus, stock options, restricted share plans, pension and other benefits. It is closely linked to the agency problems that the principals (shareholders) have in monitoring the agents (directors). Berle and Means in *The Modern Corporation and Private Property* (1932) identified the problem caused by the separation of ownership and control in US companies in the 1930s.[3] They discovered that many large companies had such widely dispersed share ownership that the board of directors, instead of the shareholders, was able to exert real control over the company. This could lead to a great danger that directors would run the company for their own benefit, rather than on behalf of the shareholders: for example, directors were likely to award themselves large pay packages. In order to address this problem, directors' remuneration and the role of remuneration committee have been subject to detailed examination by the Greenbury Report and the UK Corporate Governance Code.[4]

The Greenbury Committee was formed after widespread public concerns over the excessive amounts of remuneration paid to directors of quoted companies and newly privatised companies. When the Greenbury Report was published in 1995, it dealt specifically with the question of directors' remuneration, and many of its recommendations were developed from the earlier Cadbury Report. The Greenbury Report recommends that directors' remuneration should be linked to company performance. It also addresses the problem of the rewards for failure for directors whose performance had not been successful but still managed to leave the company with generous compensation for loss of office.

The establishment of remuneration committees aims to prevent executive directors from deciding their own remuneration levels. The Greenbury Report recommends that the remuneration committee should consist exclusively[5] of non-executive directors who have no personal financial interest, no potential conflicts of interest arising from cross-directorships and no day-to-day involvement in running the business. According to The Code (D.2.1),[6] the remuneration committee should consist of at least three, or in the case of smaller companies two, independent non-executive directors. In addition, the company chairman may also be a member of the committee if he was considered independent on appointment as chairman. The remuneration committee should recommend and monitor the level and structure of remuneration for senior management and no director should be involved in deciding his own remuneration. Moreover, there should be a formal and transparent procedure for developing policy on executive remuneration and for fixing the remuneration packages of individual directors (The Code, D.2).

It is inappropriate for the remuneration committee to decide non-executive directors' pay because it is made up of non-executives. In this regard, The Code recommends that the remuneration of non-executive directors should be decided by the board itself or, where required by the articles of association, the shareholders. Levels of remuneration for non-executive directors should reflect the time commitment and responsibilities of the role.

The performance measures are important for aligning directors' performance and their remuneration. The Code recommends that levels of remuneration should be sufficient to attract, retain and motivate directors of the quality required to run the company successfully, but a company should avoid paying more than is necessary for this purpose. A significant proportion of executive directors' remuneration should be structured so as to link rewards to corporate and individual performance (The Code, D.1). The performance-related elements of executive directors' remuneration should be designed to promote the long-term success of the company.

[7] A consideration of the compensation schemes for directors should be included in your answer because it is an important component of directors' pay packages.

In order to avoid rewarding poor performance, the remuneration committee should carefully consider what compensation commitments their directors' terms of appointment would entail in the event of early termination.[7] It should take a robust line on reducing compensation to reflect departing directors' obligations to mitigate loss (The Code, D.1.4). The compensation contracts, if designed appropriately, may help to ensure that the objectives of directors and shareholders are aligned.

The disclosure of directors' remuneration is essential to ensure a transparent and fair remuneration. The former Department of

[8] Many students are not aware of this piece of regulation. Although the provisions are now contained in the Companies Act 2006, the reference to the 2002 Regulations shows your sound knowledge and will gain you more marks.

Trade and Industry published the Directors' Remuneration Report Regulations 2002, which are now contained in the Companies Act 2006 (ss. 420–422).[8] Its main aim is to promote greater transparency and accountability of companies' remuneration policies of listed companies. The key requirement is that directors of a listed company must prepare a directors' remuneration report for each financial year of the company (s. 420). The requirements on the contents of such report are listed in section 421. The directors' remuneration report must be approved by the board of directors and signed on behalf of the board by a director or the secretary of the company (s. 422). It is debatable to what extent the disclosure of directors' remuneration has achieved the aim of improving the accountability of companies' remuneration policies.[9]

[9] Adding your own analysis makes your answer stand out from a pure narrative account.

[10] A discussion of academic argument shows your broader knowledge and will add more credit to your answer.

[11] This sentence demonstrates your analytical skills. It gains you more marks than simply describing the requirements in The Code.

The remuneration committee, composed of independent non-executive directors, plays a key role in ensuring that executive directors' remuneration packages are linked with company performance. Sykes (2002), however, is sceptical of the functions of remuneration committees. It is argued that, although remuneration committees predominantly consist of a majority of non-executive directors, they are effectively chosen by, or only with the full agreement of, senior management.[10] It is therefore doubtful how effective the remuneration committee is in ensuring a fair pay package for directors.[11] A fine balance needs to be struck between incentivising directors on the one hand and aligning directors' interests with those of shareholders on the other.[12] The difficulties, however, lie on how to ensure that the directors' pay matches up with their performance and how to establish an appropriate pay structure for this purpose.

[12] This sentence shows that you appreciate the complicated issues associated with directors' pay. A balanced view also enhances your critical analysis and helps your answers to stand out.

 Make your answer stand out

- Consider the important roles that institutional shareholders play in restraining directors' pay.
- Make reference to the provisions in Schedule A to the UK Corporate Governance Code 2014 on designing schemes of performance-related remuneration for executive directors.

> ! **Don't be tempted to . . .**
>
> ■ Only focus on the UK Corporate Governance Code. You should also discuss the Greenbury Report, which contains important recommendations on directors' remuneration.
> ■ Forget to discuss non-executive directors' pay. You should discuss the remuneration for executives and non-executive directors separately because of the different requirements.

🗨 Question 7

'A decade of debate over the future of English company law ended with the Companies Act 2006. At the heart of its conception has been a deceptively simple question – in whose interests should company law be formulated?' (Fisher, D. (2009) The enlightened shareholder – leaving stakeholders in the dark: will section 172(1) of the Companies Act 2006 make directors consider the impact of their decisions on third parties? *International Company and Commercial Law Review* 10).

In light of the above statements, critically analyse relevant corporate governance theories and recent statutory development in the UK.

Answer plan

➡ Discuss the Berle and Dodd debates in relation to shareholder primacy and stakeholder theory.

➡ Analyse the theory of shareholder primacy.

➡ Evaluate the stakeholder theory.

➡ Examine the enlightened shareholder value which is adopted in the Companies Act 2006.

Diagram plan

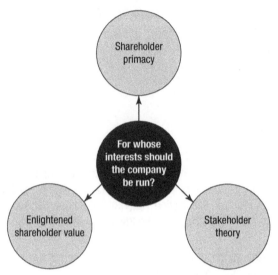

A printable version of this diagram plan is available from **www.pearsoned.co.uk/lawexpressqa**

Answer

[1] This sentence not only refers to the question but also analyses the underlying issue in corporate governance. It shows that you know what this question is about.

Fisher's statement reflects the ongoing debate on the fundamental question in corporate governance: for whose interests the company should be run.[1] Traditionally there are two most influential theories: shareholder primacy (or shareholder value theory) and stakeholder theory (or the pluralist approach). Shareholder primacy has historically been the dominant company law philosophy in the United Kingdom and the United States whilst the stakeholder theory operates in many continental European and East Asian countries such as Germany and Japan.[2] A new approach is adopted in the Companies Act 2006 in the UK.

[2] The discussion of the corporate governance issues in other countries demonstrates your broad knowledge of the international corporate governance. It will impress your examiners.

[3] It is worth learning the title of Berle's article because it is a significant argument for shareholder primacy.

The debate on shareholder primacy and stakeholder theory started from as early as 1932. Advocates of shareholder primacy such as Berle (1931)[3] argued that a company should be run to maximise profits for shareholders who invested in the company. It would be inappropriate to release directors from a strict accountability to shareholders. This theory reflects the view that shareholders are owners of the company and bear the residual risks.

Supporters of the stakeholder theory such as Dodd (1932) are concerned that concentration on share price and profits encourages short-termism. They argue that the company should be run not only for the interests of shareholders but also for all their stakeholders. Stakeholders refer to any individual group on which the activities of the company have an impact. Dodd challenged the shareholder primacy and convincingly[4] argued that public opinion in the United States increasingly regarded companies as economic institutions which have a social service as well as a profit-making function. He identified that employees, customers and the general public also had a valid interest in how the company should be run. Although the stakeholder theory is beneficial in the wider context and in the long term, it inevitably involves a fine balance of stakeholders' potentially competing interests.[5]

The traditional approach in the UK is the shareholder primacy whereby a company should be run for the wealth maximisation of its shareholders above those of other parties such as customers and suppliers. Directors were under a duty to act in the interests of the company: **Percival v Wright** [1902] 2 Ch 421. Such interests were interpreted as the best interests of present and future shareholders: **Hutton v West Cork Railway Company** (1883) LR 23 ChD 654.[6] During the recent company law reform, the stakeholder theory was considered but not adopted in the CA 2006 mainly because of the difficulties faced by directors in balancing interests of different groups and the concerns in enforcing these duties. The Company Law Review Steering Group (*The Strategic Framework*, 1999) rejected the stakeholder approach as neither workable nor desirable.[7] It argued that it was impractical to identify all the stakeholders and redefine the nature and extent of the directors' responsibilities. If the pluralist approach was adopted, the directors would not be effectively accountable to anyone since there would be no clear yardstick for judging their performance. There was also a lack of a proper measure for the enforcement of the pluralist approach. Additionally, it put forward a strong philosophical argument against the pluralist approach – it would turn directors away from business decision makers into moral, political and economic arbiters.

The new concept of enlightened shareholder value[8] is introduced into the Companies Act 2006. Section 172 not only codifies the

[4] This word demonstrates that you are analysing Dodd's argument rather than simply stating it.

[5] This sentence shows your analytical skills by evaluating the problems associated with the stakeholder theory. It will add more credit to your answer.

[6] The reference to *Hutton* shows your good knowledge of case law and will gain you more marks.

[7] The CLRSG's criticisms of the stakeholder theory demonstrate your excellent understanding of the company law reform. It will make your answer stand out from those without detailed analysis of the reasons for the rejection of stakeholder theory.

[8] Make sure that you can write this phrase accurately. Some students have a vague idea of this concept and often make the basic mistake of writing 'enlightening shareholder value'.

common law duty to act *bona fide* in what a director considers is in the interests of the company (***Re Smith & Fawcett Ltd*** [1942] Ch 304) but also introduces the enlightened shareholder value. A director must act in a way, he considers, in good faith, would be most likely to promote the success of the company for the benefit of its members as a whole. In doing so, he must also have regard to a number of factors in section 172(1)[9], including the likely consequences of any decision in the long term, the interests of the company's employees, the need to foster the company's business relationship with suppliers, customers and others, the impact of the company's operations on the community and the environment, the desirability of the company maintaining a reputation for high standards of business conduct and the need to act fairly as between members of the company.

The enlightened shareholder value is perceived to better achieve wealth generation and competitiveness for the benefit of all because it requires a long-term approach and permits directors to consider other interests as the best way of securing prosperity and welfare overall. It appears to be a compromise between shareholder primacy and stakeholder theory by maintaining the primacy of shareholders whilst considering other stakeholders' interests.[10] Despite the introduction of the non-exhaustive list in section 172(1) that a director has to consider, it is clear that shareholder primacy is still dominant because a director must act to promote the success of the company for the interests of members as a whole.

The enlightened shareholder value provides some guidance for businesses faced with the task of balancing different interests among employees, communities, environment and their own reputation. It is unclear, however, whether a director would breach this duty if he considered all the factors, except the one relating to the environment or community. It is also problematic when there is a conflict between two or more of the factors, for example, if a decision benefits the employees but detrimental to its customers.[11] While shareholders may bring a derivative action against directors for breach of this duty, there is a lack of procedure for other stakeholders such as employees or the community to hold directors accountable if the directors fail to consider their interests set out in section 172(1).[12] As derivative actions are only available to *members* of the company

[9] You should pay attention to the non-exhaustive list because it reflects the essence of the enlightened shareholder value. Although you do not need to learn the exact provision of section 172 by heart, a good understanding of this provision is essential for your answer.

[10] This sentence analyses the relationship between the enlightened shareholder value with the other two theories. It will gain you more marks.

[11] These sentences demonstrate your analytical skills by examining the problems associated with the enlightened shareholder value. They will make your answer stand out.

[12] The lack of enforcement of directors' duties by stakeholders is one of the main problems with the stakeholder theory. It should not be omitted in a sound answer.

(s. 260), it is most likely that directors will continue to ensure they exercise their power in good faith and promote the success of the company for the benefit of its members.

It is argued that the English company law has moved closer to the stakeholder theory. A company is still run to generate maximum wealth for shareholders, but directors should take a properly balanced view of the implications of decisions over time and foster effective relationships with employees, customers, suppliers and the wider community.[13] In the light of recent financial crisis and corporate failures which have drastic impact on not only shareholders but also stakeholders of the companies such as employees and communities, there may be more support for a stakeholder-oriented approach and corporate social responsibility.[14]

[13] This sentence summarises the current position in the UK in relation to the shareholder and stakeholder debate. It shows your excellent understanding of the enlightened shareholder value.

[14] You will gain more marks by expressing your views by reference to the current affairs in your conclusion.

 Make your answer stand out

- Discuss the problems associated with section 172; for instance, it is unclear which criteria should be used to assess objectively whether the action of the directors has led to success of the company.

- In relation to the test for the duty to act in good faith in section 172, consider *Fulham Football Club* v *Cabra Estates plc* [1992] BCC 863 and *Re Southern Counties Fresh Foods Ltd* [2008] EWHC 2810 (Ch).

- Further reading on shareholder primacy, stakeholder theory and enlightened shareholder value:

  - Keay, A. R. (2013) *The Enlightened Shareholder Value Principle and Corporate Governance*. Abingdon: Routledge, in particular, Chapter 7 (An Evaluation of Enlightened Shareholder Value and Its Impact)

  - Keay, A. R. (2006) Enlightened shareholder value, the reform of the duties of company directors and the corporate objective. *LMCLQ* 335.

  - Keay, A. R. (2007) Section 172(1) of the Companies Act 2006: An Interpretation and Assessment. 28 *Company Lawyer* 106.

  - Kiarie, S. (2006) At Crossroads: Shareholder Value, Stakeholder Value and Enlightened Shareholder Value: Which Road Should the United Kingdom Take? *ICCLR* 329.

! Don't be tempted to . . .

- Undertake no discussion of the debates by Dodd and Berle. You must not ignore these influential debates in the exam questions with respect to shareholder primacy and stakeholder theory.
- Provide a detailed discussion of directors' duties. This is not a question on directors' duties; you should focus on the enlightened shareholder value in section 172 instead of discussing directors' statutory duties in general.

www.pearsoned.co.uk/lawexpressqa

Go online to access more revision support including additional essay and problem questions with diagram plans, You be the marker questions, and download all diagrams from the book.

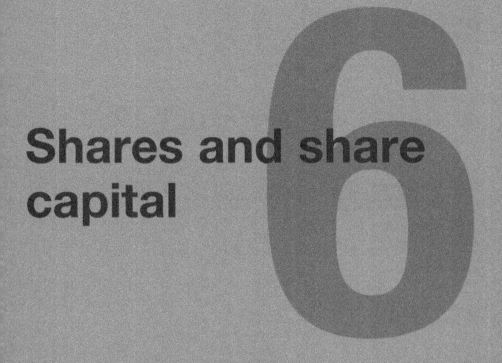

Shares and share capital

How this topic may come up in exams

Shares and share capital are complex topics and many students struggle to apply the large number of complicated statutory provisions. You are expected to show a good understanding of class rights, pre-emption rights, allotment of shares, payment of shares and transfer of shares. The procedures governing the reorganisation of share capital and the doctrine of capital maintenance are popular exam questions. The prohibition of financial assistance by a public company for the acquisition of its own shares is also frequently examined. These topics may overlap with other areas of law such as articles of association, shareholders' rights and directors' duties.

■ Before you begin

It's a good idea to consider the following key themes of shares and share capital before tackling a question on this topic.

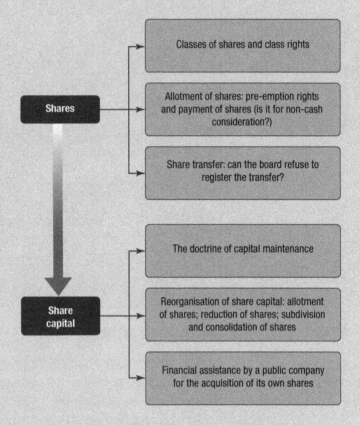

Shares

- Classes of shares and class rights
- Allotment of shares: pre-emption rights and payment of shares (is it for non-cash consideration?)
- Share transfer: can the board refuse to register the transfer?

Share capital

- The doctrine of capital maintenance
- Reorganisation of share capital: allotment of shares; reduction of shares; subdivision and consolidation of shares
- Financial assistance by a public company for the acquisition of its own shares

A printable version of this diagram is available from **www.pearsoned.co.uk/lawexpressqa**

❓ Question 1

Pesto Ltd has an issued share capital of £40,000. Peter, Jim and Emily hold 60, 30 and 10 per cent of the company's shares respectively. Peter and Jim are directors of the company. Its articles of association, which otherwise follow the Model Articles for private companies limited by shares, state that: 'Any member who intends to transfer shares to an outsider must give notice of his intention in writing to the board. The directors reserve the right to refuse to register the transfer of shares by any member for whatever reason.'

Emily has agreed to sell her shares to John. One month after the transfer was lodged with the company, the board of directors refused to register the transfer without giving any reasons for the refusal.

Advise Emily and John as to their legal positions and any possible action against the directors.

Answer plan

→ Discuss whether the shares of Pesto Ltd are freely transferable.

→ Consider whether the board of directors can refuse to register the transfer of shares without giving any reasons.

→ Examine the legal positions of Emily and John when the registration is refused.

→ Evaluate the possible legal actions against the directors.

Diagram plan

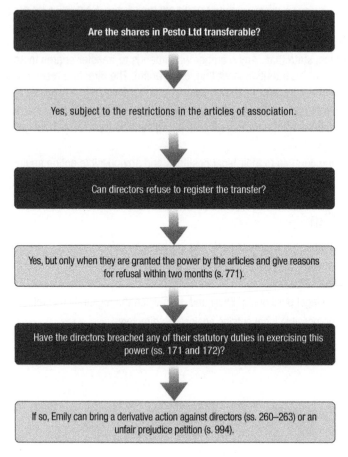

Are the shares in Pesto Ltd transferable?

⬇

Yes, subject to the restrictions in the articles of association.

⬇

Can directors refuse to register the transfer?

⬇

Yes, but only when they are granted the power by the articles and give reasons for refusal within two months (s. 771).

⬇

Have the directors breached any of their statutory duties in exercising this power (ss. 171 and 172)?

⬇

If so, Emily can bring a derivative action against directors (ss. 260–263) or an unfair prejudice petition (s. 994).

A printable version of this diagram plan is available from **www.pearsoned.co.uk/lawexpressqa**

[1] This sentence identifies the key legal issues and shows that you are engaging with the problem question.

[2] Shares are not well defined. The reference to this common law illustration shows your good understanding of the definition of shares and will gain you more marks.

Answer

In order to advise Emily and John, it is essential to analyse whether the shares in Pesto Ltd are freely transferable and whether the board of directors has the power to refuse to register the transfer of shares.[1] Shares are personal property (s. 541). Farwell J in **Borland's Trustee v Steel Bros & Co Ltd** [1901] 1 Ch 279 explained that: 'A share is not a sum of money … but is an interest measured by a sum of money, and made up of various rights contained in the contract.'[2]

3 Most students understand
that shares are transferable
but are not aware of the
conditions – subject to
the company's articles of
association. The reference to
the statutory provision shows
your precise knowledge.

4 This sentence explains why
there may be restrictions
on the transfer of shares in
private companies. It adds
more credit to your answer
than simply stating the
restrictions.

5 Make sure that your answer
refers back to the problem
question.

6 The explanation of the
rationale for pre-emption
rights will earn you more
marks.

7 This is the key phrase in
section 771. When directors
refuse to register the transfer,
reasons must be given.

8 The consequences for failure
to comply with section 771
have important implications
in a problem question. They
are often omitted in exam
answers.

9 This sentence indicates that
you are answering the part
of the question in relation to
the legal positions of Emily
and John.

A share represents a bundle of contractual rights conferred by the company's constitution and the Companies Act 2006, such as the right to vote, to declared dividends and a return of capital on winding up of the company. Shares are transferable in the manner provided by the company's articles (s. 544).3 It is common for the articles in a private company to impose restrictions on the transfer of shares because the existing members may wish to control the membership of the company.4 Any restrictions of the right to transfer must be clearly expressed in the articles: *Re Smith & Fawcett Ltd* [1942] 1 All ER 542.

The articles of Pesto Ltd state that any member who intends to transfer shares must give notice of his intention in writing to the board.5 This triggers the pre-emption rights which provide the existing shareholders with the opportunity to buy the shares for sale before they are offered outside the company. It ensures that a shareholder is able to protect his proportion of the total equity of a company.6 As a company's articles of association create contractual rights between members (s. 33), the provisions regarding the pre-emption rights are enforceable by members: *Rayfield* v *Hands* [1958] 2 All ER 194.

Although Emily and John have agreed on the sale of shares, John will not become a member of the company until he is registered. A share certificate is *prima facie* evidence that the named member has title to the shares (s. 768). When a transfer of shares has been lodged, the company must either register the transfer or give the transferee notice of refusal to register the transfer, together with its reasons for the refusal (s. 771).7 This must be done as soon as practicable and in any event within two months after the date on which the transfer is lodged with it. If the company refuses to register the transfer, it must provide the transferee with further information about the reasons for the refusal as the transferee may reasonably request (s. 771(2)). If a company fails to comply with this section, an offence is committed by the company and every officer of the company who is in default (s. 771(3)).8 Since the board of Pesto Ltd has not given any reasons for the refusal, Emily can apply to the court for rectification of the Register and the issue of a share certificate (s. 125).

It is important to clarify the legal positions of Emily and John before the transfer of shares is registered.9 If a transfer of shares is refused, the equitable title to the shares passes to the purchaser once the contract of sale is made and the legal title passes on completion and registration by the company: ***Roots*** **v** ***Williamson*** (1888) 38 Ch D 485. Such refusal will not affect John's beneficial interest in a share: for example, he is still entitled to the dividends declared on the shares and a return of capital on winding up. John, however, is not able to exercise all the membership rights: for example, he may not vote at shareholder meetings until the transfer is registered and his name is entered in the register of members. The legal title does not pass to him until his name is on the members' list but he can instruct Emily on how to vote because Emily still holds the shares as trustee for John: ***Re Rose, Rose*** **v** ***IRC*** [1952] 1 All ER 1217. If Emily did not promise to secure registration of transfer of shares, she would not be liable for damages for breach when the registration was refused.[10]

[10] This sentence analyses the terms of the contract of sale. It goes further than a discussion of the board's power to register the transfer of shares and adds more credit to your answer.

Although directors in Pesto Ltd are given absolute discretion to refuse registration of transfer of shares by its articles, they are not totally free to exercise such power. In ***Re Smith & Fawcett Ltd*** [1942] 1 All ER 542,[11] the Court of Appeal held that, when directors exercise such broad discretion, they must act *bona fide* in what they consider to be in the interests of the company and not for any collateral purpose. Emily and John may argue that directors' refusal to register the transfer is not made *bona fide* for the success of the company and therefore in breach of their duties in section 172. This duty, however, is very subjective in nature: ***Bristol & West Building Society*** **v** ***Mothew*** [1998] Ch 1. It is what a director considers, not what a court considers, would be most likely to promote the success of the company. Moreover, they can argue that the directors breached their duties in section 171 by exercising their power for improper purposes: ***Howard Smith Ltd*** **v** ***Ampol Petroleum*** [1974] AC 821.[12]

[11] This case law is very important here because it is directly relevant to the exercise of directors' power in registering the transfer of shares. The absence of this case law will negatively affect your mark.

[12] Although directors' duties are now codified in the Companies Act 2006, you should still refer to case law which is relevant in the application and interpretation of the statutory duties.

Emily may consider bringing a derivative action to challenge directors' breach of duties. She needs to establish a *prima facie* case and go through the two-stage procedure in section 261. The court will take into account a number of factors in section 263 when considering whether to give or refuse permission to continue the derivative claim. This procedure, however, is subject to tight judicial control. The court has taken a restrictive approach; for instance, it refused to grant permission if the judges did not believe that the hypothetical director would attach much importance to the claim, or if all that the claimant was seeking could be recovered by means of an unfair prejudice petition: ***Mission Capital plc*** **v** ***Sinclair*** [2008] BCC 866; ***Franbar Holding Ltd*** **v** ***Patel*** [2008] BCC 885.[13] A more practical option for

[13] These sentences analyse the merits of a derivative claim. They will gain you more marks than simply stating the possibility of bringing a derivative claim.

Emily is the unfair prejudice petition under section 994 whereby she can claim that her interests as a member have been unfairly prejudiced by the conduct of the company's affairs. If the court is satisfied that the petition is well founded, it may make any order it thinks fit for giving relief in respect of the matters complained of: for example, the court may order the board of Pesto Ltd to register the transfer of shares and issue a share certificate to John (s. 996).

Make your answer stand out

- Discuss the relevant clauses in the Model Articles, for example, the general management clause in Article 3 which provides that subject to the articles, the directors are responsible for the management of the company's business, for which purpose they may exercise all the powers of the company.
- Point out that John also has *locus standi* in the unfair prejudice petition because section 994 also applies to a person who is not a member of a company but to whom shares in the company have been transferred.

Don't be tempted to . . .

- Ignore the time limit for the refusal to register the transfer of shares. This must be done as soon as practicable and in any event within *two months* after the date on which the transfer is lodged with it.
- Undertake no discussion of directors' breach of duties. As this question asks about the legal actions available to Emily, an examination of directors' duties and shareholder remedies is essential.
- Get confused with the legal positions of Emily and John when the transfer of shares is refused. John has the *equitable* title to the shares when the contract of sale is made but Emily still has the *legal* title.

Question 2

'The doctrine of capital maintenance is designed to protect the interests of creditors. It has been relaxed in the Companies Act 2006 to accommodate modern business needs and now offers little protection for creditors.'

Undertake a critical analysis of the above statements in relation to the regime of capital maintenance in the Companies Act 2006.

Answer plan

→ Consider the rationale of the doctrine of capital maintenance.

→ Analyse the historical development of the doctrine of capital maintenance: *Trevor* v *Whitworth* (1887) 12 App Cas 409.

→ Examine the statutory provisions in the CA 2006 in relation to: reduction of share capital; company's distribution (such as dividends); purchase by a company of its own shares and redemption of shares; and prohibition of providing financial assistance in public companies.

Diagram plan

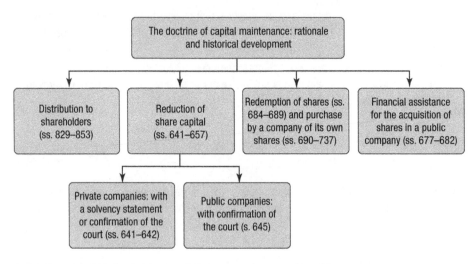

A printable version of this diagram plan is available from **www.pearsoned.co.uk/lawexpressqa**

Answer

[1] Your answer should start with an explanation of the doctrine of capital maintenance. The reference to the landmark case of *Trevor* v *Whitworth* is essential here.

[2] This part of the sentence summarises the main aspects of the doctrine of capital maintenance. It also sets a clear structure for your answer.

It was established in ***Trevor v Whitworth*** (1887) 12 App Cas 409 that a company could not return its capital to its members other than on a proper reduction of capital duly approved by the courts.[1] This doctrine of capital maintenance was originally designed to protect the interests of creditors and is now reflected in the Companies Act 2006 in relation to the company's distribution to shareholders, the reduction of capital, the redemption or purchase of a company's own shares and the prohibition of financial assistance to others for purchase of its shares.[2]

[3] The explanation as to why
the rules on distribution are
part of the doctrine of capital
maintenance adds more
credit to your answer than
simply stating the statutory
rules on distribution.

[4] Some students may
forget to discuss the legal
consequences for unlawful
distribution. The reference
to case law gains you more
marks.

[5] The historical background
for the rules on the reduction
of share capital shows your
sound knowledge and adds
more credit to your answer.

[6] You should pay attention
to the type of companies
here. Only a private company
can reduce share capital by
a special resolution and a
solvency statement; a public
company must follow the
procedure in section 645.

[7] A further explanation
of a solvency statement
demonstrates your good
understanding and will earn
you more marks.

[8] This provision is important
for the protection of creditors
and therefore it should not be
left out in your answer.

The rules on distribution are important aspects of the doctrine of capital maintenance because they protect creditors from asset-stripping by directors and shareholders of the company: *It's a Wrap (UK) Ltd* v *Gula* [2006] 2 BCLC 634.[3] A company may only make a distribution (such as dividends) to shareholders out of profits available (s. 830). Such profits are defined as its accumulated, realised profits less its accumulated, realised losses. An unlawful distribution of profits is *ultra vires* and a director who knew or ought to know that the payment amounted to a breach is liable to repay the dividends: *Bairstow* v *Queens Moat Houses plc* [2002] BCC 91.[4]

Historically, the law was strict in relation to reduction of capital for the protection of the company's creditors. The statutory rules in the Companies Act 1985 were criticised as complex by the White Paper 2005. The Companies Act 2006 seeks to deregulate this area of law for private companies by removing some burdensome measures whilst the rules for public companies remain mostly the same.[5] A private company[6] may reduce its capital by a special resolution supported by a solvency statement (s. 641). The directors should make a statement of the solvency of the company not more than 15 days before the date on which the resolution is passed (s. 642). A solvency statement is defined in section 643[7] as a statement that each of the directors has formed the opinion, as regards the company's situation at the date of the statement, that there is no ground on which the company could then be found to be unable to pay its debts. If it is intended to commence the winding up within 12 months of that date, each of the directors has formed the opinion that the company will be able to pay its debts in full within 12 months of the commencement of the winding up. If the directors make such statements without having reasonable grounds for the opinions expressed in it, an offence is committed by every director who will be liable to imprisonment on conviction and/or a fine (s. 643(4)).

Both private and public companies may reduce its share capital by a special resolution confirmed by the court (s. 645). The court has wide discretion as to whether to confirm a reduction or not; its main concerns are the protection of the interests of creditors and the fair treatment of different classes of shareholders: *Re Ratners Group plc* [1988] BCLC 685. The creditors are given the opportunities to object to the reduction of capital (s. 646).[8]

A limited company may not acquire its own shares whether by purchase or subscription (s. 658). In case of an infringement of section 658, the company will be liable to a fine and every officer of the company who is in default is liable to imprisonment or a fine, and the purported acquisition will be void (s. 658(2)). This reflects the judgment by the House of Lords in **Trevor v Whitworth** that a company could not purchase its own shares under the Companies Act, even if it was authorised by its articles of association. In the light of the modern business needs, these rigid requirements have been relaxed and some exceptions to this general rule are developed.[9] For instance, purchase by a company of its own shares is not prohibited in a reduction of capital duly made or in pursuance of an order of the court (s. 659).

[9] This sentence refers back to the statement in the question and shows that you are engaging with the question.

A company may issue shares which are to be redeemed or are liable to be redeemed at the option of the company or the shareholder under section 684. A public company must be authorised by its articles to issue redeemable shares; such authorisation is not required for private companies although the articles may exclude or restrict their issue.[10]

[10] Note that the rules which apply to private and public companies are different.

The law in relation to the financial assistance by the company for purchase of its own shares has been significantly reformed by the Companies Act 2006. The general rule that a company may not give financial assistance for the purchase of its own shares has been abolished for private companies but it still applies to public companies.[11] The scope of financial assistance is wide, including by way of gift, guarantee, security or indemnity, release or waiver. It also includes financial assistance given by way of a loan or any other agreement under which any of the obligations of the person giving the assistance are to be fulfilled (s. 677). It is unlawful for a public company or its subsidiary to give financial assistance for the acquisition of its own shares (s. 678); an infringement of this provision is a criminal offence (s. 680). A company, however, is not prohibited from doing so if its principal purpose in giving the assistance is not for the purpose of any such acquisition, or the giving of the assistance for that purpose is only an incidental part of some larger purpose of the company, and the assistance is given in good faith in the interests of the company (s. 678(2)). Despite the House of Lords' interpretation of this 'principal purpose' exception in **Brady v Brady** [1988] BCLC 20, it is still difficult to ascertain exactly what sort of

[11] This sentence demonstrates your excellent knowledge of the recent reforms introduced by the Companies Act 2006 and will impress your examiners.

[12] This brief analysis of the 'principal purpose' exception by reference to case law makes your answer stand out from a pure description of the statutory provisions.

[13] Summarise your main arguments and directly refer back to the question in your conclusion. The comments on future reforms may gain you more marks.

situations would fall within its scope: **Dyment v Boyden** [2005] 1 WLR 792.[12] The courts may take into account the commercial reality in deciding whether financial assistance has been given: **Chaston v SWP Group plc** [2003] 1 BCLC 675.

It is argued that the doctrine of capital maintenance still plays an important role in protecting the interests of creditors, despite the recent relaxation of the rules for private companies to accommodate modern business needs. The current rules, however, are still complex and wide-ranging; further reforms are desirable to clarify this area of law and reduce the costs in complying with them.[13]

 Make your answer stand out

- Discuss the rules in relation to the issue of shares. Shares may not be allotted at a discount (s. 580).

- Examine the payment of shares for non-cash consideration. If shares are issued for a non-cash consideration in a public company, the assets must be valued before allotment (s. 593).

- Further reading on the doctrine of capital maintenance: Armour, J. (2000) Share capital and creditor protection: efficient rules for a modern company law. 63 *Modern Law Review* 355; Milman, D. (2007) Share capital maintenance: current developments and future horizons. *Company Law Newsletter* 1.

! **Don't be tempted to . . .**

- Treat private companies and public companies in the same way. You should be aware that different rules may apply to these two types of companies.

- Only focus on the reduction of share capital. Your answer should include other main aspects of the doctrine of capital maintenance, including making distributions to shareholders and purchasing its own shares by a company.

- Provide an answer without reference to the relevant statutory provisions. Although the common law rules are still important, they have been modified by the statutory provisions in the Companies Act 2006.

❓ Question 3

Southsea Property Ltd has an issued share capital of 30,000 shares, divided into 10,000 £2 ordinary shares and 10,000 £1 preference shares. Its articles of association contain a term stating that the holders of the preference shares are entitled to a 5 per cent preferential dividend. They also have the right to priority in repayment of capital and the right to participate to the extent of £1 per share in any surplus assets on a winding up. Both the articles of association and the terms of issue of the preference shares are silent as to how the rights of the shareholders are to be varied. The articles grant directors unrestricted power to allot shares.

Rose and Katie are the only directors of Southsea Property Ltd. At a board meeting it was decided that the company would issue another 5,000 £2 ordinary shares and 3,000 £1 preference shares with rights identical to the existing preference shares. All these new shares were issued to the family members of Rose and Katie. Peter, who holds 10 per cent of the company's ordinary shares, is unhappy with this arrangement and he wishes to bring legal actions against Rose and Katie.

Advise Peter.

Answer plan

➜ Consider the legal procedures for the allotment of shares in a private company limited by shares.

➜ Discuss the implications of pre-emption rights.

➜ Examine whether an allotment of preference shares amounts to a variation of class rights.

➜ Assess the procedures required for a variation of class rights.

➜ Evaluate whether Rose and Katie breached their duties as directors by allotting the shares to their family members.

➜ Discuss possible legal actions that Peter can bring against Rose and Katie.

Diagram plan

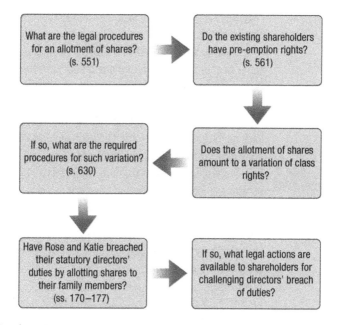

What are the legal procedures for an allotment of shares? (s. 551)

Do the existing shareholders have pre-emption rights? (s. 561)

If so, what are the required procedures for such variation? (s. 630)

Does the allotment of shares amount to a variation of class rights?

Have Rose and Katie breached their statutory directors' duties by allotting shares to their family members? (ss. 170–177)

If so, what legal actions are available to shareholders for challenging directors' breach of duties?

A printable version of this diagram plan is available from **www.pearsoned.co.uk/lawexpressqa**

Answer

[1] The introduction identifies the key legal issues that arise from the problem question. It immediately demonstrates that you understand what is asked by the question.

In order to advise Peter, it is essential to consider whether Rose and Katie followed the legal procedures by allotting the shares to their family members, whether they breached their duties as directors of Southsea Property Ltd and, if so, what actions Peter can bring against them.[1] There are two classes of shares in Southsea Property Ltd: ordinary shares and preference shares, with the latter carrying class rights. A company may alter its share capital subject to the statutory procedures in section 617 of the Companies Act 2006. Directors may exercise their power to allot shares in the company if they are authorised to do so by the articles or by resolution of the company (s. 551). Rose and Katie can allot shares because they are given unrestricted power to do so by the articles.[2]

[2] This sentence shows that you are engaging with the problem scenario instead of providing a general answer to an essay question on the allotment of shares.

When allotting shares, the directors need to consider whether the existing shareholders have pre-emption rights. These rights ensure

[3] The rationale for pre-emption rights will add more credit to your answer because it goes beyond a simple description of these rights.

[4] Some students may have the wrong understanding that pre-emption rights always apply. It is important to appreciate that such rights are subject to exceptions, exclusions and dis-applications.

[5] These sentences demonstrate your skills of analysing the problem scenario and applying the relevant law. They will gain you more marks.

[6] This sentence explains the significance of class rights because it is more difficult to alter. It shows your good understanding of class rights and will add more credit to your answer.

[7] You should pay attention to this phrase here. It refers to the holders of the issued shares with class rights instead of the holders of ordinary shares.

that a shareholder is able to protect his proportion of the total equity of a company by having the opportunity to subscribe for any new issue of shares.[3] According to section 561, a company must not allot shares to a person unless it has made an offer to each person who holds ordinary shares in the company and allot to him on the same or more favourable terms a proportion of those shares that is as nearly as practicable equal to the proportion in nominal value held by him of the ordinary share capital of the company. The offer must state a period during which it may be accepted and the offer shall not be withdrawn before the end of that period (s. 562). If these provisions on pre-emption rights are not complied with, the company and every officer of it who knowingly authorised or permitted the non-compliance are jointly and severally liable to compensate any person to whom an offer should have been made (s. 563).

The issue of pre-emption rights, however, may not always arise.[4] Pre-emption rights are subject to exceptions: for instance, they do not apply in the allotment of bonus shares (s. 564) or issue for non-cash consideration (s. 565). Pre-emption rights may be excluded by the articles of a private company (ss. 567–568); moreover, they may be dis-applied by the articles or a special resolution of a company (ss. 569–573). It is unclear whether pre-emption rights are excluded or dis-applied by the articles of Southsea Property Ltd. If they are not excluded or dis-applied, the new shares must be first offered to the existing holders of ordinary shares.[5] Since the new shares were offered only to the family members of Rose and Katie, it can be argued that the legal procedure for the allotment of shares is not complied with.

Moreover, it is essential to consider whether an allotment of preference shares varies the class rights of existing preference shareholders. Class rights confer greater security on the holder of preference shares than rights conferred merely by the articles because the latter can be altered by a special resolution under section 21.[6] Class rights may only be varied in accordance with provisions in the company's articles, or where the company's articles contain no such provisions, if the holders of shares of that class consent to the variation (s. 630). The consent must be in writing from the holders of at least three-quarters in nominal value of the issued shares of that class[7] or a special resolution passed at a separate general meeting of the holders of that class sanctioning the variation.

[8] This sentence clearly states the judicial approach to the variation of class rights. It will make your answer stand out from those which only describe the procedure in section 630 for the variation of class rights.

[9] This case is very important here for two reasons. Firstly, it illustrates what amounts to a variation of class rights by making the distinction between class rights and the enjoyment of such rights; secondly, it is the common law authority on whether an allotment of shares amounts to a variation of class rights.

[10] This provision is often missing in students' answers. It is important for the protection of class rights and therefore should be included in a good answer.

[11] The evaluation of the practicality of section 633 will gain you more marks because it shows your sound analysis.

[12] Although directors have unrestricted power to allot shares according to the articles, it does not mean they can exercise this power in any way they like. The discussion of directors' duties is essential here and it helps your answer stand out.

[13] Some students may forget to discuss section 171 on the directors' duty to exercise power for proper purposes. The reference to case law is also important because it is still relevant to the interpretation and application of the codified duties.

The court has interpreted restrictively what amounts to a variation of class rights. A distinction is made between matters affecting the rights attached to each share and matters affecting the enjoyment of these rights.[8] If only the enjoyment of the right is affected, it does not attract the protection under section 630 for the variation of class rights because the right remains the same. In *White v Bristol Aeroplane Co Ltd* [1953] Ch 65,[9] it was held that an issue of preference shares to the existing ordinary shareholders was not a variation of class rights although it would dilute the control of the existing preference shareholders. It was concluded that the new issue did not affect the rights of the existing preference shareholders which remained exactly as they were before. As the court is very likely to follow the approach in *White v Bristol Aeroplane Co Ltd*, the board of directors in Southsea Property Ltd, when allotting preference shares, does not need the consent of the holders of preference shares as required by section 630.

It should be noted that, even when a majority of the class has consented to a variation, the holders of not less than 15 per cent of the issued shares of the class in question may apply to the court to have the variation cancelled, provided that they did not consent to or vote in favour of the resolution for the variation (s. 633).[10] If the court is satisfied that the variation would unfairly prejudice the shareholders of the class represented by the applicant, it may disallow the variation: otherwise, it must confirm it and the decision of the court is final. This provision is rarely used in practice because it is unlikely that the court would overturn a decision which was made by a majority of the class. It may be easier to bring an unfair prejudice petition under section 994 if a member of the class feels that his rights have been unfairly prejudiced.[11]

When directors exercise the power to allot shares, they must ensure that they do not breach their statutory duties to the company[12]. In particular, the exercise of this power must be made *bona fide* in a way that is likely to promote the success of the company (s. 172). It adopts a subjective test in the sense that directors are not in breach of this duty if they honestly believe that they are acting properly: *Re Smith and Fawcett* [1942] 1 All ER 542. Directors must also ensure that the power is exercised for a proper purpose for which it is conferred (s. 171): *Howard Smith Ltd v Ampol Petroleum Ltd* [1974] AC 821.[13] If the allotment is for improper purposes such as diluting the control of existing shareholders, an unfair prejudice petition may be brought under section 994: ***Dalby* v *Bodilly*** [2005] BCC 627. Moreover, Peter may bring a derivative claim against the directors' breach of duties under sections 260–263.

 Make your answer stand out

■ Consider the derivative claim in more depth by reference to the statutory provisions and recent case law.
■ Further reading on pre-emption rights and class rights:
  – MacNeil, I. (2002) Shareholders Pre-emptive Rights. *JBL* 78.
  – Reynolds, B. (1996) Shareholders' Class Rights: A New Approach. *JBL* 554.

Don't be tempted to . . .

■ Apply the procedure in section 550 to the allotment of shares in Southsea Property Ltd. Section 550 applies to a private company with only one class of shares. It is not applicable here because the company has two classes of shares.
■ Forget to discuss whether an allotment of preference shares varies class rights of existing preference shareholders. This is an important issue raised in the question and therefore it should be sufficiently addressed.

❓ Question 4

Nottinghill plc issued 400,000 £1 ordinary shares in November 2009. Ella was allotted 100,000 shares for her services as an IT consultant for six years at the rate of £20,000 per annum. Ella then transferred all her shares to her friend Lisa.

In January 2010, the board of directors paid a dividend of 50p per share although they were aware that the company had no profits for distribution.

Advise the board of directors as to the validity of these arrangements.

Answer plan

→ Consider the rules on payment of shares for non-cash consideration in a public company (s. 593).
→ Discuss the restrictions on the issue of shares against performance of future personal services (s. 585).
→ Examine the rules with regard to payment of dividends (s. 830).

Diagram plan

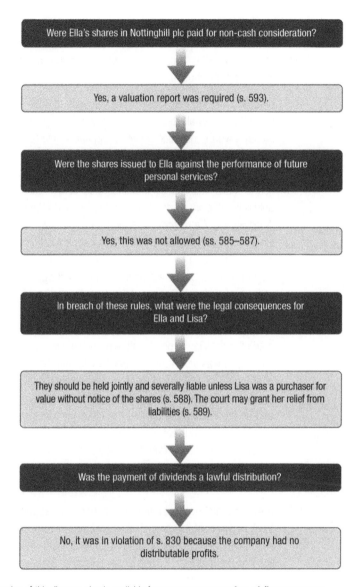

Were Ella's shares in Nottinghill plc paid for non-cash consideration?

Yes, a valuation report was required (s. 593).

Were the shares issued to Ella against the performance of future personal services?

Yes, this was not allowed (ss. 585–587).

In breach of these rules, what were the legal consequences for Ella and Lisa?

They should be held jointly and severally liable unless Lisa was a purchaser for value without notice of the shares (s. 588). The court may grant her relief from liabilities (s. 589).

Was the payment of dividends a lawful distribution?

No, it was in violation of s. 830 because the company had no distributable profits.

A printable version of this diagram plan is available from **www.pearsoned.co.uk/lawexpressqa**

Answer

In order to advise the board of directors in Nottinghill plc, it is essential to examine whether the allotment of shares to Ella for non-cash consideration is legal and whether the payment of dividend is a lawful distribution.[1]

Shares must not be issued at a discount to their nominal value (s. 580). Shares allotted by a company may be paid up in money or money's worth, including goodwill and know-how (s. 582). If shares are paid in non-cash consideration such as goods or services, there may be a danger that they are undervalued. At common law, the courts make little inquiry into the value of non-cash consideration unless it is illusory or manifestly inadequate. Lord Waton in **Ooregum Gold Mining Co of India v Roper** [1892] AC 125 held that 'so long as the company honestly regards the consideration given as fairly representing the nominal value of the shares in cash, its estimate ought not to be critically examined'.[2] In **Re Wragg Ltd** (1897) 1 Ch 796, it was alleged that the defendant directors sold their business to the company they had incorporated at an overvalue and these shares should be treated as unpaid. The court held that the directors made the decision in good faith and the benefit received in return for the shares was worth their nominal value and therefore not open to challenge. Lindley LJ held that the agreements by a limited company to pay for property or services were valid and binding on the company and its creditors, provided that the company 'does so honestly and not colourably and that it has not been so imposed upon as to be entitled to be relieved from its bargain'. This common law approach still applies to a private company; however, more restrictions are imposed on a public company such as Nottinghill plc.[3]

A public company must not allot a share except as paid up at least as to one-quarter of its nominal value and the whole of any premium on it (s. 586). It must not allot shares as fully or partly paid up otherwise than in cash unless it meets the following three requirements in section 593.[4] First, the consideration for the allotment has been independently valued; secondly, the valuer's report has been made to the company during the six months immediately preceding the allotment of the shares; and thirdly, a copy of the report has been sent to the proposed allottee. A copy of the valuation report must also be filed by the company with the registrar of companies. As Nottinghill

---

² The reference to Lord Waton and his judgment shows your precise knowledge. It will gain you more marks than only stating the name of the case.

³ This sentence shows that you appreciate the different requirements for private companies and public companies. The reference to Nottinghill plc indicates that your answer focuses on the rules applicable to public companies.

⁴ Section 593 is very important for any question on payment of shares for non-cash consideration. You will lose some marks if it is omitted in your answer.

plc allotted shares to Ella for her services instead of in cash, the board of directors had to ensure these conditions in section 593 were met.[5]

Moreover, in payment of its shares, a public company must not accept an undertaking given by any person that he should do work or perform services for the company (s. 585). In particular, it must not allot shares for a non-cash consideration which includes an undertaking which is to be performed more than five years after the date of the allotment (s. 587).[6] As it accepted an undertaking from Ella to perform services as a consideration for the allotment of shares and the services would be provided over six years (longer than five years), Nottinghill plc was in breach of the requirements in sections 585 and 587. Moreover, the company and its officers committed criminal offences for contravention of these provisions and they are liable to a fine on conviction (ss. 590 and 607). The allottee, Ella, is liable to pay the company in respect of those shares an amount equal to the aggregate of the nominal value of the shares, with interest at the appropriate rate which is fixed at 5 per cent per annum (s. 592).[7]

As Ella transferred her shares to Lisa, both will be jointly and severally liable in respect of the amount for which Ella is liable unless Lisa was a purchaser for value without notice of the shares (s. 588).[8] The court has the power to grant relief from liability of Ella and Lisa where it is just and equitable to do so (ss. 589 and 606): ***Re Bradford Investments plc (No. 2)*** [1991] BCLC 688. In ***Re Ossory Estates plc*** [1988] BCLC 213,[9] the property was sold to the company as part of the consideration for the purchase of shares. It was not valued as required by section 103, CA 1985 (now s. 593, CA 2006) and a claim was made against the allottee for payment for the price of the shares. The court granted relief under section 113, CA 1985 (now s. 606, CA 2006) on the grounds that the company had sold the property at a substantial profit and received at least money or money's worth equal to the aggregate nominal value of the shares and any premium. There was therefore manifestly no issue at a discount. If the agreement between Nottinghill plc and Ella is likely to be honoured, Ella and Lisa may be exempt from their liabilities provided that they can prove that the company has received total or partial consideration for the share allotment.[10]

Another legal issue is whether Nottinghill plc has made unlawful distribution by paying dividends when it had no distributable profits.

[5] Apply to the question after discussing the relevant law.

[6] Some students may forget to discuss section 587 in relation to the restrictions on long-term undertaking. The application of section 587 to the problem question will make your answer stand out.

[7] The legal consequences for breach of these provisions on the allotment against non-cash consideration (s. 593) and the restrictions on undertaking (s. 587) are the same. You do not need to repeat them or state them separately.

[8] An analysis of the circumstances where the transferee is not jointly and severally liable will gain you more marks.

[9] This case law illustrates the court's power to grant relief and adds more credit to your answer.

[10] Again, apply the law to the problem scenario.

[11] The case law illustration is essential for a good answer because it shows your sound knowledge of the common law approach.

A company may pay dividends only out of distributable profits (s. 830). A breach of these rules makes a payment unlawful and *ultra vires*; a director who knew or ought to know that the payment amounted to a breach is liable to repay the dividends. In ***Bairstow v Queens Moat Houses plc*** [2002] BCC 91, directors were held liable for unlawfully paying dividends that exceeded the distributable reserves.[11] In ***Re Exchange Banking Co, Flitcroft's case*** (1882) 21 Ch D 519, the former directors of the company were sued for paying half-yearly dividends when they knew that some items in the accounts were bad debts and that the company had no distributable profits. The directors were held jointly and severally liable for the amount of the dividends. The distribution of dividends in Notthinghill plc was unlawful because directors knew that the company had no distributable profits. Thus the directors should be liable to repay the dividends. If, at the time of the distribution, the shareholders know or have reasonable grounds for believing that it is so made, they should also be liable to repay it to the company (s. 847).[12]

[12] A discussion of the potential liabilities of other shareholders goes beyond the liabilities of the directors, Ella and Lisa. It will add more credit to your answer.

 Make your answer stand out

- Show your wider understanding by relating the rules on payment of shares to the doctrine of capital maintenance.
- Point out that your answer will be different if it is a private company. If the shares are paid in non-cash consideration, there is no requirement for valuation report and the court will treat such consideration as fully paid unless it is manifestly inadequate or illusory (*Re Wragg Ltd* (1897)).

! Don't be tempted to . . .

- Fail to discuss whether Lisa should be held jointly and severally liable for the repayment of dividends.
- Forget to examine the court's power to grant relief for Ella and Lisa where it is just and equitable to do so under section 589.
- Only focus on the issue in relation to the payment of shares for non-cash consideration. You should address all the issues that arise from the question and discuss whether the payment of dividends amounts to unlawful distribution.

❓ Question 5

John and Peter are directors of Johnson plc. Peter, who owns 15 per cent of the company's shares, wishes to sell them. John is interested in purchasing them but does not have sufficient funds. In order to purchase Peter's shares, John has authorised a private loan with the bank which is guaranteed by Johnson plc.

Emma, who owns 1 per cent of the company's shares, is unhappy about the arrangement in relation to the guarantee.

Advise Emma.

Answer plan

→ Discuss the statutory provisions on the prohibition of financial assistance by a public company for the acquisition of its own shares (ss. 677–683).

→ Analyse whether the 'principal purpose' exception applies.

→ Examine the consequences of a breach of the statutory provisions on financial assistance.

→ Consider whether John has breached his director's duties in authorising the arrangement.

→ Evaluate what actions Emma can take to challenge the arrangement.

Diagram plan

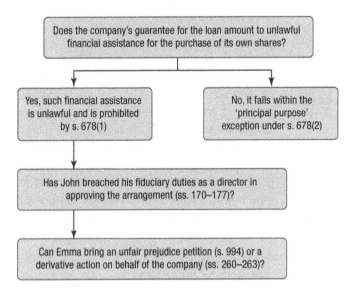

A printable version of this diagram plan is available from **www.pearsoned.co.uk/lawexpressqa**

Answer

[1] The introduction clearly
identifies the important issues
that you are going to address
in your answer. It immediately
shows that you know this
question is in relation to
financial assistance, directors'
duties and shareholders'
remedies.

[2] By pointing out that Emma is
a minority shareholder here, it
indicates that your answer will
deal with the issues in relation
to minority shareholder
remedies.

[3] This is the main provision
on the prohibition of financial
assistance in a public
company. You will lose some
marks if it is not referred to.

[4] This sentence demonstrates
your ability to apply the
relevant law to the problem
scenario.

[5] Note here that both
requirements must be met for
the exception to apply. This
is another essential provision
on financial assistance and it
must not be omitted in your
answer.

[6] This sentence shows
that you appreciate the
complicated nature of the
principal purpose exception.
It also demonstrates your
analytical skills and makes
your answer stand out.

[7] This case is important here
because it is the House of
Lords' interpretation of the
principal purpose exception. It
will gain you more marks.

In order to advise Emma on any legal action against the guarantee provided by the company, it is essential to consider three key issues:[1] first, whether the guarantee for the private loan amounts to unlawful financial assistance by the company for the purchase of its own shares; secondly, whether John has breached his statutory duties as a director; and, thirdly, what legal actions are available to Emma, who is a minority shareholder of the company.[2]

The guarantee, which is provided by the company for the loan for John's purchase of shares, falls within the definition of financial assistance in section 677. It states that financial assistance can be given by way of gift, guarantee, security or indemnity, a loan or any other agreement. The assistance must also be given for the purpose of the acquisition or to reduce or discharge a liability incurred for the purpose of the acquisition: **Dyment v Boyden** [2005] 1 BCLC 163. Where a person is acquiring or proposing to acquire shares in a public company, it is unlawful for that company or its subsidiary, to give financial assistance directly or indirectly for the purpose of the acquisition (s. 678(1)).[3] As John is purchasing shares in Johnson plc, the financial assistance is given directly for the purpose of the purchase and therefore it is unlawful.[4]

There are, nevertheless, exceptions to the prohibition in section 678(1). Financial assistance is not prohibited in a public company if both the requirements in section 678(2) are met.[5] First, if it is given in good faith and in the interests of the company; secondly, if the company's principal purpose is not the acquisition of shares or it is only an incidental part of some larger purpose of the company. Thus, if John can convince the court that the guarantee is given in good faith and in the interests of the company and that the company's principal purpose in granting the guarantee is not for the purchase of shares or it is only an incidental part of some larger purpose, it is likely that the court will not consider the guarantee as unlawful financial assistance.

It is difficult to determine what the principal purpose is or whether the purpose of an acquisition of shares is an incidental part of some larger purpose.[6] In **Brady v Brady** [1988] BCLC 20,[7] the House of Lords interpreted the principal purpose narrowly and distinguished between a purpose and the reason why a purpose was formed. This approach appears to restrict unduly the scope of the principal purpose exception; it also makes it very difficult to ascertain exactly what sort of situations would fall within its scope. Nevertheless, it appears that in some cases a more pragmatic approach is adopted towards the prohibition by looking at the commercial realities surrounding a financial assistance claim: *Charterhouse Investment Trust Ltd v Tempest Diesels Ltd* [1986] BCLC 1; *Anglo Petroleum Ltd v TFB (Mortgages) Ltd* [2008] 1 BCLC 185.[8] In *Chaston v SWP Group plc* [2003] 1 BCLC 675, it was alleged that Chaston, as a director of a subsidiary company, had breached his fiduciary duties by giving financial assistance for the purpose of the acquisition by the purchaser of the shares in its parent company. The alleged financial assistance was that the subsidiary paid the accountants' fees for the reports in respect of the transaction.[9] Arden LJ considered the commercial substance of the transaction and held that the transaction amounted to unlawful financial assistance and Chaston was liable for damages for breach of his statutory duties.

If the court is of the opinion that the guarantee by Johnson plc amounts to unlawful financial assistance by looking at the commercial realities behind the arrangement, the company is liable to a fine and every officer who is in default is liable to imprisonment or a fine or both (s. 680); the guarantee agreement will be unenforceable by either party to it: *Heald v O'Connor* [1971] 2 All ER 1105.[10]

John, as a director of Johnson plc, has authorised the giving of unlawful financial assistance, so it can be argued that he has breached his fiduciary duties to the company in sections 171, 172 and 175.[11] A director must exercise powers for the purposes for which they are conferred (s. 171): *Howard Smith Ltd v Ampol Petroleum* [1974] AC 821.[12] He must also act in the way he considers, in good faith, would be most likely to promote the success of the company for the benefit of its members as a whole (s. 172): *Re Smith & Fawcett* [1942] 1 All ER 542. Moreover, a director must avoid a situation in which he has, or can have, a direct or indirect interest that conflicts, or possibly may conflict, with the interests of the company (s. 175): *Aberdeen Railway Co v Blaikie Bros* (1854) 1 Macq 461.[13] It appears that John did not exercise

[8] A discussion of the judicial approach of respecting commercial realities demonstrates your excellent understanding of the common law on financial assistance. It adds more analysis and more credit to your answer.

[9] Although the facts of a case are not usually required, a brief summary of the facts of *Chaston* here illustrates the court's pragmatic approach and shows your sound knowledge.

[10] Some students forget to discuss the legal consequences for the company and its officers as well as the validity of the guarantee agreement.

[11] This sentence refers back to the problem question and leads on to the discussion of directors' duties. It shows that your answer is clearly structured.

[12] The reference to common law will gain you more marks because it demonstrates that you are aware of its relevance in the interpretation of the statutory duties.

[13] Most students are familiar with the duties under sections 171 and 172 but not section 175. Your sound knowledge of section 175 may impress your examiner.

his power of authorising transactions for proper purposes or act in the interests of the company. Besides, he did not avoid a situation where there was a conflict of interest between him and the company in relation to the guarantee agreement. John is therefore liable to account for the full amount of the financial assistance: *JJ Harrison (Properties) Ltd* v *Harrison* [2002] 1 BCLC 162.

[14] Although the most popular remedy for the unfair prejudice petition is the buy-out order, the court has very wide discretion and can make any order it thinks fit under section 996, in particular, to 'require the company to refrain from doing or continuing an act complained' under section 996(2)(b).

Emma may bring an unfair prejudice petition under section 994 and claim that her interests as a member have been unfairly prejudiced by the guarantee agreement. If the court is satisfied that the petition is well founded, it may issue an injunction to restrain the giving of financial assistance in breach of the statutory provisions (s. 996(2)(b)).[14] Emma may also bring a derivative action on behalf of the company under sections 260–263 to challenge John's breach of duties. She needs to establish a *prima facie* case and go through the two-stage procedure in section 261. The court will take into account a number of factors in section 263 when considering whether to give or refuse permission to continue the derivative claim. It should be noted that the court has taken a restrictive view towards this procedure and it is likely that permission to continue the claim would be refused if all that the claimant was seeking could be recovered by means of an unfair prejudice petition: *Mission Capital plc* v *Sinclair* [2008] BCC 866.

✓ **Make your answer stand out**

- Consider the issue of pre-emption rights. Peter's shares may need to be offered to all of the existing shareholders if there is a pre-emption clause in the company's articles of association.
- Point out that the answer would be different if it is a private company limited by shares. The rules on the prohibition of financial assistance by a private company for the acquisition of its own shares are abolished by the Companies Act 2006.

🖋 Question 6

'A public company is prohibited from providing financial assistance to a purchaser of its own shares. The prohibition is wide-ranging but it appears that the courts have adopted a pragmatic approach in defining financial assistance.'

Critically analyse the above statements by reference to the common law and statutory provisions.

Answer plan

→ Consider the rationale and historical background of the rules on the prohibition of financial assistance by a company for the acquisition of its own shares.

→ Examine the circumstances where financial assistance is prohibited (s. 678).

→ Analyse the 'principal purpose' exception in section 678(2).

→ Evaluate the House of Lords' judgment in *Brady* v *Brady* [1988] BCLC 20.

Diagram plan

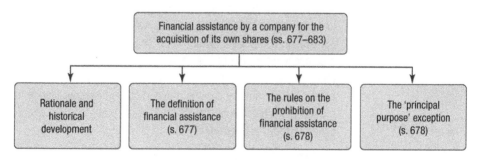

A printable version of this diagram plan is available from **www.pearsoned.co.uk/lawexpressqa**

Answer

[1] The reference to the doctrine of capital maintenance shows your understanding of the wider context. It will impress your examiner at the beginning of your answer.

[2] This sentence explains the main reasons why the financial assistance is prohibited. It demonstrates your good understanding of its rationale.

[3] The detailed understanding of the whitewash procedure will gain you more marks than simply referring to the procedure without explaining it.

[4] The reference to the *Modern Company Law for a Competitive Economy* demonstrates your excellent knowledge of the problems in relation to the provisions in the CA 1981. It will add more credit to your answer.

[5] This shows your knowledge of the relevant EU legislation and helps your answer stand out.

As a general rule, a company is prevented from providing financial assistance in purchasing its own shares. This reflects the doctrine of capital maintenance that a company must maintain its share capital in order to protect the interests of creditors: *Trevor* v *Whitworth* (1877) 12 App Cas 409.[1] The prohibition on financial assistance aims to prevent the abuse of asset-stripping whereby a bidder, after taking control of the company, uses the assets of the company to pay for the price of the shares.[2] Such abuse may prejudice the interests of the creditors of the company and the interests of any shareholder who does not accept the offer to acquire the shares.

The prohibition on financial assistance was first introduced by section 45 of the Companies Act 1929 as a result of the recommendations of the Greene Committee (1926). The whitewash procedure was then introduced for private companies in the Companies Act 1981, where financial assistance was permitted subject to certain conditions (ss. 155–158). It essentially required a special resolution and a directors' statement backed up by an auditors' statement.[3] These statutory procedures were criticised as expensive and time-consuming because substantial professional fees were incurred when the company attempted to ensure that innocent and worthwhile transactions did not breach the rules (*Modern Company Law for a Competitive Economy: Completing the Structure,* 2000).[4] It was proposed that these rules should be abolished completely for private companies. This proposal is adopted in the Companies Act 2006, but the rules on financial assistance still remain for public companies as a result of the implementation of the Second Company Law Directive (Art. 23).[5]

Financial assistance can be given by way of gift, guarantee, security or indemnity, or by way of release or waiver, a loan or any other agreement. It also includes any other financial assistance given by a company where the net assets of the company are reduced to a material extent by the giving of the assistance (s. 677). In addition, the assistance must be given for the purpose of the acquisition or to reduce or discharge a liability incurred for the purpose of the acquisition: *Dyment* v *Boyden* [2005] 1 BCLC 163.

The scope of the prohibition is wide, but it appears that the courts have adopted a pragmatic approach by looking at the commercial

[6] This sentence echoes the statement in the question and demonstrates that you are engaging with the question.

[7] The name of the leading judge shows your detailed and precise knowledge of this case.

[8] Note that there are three main provisions in relation to the prohibition. Many students only make reference to the first one.

[9] You must pay attention to the word 'both' instead of 'either'. Students tend to make the careless mistake of stating that financial assistance is allowed in a public company if one of the requirements in section 678(2) is met.

[10] It is important to point out the problems with these exceptions here because they are the main difficulties faced by the courts in interpreting this provision.

[11] The case of *Brady* v *Brady* (1988), which was decided by the House of Lords, should not be omitted in your answer.

realities surrounding a financial assistance claim instead of focusing on whether a transaction may technically be classified as financial assistance.[6] Hoffmann J[7] in ***Charterhouse Investment Trust Ltd* v *Tempest Diesels Ltd*** [1986] BCLC 1 emphasised that the commercial realities of the transaction as a whole must be considered when deciding whether a transaction could properly be described as the giving of financial assistance by the company. This view has been accepted by the Court of Appeal in ***MT Realisations Ltd* v *Digital Equipment Co Ltd*** [2003] 2 BCLC 117 and ***Chaston* v *SWP Group plc*** [2003] 1 BCLC 675. The emphasis on commercial realities has enabled the courts to narrow the scope of the prohibition.

In relation to the statutory provisions in the Companies Act 2006, there are three main rules in relation to the prohibition on financial assistance.[8] First, where a person is acquiring or proposing to acquire shares in a public company, it is unlawful for that company or its subsidiary to give financial assistance directly or indirectly for the purpose of the acquisition (s. 678(1)). Secondly, where a person has acquired shares in a company and a liability has been incurred for the purpose of the acquisition, it is unlawful for that company, or its subsidiary, to give financial assistance directly or indirectly for the purpose of reducing or discharging the liability (s. 678(3)). Thirdly, where a person is acquiring or proposing to acquire shares in a private company, it is not lawful for a public company that is a subsidiary of that company to give financial assistance directly or indirectly for the purpose of the acquisition (s. 679(1)).

Financial assistance is not prohibited in a public company if both of the requirements in section 678(2) are met:[9] first, if it is given in good faith and in the interests of the company; and secondly, if the company's principal purpose is not the acquisition of shares or it is only an incidental part of some larger purpose of the company. The exceptions are designed to ensure that genuine commercial transactions which are in the interests of the company are not prohibited. It is, however, often difficult to determine what the company's principal purpose is or whether the purpose of an acquisition of shares is an incidental part of some larger purpose.[10]

The 'principal purpose' exception is illustrated in ***Brady* v *Brady*** [1988] BCLC 20,[11] where the House of Lords held that the purpose of the transaction was to assist in financing the acquisition of the shares, and the acquisition of the shares was not incidental to the reorganisation but the essence of it. It interpreted the principal purpose narrowly and distinguished between a purpose and the reason why a purpose was formed. It found that the purpose of the transaction in this case was to assist financing the acquisition of the shares although the reason for the transaction was to facilitate the division of the business. The financial assistance was not incidental to a larger purpose and therefore illegal. This interpretation of the principal purpose exception has been criticised, as it appears to restrict its scope of application unduly and makes it very difficult to ascertain exactly what sort of situations would fall within its scope.[12]

[12] This sentence shows your analytical skills and will gain you more marks.

[13] The discussion of the consequences for the breach of the statutory provisions is essential for a sound answer.

A breach of these provisions is a criminal offence and the company is liable to a fine and every officer in default is liable to imprisonment or a fine or both (s. 680).[13] An agreement which provides unlawful financial assistance is unenforceable by either party to it: **Heald v O'Connor** [1971] 2 All ER 1105. Moreover, a director who authorises the giving of unlawful financial assistance is in breach of his duties and liable for the full amount of the improper financial assistance: **JJ Harrison (Properties) Ltd v Harrison** [2002] 1 BCLC 162. It can be concluded that the pragmatic approach in defining financial assistance by looking at the commercial realities is helpful in ensuring that genuine commercial transactions are not prohibited. The current rules on the prohibition of financial assistance, however, are still complex despite the reform in the Companies Act 2006.[14]

[14] Your conclusion should refer back to the question and summarise the main arguments.

✓ **Make your answer stand out**

- Consider the exceptions to the prohibition where certain transactions do not amount to unlawful giving of financial assistance: conditional exceptions (s. 682) and unconditional exceptions (s. 681).
- Make reference to academic opinions on financial assistance, in particular, in relation to the interpretation of the 'principal purpose' exception: Ferran, E. (2004) Corporate transactions and financial assistance: shifting policy perceptions but static law. *Cambridge Law Journal* 225; Ho, L. C. (2003) Financial assistance after *Chaston* and *MT Realisations*. JIBLR 424; Hirt, H. C. (2004) The scope of prohibited financial assistance after *MT Realisations Ltd v Digital Equipment Co Ltd.* 25 *Company Lawyer* 9; Luxton, P. (1991) Financial assistance by a company for the purchase of its own shares – the principal or larger purpose exception. *Company Lawyer* 18.

❓ Question 7

Sunshine Ltd has an issued share capital of £40,000, divided into 30,000 £1 ordinary shares and 10,000 £1 preference shares. Its articles of association provide that: 'The holders of preference shares are entitled to a 5 per cent fixed dividend and prior repayment of capital on a winding up of the company.'

Advise the board of directors as to the procedures required to achieve the following schemes:

1   Reducing the preferential dividend from 5 to 3 per cent.

2   Paying off the whole preference shares.

Answer plan

➜ Examine whether a reduction of the dividend attached to the preference shares constitutes a variation of class rights.

➜ Consider the procedure for the reduction of share capital.

➜ Evaluate whether the cancellation of the whole class of preference shares amounts to a variation or abrogation of class rights.

Diagram plan

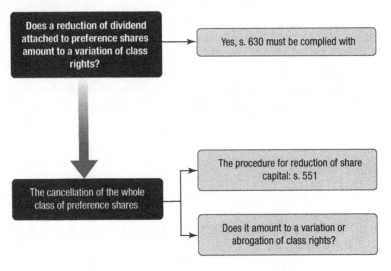

A printable version of this diagram plan is available from **www.pearsoned.co.uk/lawexpressqa**

Answer

This question concerns the legal procedures required for a variation of class rights and the reduction of share capital. The rights attached to preference shares as stated in the articles are class rights and they are presumed to be exhaustive: *Re National Telephone Co* [1914] 1 Ch 755.[1]

[1] This sentence explains the presumption that any rights attached to a share are deemed to be exhaustive. It is a good starting point to discuss class rights.

1. A reduction of dividend from 5 to 3 per cent[2]

[2] In an exam question like this, the use of headings may help examiners follow your answer and allocate marks accordingly.

If the board decides to reduce the dividend of the preference shares from 5 to 3 per cent, it needs to consider whether the reduction constitutes a variation of class rights. If it is not a variation of class rights, a special resolution is required for an alteration of the articles of association (s. 21): otherwise, the procedure in section 630 must be followed for a variation of class rights.[3] Class rights may only be varied in accordance with provisions in the company's articles, or, where the articles contain no such provisions, if the holders of shares of that class consent to the variation (s. 630(1)). The consent must be in writing from the holders of at least three-quarters in nominal

[3] Section 630 is a very important provision for the protection of class rights. It must not be omitted in your answer.

value of the issued shares of that class⁴ or a special resolution passed at a separate general meeting of the holders of that class sanctioning the variation (s. 630(4)). It appears that the articles of Sunshine Ltd do not contain provisions on the variation of class rights: thus, the consent of the holders of at least three-quarters in nominal value of the issued shares of that class is required.⁵

Section 630 only applies to variation or abrogation of class rights; however, there is no definition of variation or abrogation of class rights. A distinction is made at common law between matters affecting the rights attached to each share and matters affecting the enjoyment of these rights: **White v Bristol Aeroplane Co Ltd** [1953] Ch 65.⁶ If only the enjoyment of the right is affected, it does not attract the protection under section 630 because the class rights remain the same. Moreover, the courts have adopted a narrow⁷ view by comparing the right which would attach to a share before and after the proposed amendment of the class right. If the right remains the same, no variation occurs: **Re Mackenzie and Co Ltd** [1916] 2 Ch 450. The dividend of preference shares in Sunshine Ltd is reduced from 5 to 3 per cent and it is clearly a variation of class rights.

It should be noted that where a class has consented to a variation, the holders of not less than 15 per cent of the issued shares of the class in question may apply to the court to have the variation cancelled, provided that they did not consent to or vote in favour of the resolution for the variation (s. 633(2)).⁸ If the court is satisfied that the variation would unfairly prejudice the shareholders of the class represented by the applicant, it may disallow the variation (s. 633(5)). This provision is rarely used in practice because it is unlikely that the court would overturn a decision which was made by a majority of the class. An unfair prejudice petition under section 994 may be preferable if a member of the class feels that his rights have been unfairly prejudiced.⁹

2. Cancellation of the whole class of the preference shares

The cancellation of the preference shares involves a reduction of share capital. A reduction of share capital is subject to strict conditions because it goes against the doctrine of capital maintenance

[10] The reference to the rule of capital maintenance shows your wider understanding of the reduction of share capital. It may impress your examiners.

[11] Most students are aware of the requirements of special resolution and solvency statement in section 641 but many forget to discuss the alternative procedure in section 645.

[12] The reference to case law here will gain you more marks because it shows your good understanding of the general rule by illustrating how it works.

[13] This analysis is essential for a good answer because it addresses one of the core issues raised in the problem question. The reference to the case law authority should not be omitted.

[14] This sentence shows that your analysis has progressed from a reduction of share capital generally (which is discussed in the previous paragraph) to an abolition of the whole class of preference shares.

[15] This is a House of Lords' authority on whether a cancellation of a whole class of shares amounts to variation of class rights. It will add more credit to your answer.

which is designed to protect the interests of creditors.[10] A private company may reduce its capital by special resolution supported by solvency statement (s. 641(a)). The directors should make a solvency statement not more than 15 days before the date on which the resolution is passed (s. 642). If they make such statements without having reasonable grounds for the opinions expressed in it, an offence is committed by every director who will be liable to imprisonment on conviction and/or a fine (s. 643(4)). A private company may also reduce its share capital by special resolution confirmed by the court (s. 645).[11] The court has discretion to confirm or reject a proposed reduction of capital. Its main concern in approving reduction is the protection of creditors and fair treatment of different classes of shareholders: *Re Ratners Group plc* [1988] BCLC 685. Creditors are given the opportunities to object to the reduction of capital if a reduction involves any diminution of liability or any repayment of capital (s. 646).

The general rule on the repayment of capital is that money should be paid in the order in which the classes of shares would rank on a winding up. In *Re Chatterley-Whitfield Collieries Ltd* [1948] 2 All ER 593,[12] the company decided to reduce its capital by paying off preference capital but keeping its ordinary shareholders. It was held that the reduction was fair because it was carried out in accordance with the rights of the two classes of shareholders on a winding up.

When considering whether a reduction of capital amounts to a variation of the class rights of preference shareholders, the courts will compare the rights of the preference shareholders on a winding up with their rights under the proposed reduction. If the proposed reduction is in accordance with the class rights on a winding up, there is no variation of the class rights: *Re Saltdean Estate Co Ltd* [1968] 3 All ER 829.[13] Buckley J in this case noted that, although the preference shareholders hoped to retain their interest in the company, this expectation was always vulnerable to a future winding up or a reduction of capital.

In relation to the abolition of the whole class of preference shares, the courts have been generally reluctant to treat it as a variation of class rights.[14] In *House of Fraser plc v ACGE Investments Ltd* [1987] AC 387,[15] the ordinary shareholders passed a special resolution which approved the paying off of the whole preference shares of the company. The House of Lords held that the proposed reduction of capital which led to the extinction of the preference shares was not a variation of the class rights attached to these shares and therefore the consent of the preference shareholders was not required. The preference shareholders had a right to a return of capital prior to other shareholders and that right was not affected. As the preference shareholders in Sunshine Ltd are entitled to prior repayment of capital on a winding up, the capital of the preference shares should be repaid first and a proposed cancellation is not a variation of class rights.

 Make your answer stand out

- Consider whether directors have breached their duties in sections 171 and 172 in exercising their power to reduce the dividend and to pay off the whole class.
- Discuss in more detail the protection of shareholders' rights by way of unfair prejudice petition under section 994 or a derivative claim under section 260 against a director's breach of duties.
- Explain the solvency statement as defined in section 643 in more detail.

! Don't be tempted to . . .

- Only answer part of the question. Although the first part of the question on the reduction of dividend from 5 to 3 per cent appears simple and straightforward, it still requires a detailed analysis of class rights and the procedures for a variation of class rights.
- Reach the wrong conclusion that a cancellation of a whole class of preference shares amounts to a variation of class rights. Contrary to what many students may think, the abolition of a whole class does not vary class rights in this question.

www.pearsoned.co.uk/lawexpressqa

 Go online to access more revision support including additional essay and problem questions with diagram plans, You be the marker questions, and download all diagrams from the book.

Loan capital

7

How this topic may come up in exams

Students often find the questions on loan capital complex and confusing. The legal distinctions between fixed charges and floating charges are often examined in an essay question; in particular, you should focus on the nature of charges over book debts. Other popular areas for examination include the requirements for the registration of charges, the conclusive nature of the registration certificate, and the consequences and remedies for non-registration or late registration. This topic overlaps with corporate insolvency where the liquidator needs to consider the validity of charges and their order of priority when the company goes into liquidation.

■ Before you begin

It's a good idea to consider the following key themes of loan capital before tackling a question on this topic.

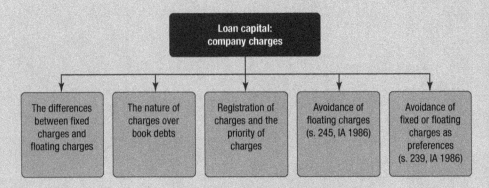

A printable version of this diagram is available from **www.pearsoned.co.uk/lawexpressqa**

 # Question 1

Critically evaluate the distinctions between fixed charges and floating charges, in particular, the nature of charges over book debts.

Answer plan

→ Explain the definitions of a fixed charge and a floating charge.
→ Examine the differences between a fixed charge and a floating charge.
→ Analyse the nature of charges over the company's book debts.

Diagram plan

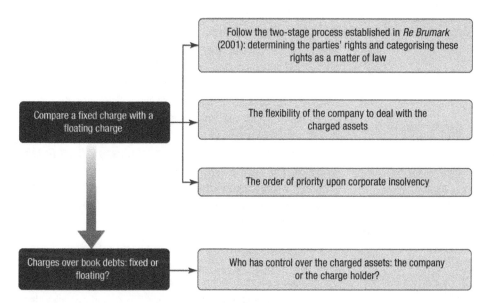

A printable version of this diagram plan is available from **www.pearsoned.co.uk/lawexpressqa**

Answer

This question requires an examination of the legal distinctions between a fixed charge and a floating charge with particular reference to the nature of the charge over book debts. A fixed charge is created over a specific asset of a company such as its land and buildings. It gives the charge holder an immediate proprietary interest in the assets and restricts the company's ability to deal with the asset: for example, the company would not be able to sell the asset without the consent of the charge holder.[1]

A floating charge is not attached to any particular assets and it is typically taken over the entire undertaking of the company, including removable plant and equipment, stock-in-trade, work in progress and book debts. It is an extremely flexible device because it enables the company to deal with the charged assets without the need to obtain the consent of the charge holder.[2] Its main characteristics are illustrated by Romer LJ in **Re Yorkshire Woolcombers Association** [1903] 2 Ch 284: a floating charge is a charge on a class of assets of a company, present and future; that class of assets would be changing from time to time in the company's ordinary course of business; and the company may carry on its business in the ordinary way until some future step is taken such as crystallisation.[3] Once it is crystallised, the floating charge becomes a fixed charge and the company is no longer free to deal with the assets in the normal course of business. When the company is in liquidation, a floating charge is still treated as a floating charge notwithstanding it has been crystallised. A floating charge may crystallise in the events expressly specified in the charge document, or upon the appointment of a receiver or administrator (**Evans v Rival Granite Quarries Ltd** [1910] 2 KB 979), or upon a winding up order (**Wallace v Universal Automatic Machines** [1894] 2 Ch 547), or the company's ceasing to carry on business (**Re Woodroffes (Musical Instruments) Ltd** [1986] Ch 366).[4]

[2] This is the most important feature of a floating charge. You will lose some marks if it is omitted in your answer.

[3] The reference to the case law and Romer LJ's classic statement of the characteristics of a floating charge will make your answer stand out because they go beyond a simple description of a floating charge.

[4] A discussion of the events for crystallisation with the support of relevant case law shows your sound understanding. It will add credit to your answer.

[5] Your answer should go beyond a basic description of the definitions of fixed charges and floating charges. An analysis of the advantages of a fixed charge over a floating one is essential for a sound answer. Also try to adopt a clear and logical list rather than stating everything you know about the differences between the two types of charges.

[6] The discussion of the avoidance of floating charges adds more credit to your answer. It is often ignored by students when comparing fixed and floating charges.

It is more advantageous for a creditor to hold a fixed charge than a floating charge for four main reasons.[5] First, a fixed charge offers greater security. Although the holder of a floating charge has considerable control over the company's affairs and can take steps to enforce the charge, there is always the danger that the assets will be dissipated. Secondly, a floating charge is open to challenge by a liquidator or an administrator under section 245 of the Insolvency Act 1986 whilst a fixed charge is not subject to this provision.[6] Thirdly, when the company goes into liquidation, a floating charge ranks before unsecured creditors but is subject to the prior claims of the expenses of liquidation, the preferential debts and the prescribed part of the floating charge assets. By contrast, the fixed charge holder ranks above all other creditors, including the expenses of the liquidation. Finally, the holder of a floating charge over a company's assets is vulnerable to the company granting another lender a fixed charge over the same assets at a later date. In order to prevent this, it is common to include a negative pledge clause[7] in the charge instrument, which states that the company will not grant another charge over the same assets or any attempt to grant another charge will be regarded as a crystallising event for the first floating charge.

The nature of a charge over the proceeds of book debts has been subject to a considerable amount of litigation.[8] Book debts are sums due to the company by its debtors and they would ordinarily be entered in the books of the company for accounting purposes. The nature of the charge is determined by who has control of the proceeds of the book debts, as demonstrated by *Agnew* v *IRC (Re Brumark)* [2001] 2 BCLC 188 and *National Westminster Bank plc* v *Spectrum Plus Ltd* [2005] 2 BCLC 269 *(Re Spectrum Plus Ltd)*.[9]

In *Re Brumark* the dispute arose in relation to the nature of the charge on the book debts which were uncollected at the time of the appointment of the receivers. The New Zealand Court of Appeal considered that the company was free to collect the book debts and deal with the proceeds in the normal course of business and therefore held that it was a floating charge. This decision was confirmed by the Privy Council, where a two-stage process was established: first, the court must construe the charge instrument and seek to ascertain the intention and the rights of the parties; and then it is a matter of law for the courts to determine whether the charge is fixed or floating.[10] Thus, neither the intention of the parties nor the terms which they use to describe the charge are conclusive in determining whether a charge is fixed or floating. The key issues are whether the company has control of the asset and whether it is free to remove it from the security without the consent of the bank. This approach was adopted by the House of Lords in *Re Spectrum Plus*.

In *Re Spectrum Plus* the company collected its book debts and paid them into a bank account. It was free to draw on the account for its business purposes, provided that the overdraft limit was not exceeded. At first instance, the court held that it was a floating charge over book debts. The Court of Appeal overturned this decision and held that it was a fixed charge because the bank

[7] Some students do not understand, or are not aware of, the negative pledge clause. It is very common in relation to a floating charge and therefore should be included in your answer.

[8] This shows your understanding of the complicated issues in relation to book debts. It also indicates that your answer is moving on to the legal issues of book debts. Try to signpost your answer so that it is easier for your examiners to follow.

[9] These are the two most important cases on the nature of charges over book debts. They should be discussed in detail in a good answer.

[10] The two-stage process for determining the nature of the charge enhances your understanding of the judgment of *Re Brumark*. It will gain you more marks.

[11] Some students only focus on the decision by the House of Lords. As this is a very important case, you should also discuss the judgments by the court of first instance and the Court of Appeal which will demonstrate your excellent knowledge of this case.

[12] The reference to this case demonstrates your sound understanding of the case law in relation to the nature of charges over book debts. It will gain you more marks.

was in control of the proceeds. The House of Lords concluded that it was only a floating charge because the company was free to withdraw the proceeds of the book debts in the ordinary course of business despite the restrictions.[11] The decision in **Siebe Gorman & Co Ltd v Barclays Bank Ltd** [1979] 2 Lloyd's Rep 142 was overruled.[12]

In most cases charges on book debts are floating charges; nevertheless, it is still possible to create a fixed charge over book debts. In **Re Keenan Bros Ltd** [1986] BCLC 242 the funds collected by the company were required to be paid into a blocked account with the charge holder and the consent of the bank was required for each withdrawal from that account. It was held that the charge was a fixed charge as the debts were unavailable to the company. It can be concluded from the above discussion that a charge over book debts is a floating charge if the company is free to collect the debts and deal with the proceeds without the consent of the holder of the charge.

Make your answer stand out

- Discuss the effect of the negative pledge clause. Registration of a floating charge does not by itself give constructive notice of the negative pledge clause: *Wilson* v *Kelland* [1910] 2 Ch 306.
- Examine in detail the judgments in *Re Spectrum Plus* (2005).
- Analyse in more detail the avoidance of a floating charge under section 245 of the Insolvency Act 1986.
- Explain the judgment in *Siebe Gorman & Co Ltd* (1979), where it was held that the charge was a fixed charge over book debts because the restrictions on the book debts and on their proceeds gave the lender some control.
- Make reference to academic opinions on fixed charges and floating charges: Capper, D. (2003) Fixed charges over book debts – the future after *Brumark*. 24 *Company Lawyer* 325; Smart, P. (2004) Fixed or floating? Siebe Gorman post-Brumark. 25 *Company Lawyer* 331; Sheehan, D. and Arvind, T. T. (2006) Prospective overruling and the fixed-floating charge debate. 122 *Law Quarterly Review* 20; Pennington, R. (2009) Recent developments in the law and practice relating to the creation of security for companies' indebtedness. 30 *Company Lawyer* 163.

> ## ! Don't be tempted to . . .
>
> ■ Forget to discuss the nature of a charge over book debts. You need to show a good understanding of the circumstances when it is categorised as a fixed charge or a floating one.
>
> ■ Provide an answer without reference to cases such as *Re Brumark* [2001] 2 BCLC 188 and *Re Spectrum Plus Ltd* [2005] 2 BCLC 269. These are very influential cases and should not be ignored in your answer.

❓ Question 2

Park Ltd obtained a loan of £10,000 from M Bank plc and a floating charge was created on 5 January 2011 in favour of M Bank plc over its entire undertakings, both present and future, to secure the loan. The charge instrument prohibits the creation of any subsequent charges which rank in priority to the floating charge. It was discovered on 25 February 2011 that the charge was not registered with the Registrar.

In March 2011, Park Ltd borrowed £20,000 from N Bank plc. On 2 May 2011, a fixed charge was created over Park Ltd's office buildings in favour of N Bank plc for this loan and it was registered on 20 May 2011. Park Ltd went into insolvent liquidation on 3 October 2011.

Discuss the validity of both charges and their order of priority.

Answer plan

→ Analyse the legal requirements for the registration of both charges (s. 860, CA 2006).

→ Examine the remedies for late registration or non-registration of the floating charge in favour or M Bank plc (s. 873, CA 2006).

→ Evaluate the effect of the negative pledge clause in the floating charge instrument.

→ Consider whether the floating charge in favour of M Bank plc can be avoided under section 245, IA 1986.

→ Discuss whether the floating charge or the fixed charge can be set aside as a preference under section 239, IA 1986.

Diagram plan

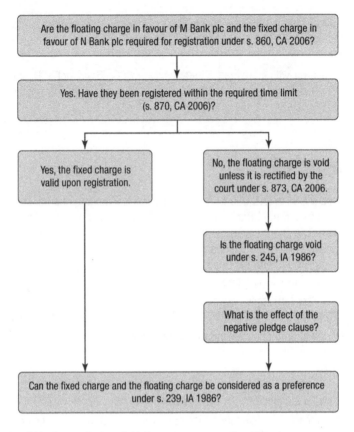

Are the floating charge in favour of M Bank plc and the fixed charge in favour of N Bank plc required for registration under s. 860, CA 2006?

↓

Yes. Have they been registered within the required time limit (s. 870, CA 2006)?

Yes, the fixed charge is valid upon registration.

No, the floating charge is void unless it is rectified by the court under s. 873, CA 2006.

Is the floating charge void under s. 245, IA 1986?

What is the effect of the negative pledge clause?

Can the fixed charge and the floating charge be considered as a preference under s. 239, IA 1986?

A printable version of this diagram plan is available from **www.pearsoned.co.uk/lawexpressqa**

Answer

[1] This sentence identifies the main legal issues that arise in the problem question. It clearly indicates that your answer is going in the right direction.

[2] Note that this statutory provision is included in the Companies Act 2006, not the Insolvency Act 1986.

This question concerns whether both charges are registered according to section 870 of the Companies Act 2006, whether the charges are valid under sections 245 and 239 of the Insolvency Act 1986, and whether the floating charge has priority over the fixed charge in light of the negative pledge clause.[1] Two charges were created by Park Ltd: one is a floating charge over its entire undertakings and the other is a fixed charge over its office buildings. Both charges are required for registration with the registrar. According to section 860 of the Companies Act 2006,[2]

[3] Some students may assume that all fixed charges must be registered. You should understand that registration is only required for those charges listed in section 860(7).

all floating charges must be registered; fixed charges need only be registered if they are over one of the specified classes of assets listed in section 860(7).[3] The list covers most classes of charges commonly given by companies, such as a charge on land, book debts, or any intellectual property; the charges on shares are not required to be registered. The purpose of registration is to give potential lenders more accurate information about the company and warn other creditors of the company's charged assets.[4]

[4] The reason for registration of charges adds more credit to your answer because it shows your good understanding.

[5] You should pay attention to the 21-day period for registration. Many students are aware of the requirement for 21 days but are not sure when it starts to run.

The particulars and the instrument of a charge must be delivered to the registrar of companies within 21 days beginning with the day after the day on which the charge is created[5] (s. 870(1)). If a company fails to comply with it, an offence is committed by the company and every officer in default who is liable to a fine (s. 860(4)) and the charge is void against the liquidator or administrator and any creditor of the company (s. 874(1)). It loses all priority it would otherwise possess and the charge holder will become an unsecured creditor. The charge, however, is still valid against the chargee and the money secured by it immediately becomes payable (s. 874(3)).[6] The fixed charge in favour of N Bank plc was registered within the 21-day limit. The floating charge in favour of M Bank plc, however, was not registered within 21 days of its creation and was therefore void unless it was successfully registered out of time.[7] This may have some implications in relation to the priority of the charges which have been registered in the period during which the floating charge was void.

[6] These sentences analyse the importance of registration and the consequences for non-registration. You should understand that the charge is only void against the liquidator or administrator and any creditor of the company; it is not void against the charge holder.

[7] Apply the law on registration to the question by discussing the charges in favour of M Bank plc and N Bank plc. As this is a problem question, you should apply the law to the question throughout your answer instead of only applying it in your conclusion.

The court, on the application of Park Ltd or M Bank plc, may order that the period allowed for registration shall be extended on such terms and conditions as seem to the court just and expedient (s. 873). The court will only make the order if it is satisfied with one of the following three conditions:[8] first, the failure to register a charge on time was accidental or due to inadvertence or to some other sufficient cause; secondly, the failure to register is not of a nature to prejudice the position of creditors or shareholders of the company; thirdly, it is just and equitable to grant relief. The jurisdiction of the court is very wide; however, the chargee must act expeditiously once the failure to register is discovered: *Re Teleomatic* [1994] 1 BCLC 90. Moreover, the court will not normally make an order under section 873 once a

[8] Ensure you don't make the mistake of some students by suggesting that all three conditions need to be met at the same time, as this is not the case.

[9] These sentences discuss the circumstances where the registration out of time will not be allowed. The reference to case law demonstrates your detailed knowledge and will make your answer stand out.

[10] Not all charges created within the specified period of time are invalid. It is essential that you know the exception.

[11] Some students are not aware of the different time limits which apply to the connected and unconnected persons. You will lose some marks in case of failure to make this important distinction.

winding up has commenced: *Barclays Bank plc* v *Stuart London Ltd* [2001] 2 BCLC 316.[9]

It should be noted that a floating charge on the company's undertaking or property shall be invalid if it is created in favour of an unconnected person within 12 months (two years for a connected person) ending with the onset of insolvency, unless the company was able to pay its debts at the time the charge was created[10] (s. 245, IA 1986). A person is connected with the company if he is a director, a shadow director or an associate of such a director or shadow director, or if he is an associate of the company (s. 249, IA 1986). It appears that M Bank plc does not fall within this definition of a connected person. The floating charge in favour of M Bank plc was created within 12 months of the commencement of the winding up; it was therefore invalid unless Park Ltd was solvent when granting the floating charge.

The floating charge or the fixed charge may be avoided under section 239 of the IA 1986 on the basis that the transaction has given one of the company's creditors an unfair advantage to increase their chances of repayment over the other creditors. The liquidator can apply to the court challenging the alleged preference, if a company has, within six months prior to the onset of insolvency (two years for connected person) given a preference to an unconnected person.[11] The court may make such order as it thinks fit for restoring the position to what it would have been if the company had not given that preference. It shall not make an order unless the company which gave the preference was influenced in deciding to give it by a desire to put that person in a better position. The floating charge in favour of M Bank plc was not created within six months prior to the onset of insolvency and therefore section 239 does not apply to it. As the fixed charge in favour of N Bank plc was created within six months before the commencement of the winding up, it should be set aside if the court is satisfied that Park Ltd was influenced in deciding to give it by a desire to give N Bank plc an unfair advantage over other creditors.

The priority between charges is subject to common law. In principle, a fixed charge takes priority over the equitable floating charge on the assets concerned. This means that a floating charge will be postponed to any subsequently created fixed charge over the same assets. In order to prevent this, a negative pledge clause is often included in the floating charge instrument which expressly prohibits the creation of charges in priority to the floating charge, which is the

[12] This part of the sentence identifies the negative pledge clause in the problem question.

[13] A discussion of the effect of this clause by reference to case law gains you more marks.

case with the floating charge in favour of M Bank plc.[12] Although registration is held to give constructive notice of the charge, it does not constitute notice of the terms and conditions contained in the charge document: **Wilson v Kelland** [1910] 2 Ch 306.[13] Thus, registration of a floating charge does not by itself give constructive notice of the negative pledge clause. It appears that N Bank plc did not know this clause and therefore the fixed charge (if it is not considered as a preference under section 239, IA 1986) ranks in priority to the floating charge in the event of insolvency (even if the floating charge was allowed to be registered out of time).

✓ Make your answer stand out

- Discuss that the charge which is caught by section 245 is valid only to the extent of any new value in the form of cash, goods or services supplied to the company, or the discharge of any liability of the company, if these take place at the same time as, or after, the creation of the charge (s. 245(2), IA 1986).
- In your discussion of section 245, IA 1986, make reference to the case of *Power* v *Sharpe Investments Ltd* [1994] 1 BCLC 111, where it was held that the new value must be provided at the same time with the creation of the charge.
- Consider the order of priority of charges when the company goes into insolvency. The fixed charge holder ranks above all other creditors, including the expenses of the liquidation and the preferential debts. By contrast, the floating charge ranks in a lower position, just above the unsecured creditors.

! Don't be tempted to . . .

- Assume that the floating charge was void because it was not registered within 21 days under section 870, CA 2006. You should discuss the possibility of a court order for registration out of time under section 873, CA 2006.
- Come to the conclusion that the fixed charge ranks after the floating charge because of the negative pledge clause. You should be aware that the negative pledge clause does not take effect unless the holder of the later charge has actual notice of it: in other words, unless he knows the clause in the charge instrument.
- Only focus on the requirements for registration of charges in the Companies Act 2006. You should also examine whether the floating charge can be avoided and whether the fixed charge or the floating charge can be considered as a preference in the Insolvency Act 1986.

❓ Question 3

Copnor Retailers Ltd obtained a loan from Cathy Bank plc and a charge was created in favour of the bank over all its book debts arising from its ordinary business. Copnor Retailers Ltd collected the book debts and paid them in a bank account with Cathy Bank plc. Copnor Retailers Ltd was free to withdraw money from the account for its business purposes on the condition that the overdraft limit was not exceeded.

Copnor Retailer Ltd went into liquidation in May 2014. Cathy Bank plc claimed that the proceeds over the book debts were subject to a fixed charge in its favour.

Advise Cathy Bank plc as to the nature of the charge over the book debts.

Answer plan

→ Discuss the differences between a fixed charge and a floating one.

→ Examine earlier authorities in relation to the nature of charges over book debts in *Siebe Gorman & Co Ltd v Barclays Bank Ltd* [1979] 2 Lloyd's Rep 142 and *Re New Bullas Trading Ltd* [1993] BCC 251.

→ Analyse recent authorities in relation to charges over book debts in *Agnew* v *Commissioner of Inland Revenue (Re Brumark)* [2001] 2 BCLC 188 and *National Westminster Bank plc* v *Spectrum Plus Ltd (Re Spectrum Plus Ltd)* [2005] 2 BCLC 269.

→ Apply the relevant law to the problem question with regard to the nature of the book debts.

Diagram plan

The key issue: who has control over the proceeds of the book debts?

Recent authorities: *Re Brumark; Re Spectrum Plus*

The charge over book debts in favour of Cathy Bank Plc: fixed or floating?

The distinction between a fixed charge and a floating charge

Earlier authorities: *Siebe Gorman & Co Ltd v Barclays Bank Ltd; Re New Bullas Trading Ltd*

A printable version of this diagram plan is available from **www.pearsoned.co.uk/lawexpressqa**

[1] In a problem question, you need to engage with the problem scenario in your introduction.

[2] Some students do not understand what is meant by book debts. This explanation shows that you know the basic concept of this topic.

Answer

Cathy Bank plc may have difficulties in seeking to enforce the fixed charge over the book debts of Copnor Retailers Ltd.[1] Book debts are sums due to the company by its debtors and would ordinarily be entered in the books of the company.[2] The nature of a charge over book debts has been subject to a considerable amount of litigation. This complex area of case law has recently been clarified by the Privy Council in *Re Brumark* and the House of Lords in *Re Spectrum Plus Ltd*. Earlier authorities such as *Siebe Gorman & Co Ltd* (1979) and *Re New Bullas Trading Ltd* (1993) were overruled.[3]

A fixed charge is created over a specific asset of a company, for example, its land and buildings and fixed plant. The charge restricts the company's ability to deal with the asset. By contrast, a floating charge is not attached to any particular assets identified when the charge is created; the company is free to deal with the charged assets in the ordinary course of business without the need to obtain the consent of the chargee: *Re Yorkshire Woolcombers Association* [1903] 2 Ch 284.

[4] Although *Siebe Gorman & Co Ltd* has been overruled, a discussion of the judgment is still essential because it shows how the law has developed. It will gain you more marks.

In *Siebe Gorman & Co Ltd* (1979),[4] the charge instrument required that the proceeds of the book debts be credited to a specific account held with the lender. This effectively prevented the company from withdrawing the monies in the course of its business. It was held that the charge was a fixed charge over book debts because the restrictions on the proceeds gave the lender some control. In *Re New Bullas Trading Ltd* (1993), the Court of Appeal accepted the arrangement which created a fixed charge over the uncollected book debts and a floating charge over their collected proceeds in the bank account. It was overruled by the House of Lords in *Re Spectrum Plus* on the basis that, since the company was free to deal with the book debts and their proceeds without the consent of the chargee, it was a floating charge.[5]

[5] The reason why *Re New Bullas Trading Ltd* was overruled shows your excellent understanding. It will add more credit to your answer.

In *Re Brumark*, a fixed charge was created in favour of a bank over all book debts of the company arising in its ordinary course of business. The dispute was in relation to the nature of the charge on the book debts which were uncollected at the time of the appointment of the receivers.[6] The Privy Council held that a charge over uncollected book debts was a floating charge because the company was free to collect the debts and use the proceeds in the ordinary course of its business. Lord Millett established a two-stage process: first, the court must construe the charge instrument and gather the intention of the parties from the language used in order to ascertain the nature of the rights and obligations which the parties intended to; secondly, it is a matter of law for the courts to determine

[6] The facts of this case are complicated and a detailed description will add little to your answer. A brief summary, however, shows your good understanding of the case and may impress your examiners.

whether the charge is fixed or floating; neither the intention of the parties nor the terms which they use to describe the transaction are conclusive. The crucial question is therefore whether the company has control of the asset and is free to remove it from the security without the consent of the bank.

[7] The reference to the House of Lords indicates that you appreciate the significance of this case.

This approach was confirmed by the House of Lords[7] in *Re Spectrum Plus* where an overdraft had been secured by a charge and the company was required to pay the proceeds from its book debts into that bank account. The company, however, was free to draw on the account for its business purposes provided the overdraft limit was not exceeded.[8] The charge over book debts was expressed in the same terms as that in *Siebe Gorman* which had been accepted as a fixed charge.[9] Upon the liquidation of the company, the bank claimed that the proceeds of the book debts were the subject of a fixed charge in its favour. The courts had to consider whether the charge was fixed or floating.

[8] The brief fact of this case is included here because it is similar to the problem scenario.

[9] This sentence shows you understand the link between *Re Spectrum Plus* and *Siebe Gorman*. It also lays the foundation for your discussion of the overruling of *Siebe Gorman* in the next paragraph.

At first instance, the court ruled that *Siebe Gorman* had been wrongly decided and it was held that the charge was a floating charge over book debts. The Court of Appeal, however, held that it was a fixed charge because the bank was in control of the proceeds.[10] The House of Lords confirmed that it was a floating charge despite that it was expressed to grant the bank a fixed charge over the company's book debts. The restrictions imposed were insufficient because the company was still free to withdraw the proceeds of the book debts in the ordinary course of business. The decision in *Siebe Gorman* was overruled.

[10] Some students only discuss the judgment of the House of Lords. The decisions by the Court of First Instance and the Court of Appeal demonstrate your excellent understanding of this case and will improve your grade.

[11] This part of the sentence, although short, will add more credit to your answer because it analyses the reasons why most charges over book debts are floating charges

In most cases charges on book debts are floating charges because it may be impossible in practice to give lenders complete control over the company's book debts.[11] In *Re Brightlife Ltd* [1986] BCLC 418, the company was free to collect the debts and pay the proceeds into its bank account and use them in the ordinary course of business. It was held that the charge was a floating charge despite some restrictions on the company. In *Royal Trust Bank v National Westminster Bank plc* [1996] 2 BCLC 682, the charge instrument required that the company pay all the proceeds of the book debts into a separate account. The charge was held to be a floating charge because the company was free to withdraw the proceeds collected which were deposited into the company's ordinary trading account.

It is still possible, nevertheless, to create a fixed charge over book debts if the lender prohibits the company from collecting the debts, for example, when there is requirement that the proceeds must be placed in a blocked account under the control of the lender. In **Re Keenan Bros Ltd** [1986] BCLC 242, the funds collected by the company were required to be paid into a blocked account with the charge holder and prior consent of the bank was required for each withdrawal from that account. The Privy Council held that the charge was a fixed charge because the debts were not available to the company.[12] Similarly in **William Gaskell Group Ltd v Highley** [1994] 1 BCLC 197, it was held that a charge over a company's book debts was a fixed charge because the proceeds of the book debts were required to be paid into an account and the company could not make withdrawal without the chargee's consent.

[12] These two sentences illustrate the circumstances where fixed charges can be created over book debts. The reference to case law will gain you more marks.

It is concluded that the key issue in determining the nature of the charge over book debts is who has control of the proceeds of the book debts. In relation to the charge over the book debts of Copnor Retailers Ltd, following **Re Spectrum Plus**, it is very likely that the court will consider it as a floating charge because Copnor Retailers Ltd, instead of Cathy Bank plc, is in control of the proceeds of the book debts.[13]

[13] Your conclusion should clearly state the legal position of the charge over the book debts of Copnor Retailers Ltd.

 Make your answer stand out

- Consider the characteristics of a floating charge which were stated by Romer LJ *Re Yorkshire Woolcombers Association* [1903] 2 Ch 284.
- Discuss whether the charge has been registered within the required time limit in section 860, CA 2006.
- Examine whether the floating charge over book debts can be avoided under section 245, IA 1986.
- Evaluate whether the floating charge can be set aside as a voidable preference under section 239, IA 1986.
- Analyse the circumstances where the floating charge crystallises.

> ## ! Don't be tempted to . . .
>
> ■ Make no reference to the House of Lords' decision in *Re Spectrum Plus*. This is a highly significant case on the nature of a charge over book debts and it must be included in your answer.
>
> ■ Wrongly believe that the decisions in *Siebe Gorman & Co Ltd* v *Barclays Bank Ltd* [1979] 2 Lloyd's Rep 142 and *Re New Bullas Trading Ltd* [1993] BCC 251 are still valid. You should know that they have been overruled by *Re Spectrum Plus*.
>
> ■ Reach the wrong conclusion that all charges over book debts are floating charges. You should also examine the circumstances where they are considered as fixed charges.

? Question 4

David was the majority shareholder and director of WL Tea Ltd. In February 2009, David lent £50,000 to WL Tea Ltd. In April 2010, David was worried about the financial situation of the company and obtained a floating charge over the entire undertaking of WL Tea Ltd for his loan. WL Tea Ltd was wound up in September 2010.

Advise the liquidator as to the validity of the floating charge.

Answer plan

➡ Consider the registration requirements for the floating charge in section 870, CA 2006.

➡ Examine whether the floating charge can be avoided under section 245, IA 1986.

➡ Analyse whether the floating charge can be set aside as a voidable preference under section 239, IA 1986.

Diagram plan

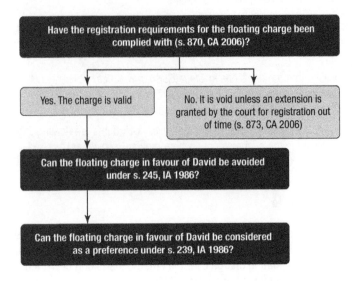

Have the registration requirements for the floating charge been complied with (s. 870, CA 2006)?

Yes. The charge is valid

No. It is void unless an extension is granted by the court for registration out of time (s. 873, CA 2006)

Can the floating charge in favour of David be avoided under s. 245, IA 1986?

Can the floating charge in favour of David be considered as a preference under s. 239, IA 1986?

A printable version of this diagram plan is available from **www.pearsoned.co.uk/lawexpressqa**

Answer

[1] These sentences not only identify the key legal issues arising from the question but also summarise the main areas of law which are relevant to the question. They immediately show your sound knowledge and clear structure of your answer. They will impress your examiners from the start.

This question concerns the validity of the floating charge created in favour of David, who was a director of WL Tea Ltd. A floating charge may be void if the registration requirements in section 870 of the Companies Act 2006 are not met. It may be avoided under section 245 of the Insolvency Act 1986 or set aside as a voidable preference by the liquidator under section 239, IA 1986.[1]

[2] You should discuss the serious consequences for non-registration. Many students are not aware that the charge is still valid against the chargee and the debt becomes payable. You will lose some marks if this issue is not included in your answer.

The floating charge over the company's undertaking must be registered with the registrar within 21 days, beginning with the day after the day on which the charge is created (s. 870, CA 2006). If a company fails to comply with it, an offence is committed by the company and every officer in default who is liable to a fine (s. 860) and the charge is void against the liquidator or administrator and any creditor of the company (s. 874). It loses all priority it would otherwise possess and the charge holder will become an unsecured creditor. The charge is, however, not void against the chargee and the money secured by it immediately becomes payable (s. 874).[2]

If the charge is not registered within the required 21 days of its creation, the company or a person interested may apply to the court for registration out of time (s. 873, CA 2006). The court may order that the period allowed for registration shall be extended on such terms and conditions as seem to the court just and expedient. The court will only make such an order if it is satisfied with one of the following three circumstances: first, the failure to register a charge on time was accidental or due to inadvertence or to some other sufficient cause; secondly, the failure to register is not of a nature to prejudice the position of creditors or shareholders of the company; thirdly, it is just and equitable to grant relief.[3] When the registration period is extended, the charge is regarded void until registered.

David obtained a floating charge over his unsecured loan shortly before the company was wound up. It is likely that he had early warnings of the company going into insolvency. Section 245 of the Insolvency Act 1986 is designed to prevent this and protect the interests of other creditors.[4] If a floating charge on the company's undertaking or property is created in favour of a connected person within two years, ending with the onset of insolvency, it shall be invalid unless some value has been given to the company. The connected person is defined in section 249 and it includes a director, a shadow director and the associates of the director. David, who was the company director, is therefore a connected person.[5] The onset of insolvency refers to the commencement of the winding up or the making of an administration order (s. 245). If the charge is created for an unconnected person within 12 months ending with the onset of insolvency, it shall be invalid unless the company is able to pay its debts at the time the charge was created (s. 245(4)). The charge caught by section 245 is valid only to the extent of any new value in the form of cash, goods or services supplied to the company, or the discharge of any liability of the company, if these take place at the same time as, or after, the creation of the charge (s. 245(2)).[6] In *Power* v *Sharpe Investments Ltd* [1994] 1 BCLC 111, it was held that the new value must be provided at the same time with the creation of the charge. As the floating charge in favour of David was created within five months (less than two years) of the commencement of the winding up and new value was not provided either at the time or after the charge was created, it can be argued that the charge should be void.[7]

[3] A discussion of the circumstances where the charge can be registered out of time shows your sound understanding. It will gain you more marks than only stating that the court may allow registration out of time.

[4] The rationale of section 245 goes beyond a simple description of the statutory provision and will add credit to your answer.

[5] Try to apply the relevant law to the problem question as you go along. Some students discuss the law with little or no application to the problem question, or only start to apply to the question in the conclusion. Your examiners are keen to see not only your good understanding of the law but also your ability to apply the law.

[6] Section 245(2) is often missing in students' answers. Many students have the wrong idea that the floating charge, if caught under section 245 of the IA 1986, will definitely be void. You need to understand that if any new consideration is provided, the charge is valid to the extent of the new value.

[7] Again, apply to the problem question after discussing the relevant law.

The floating charge may also be avoided under section 239 of the IA 1986 on the basis that the transaction has given one of the company's creditors a preference, for example, an unfair advantage in order to increase their chances of repayment over the other creditors. Where a company has, within two years prior to the onset of insolvency (six months for an unconnected person),[8] given a preference to a connected person, the liquidator can apply to the court challenging the alleged preference. If the court finds that a preference has been given, it can make such order as it thinks fit for restoring the position to what it would have been if the company had not given that preference.

[8] Note the different time limits for connected and unconnected persons. Failure to show an accurate understanding of this will lead to a reduction of marks.

A company is considered to have given a preference if both of the following conditions are met.[9] First, if that person is one of the company's creditors or a surety or guarantor for any of the company's debts or other liabilities; secondly, in the event of the company going into insolvent liquidation, the person is put into a better position by what the company has done (s. 239(4)). Both conditions are satisfied here, as David was the company's creditor and he was put into a better position by way of the creation of the floating charge.

[9] You need to pay more attention here. 'Both' of the conditions must be met. If only one is met, the transaction will not be considered as a preference.

The court shall not make an order unless the company which gave the preference was influenced in deciding to give it by a desire to put that person in a better position (s. 239(5)).[10] The essential element in establishing the existence of a preference is the desire to prefer that creditor on an insolvent liquidation. In *Re MC Bacon Ltd* [1990] BCLC 324,[11] the overdraft was secured by a debenture granted by the company within six months prior to the onset of insolvency when the company was unable to pay its debts. The court held that the company gave the security to the bank out of a desire to continue trading rather than positively wishing to improve the bank's position; the debenture was not held void as a preference. This case emphasised that the key test was whether the company desired to improve the creditor's position in the event of its insolvency.

[10] This is another condition for the court to set aside the preference. It is not often discussed in exam answers.

[11] A discussion of the case law which interprets the application of the statutory provisions makes your answer stand out from those which focus only on the statutory provisions.

If a company has given a preference to a person connected with the company, it is presumed to have been influenced in deciding to give it by a desire to prefer that creditor unless the contrary is shown (s. 239(6)). In *Re Exchange Travel (Holdings) Ltd* [1996] 2 BCLC 524 the company repaid loans made by the directors to the company two months before it went into administration. Such payments were held to be voidable preferences. It can therefore be presumed that

WL Tea Ltd had been influenced in deciding to give the floating charge by a desire to prefer David because David is considered as a connected person. Unless the contrary is shown, the floating charge will be set aside as voidable preference.

 Make your answer stand out

- Consider whether David has breached any of his fiduciary duties owed to the company, in particular, the duty to act to promote the success of the company (s. 172, CA 2006) and the duty to avoid conflicts of interests (s. 175, CA 2006).
- Examine whether David may be liable for wrongful trading under section 214 of the Insolvency Act 1986. A director is liable to contribute to the assets of the company if, at some time before the commencement of the winding up of the company, he knew or ought to have concluded that there was no reasonable prospect that the company would avoid going into insolvent liquidation, and he did not take every step to minimise the potential loss to the company's creditors.
- Consider section 10 of the Company Directors Disqualification Act 1986 where the court can make a disqualification order against a director who has been liable for wrongful trading.

¡ Don't be tempted to . . .

- Mix up the reference to the Companies Act 2006 and the Insolvency Act 1986. The requirements for registration are contained in the CA 2006 whilst the provisions in relation to the avoidance of a floating charge and the voidable preference are contained in the IA 1986.
- Assume that the floating charge is duly registered and forget to discuss the legal requirements for registration of charges. The rules on registration, in particular with respect to registration of charges out of time, are an essential part of your answer because a failure to meet these requirements will make the charge void.
- Forget to discuss whether the floating charge can be set aside as a voidable preference in section 239 of the IA 1986.

www.pearsoned.co.uk/lawexpressqa

 Go online to access more revision support including additional essay and problem questions with diagram plans, You be the marker questions, and download all diagrams from the book.

Shareholder remedies

How this topic may come up in exams

Shareholder remedies are broad, complicated and important topics in company law and are often favoured by examiners. The main remedies are personal actions, unfair prejudice remedies, derivative actions and winding-up remedies. Each type of remedy is likely to be examined by way of an essay or problem question on its own or with other types of remedies. You should pay special attention to statutory derivative actions and unfair prejudice remedies. In most problem questions, shareholder remedies are related to the topics on directors' duties. You should be able to apply the relevant law on directors' duties and shareholder remedies to complex problem questions.

■ Before you begin

It's a good idea to consider the following key themes of shareholder remedies before tackling a question on this topic.

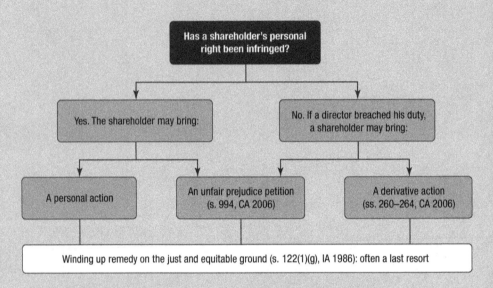

A printable version of this diagram is available from **www.pearsoned.co.uk/lawexpressqa**

 **Question 1**

'Statutory derivative actions have been introduced by the Companies Act 2006 to replace those at common law. They have removed the obstacles which prevented shareholders from bringing derivative actions at common law. It is without doubt that they will open the floodgates for vexatious claims against directors by disgruntled minority shareholders.'

Critically analyse the above statements.

Answer plan

→ Discuss derivative actions at common law and the difficulties faced by shareholders in bringing such actions.

→ Focus on statutory derivative actions (ss. 260–264) in relation to the procedure and the factors that the courts must take into account in granting permission to continue a derivative claim.

→ Compare derivative actions at common law and those in the Companies Act 2006.

→ Discuss whether the new rules provide shareholders with easier access to derivative actions and whether they will open the floodgates for vexatious litigation.

Diagram plan

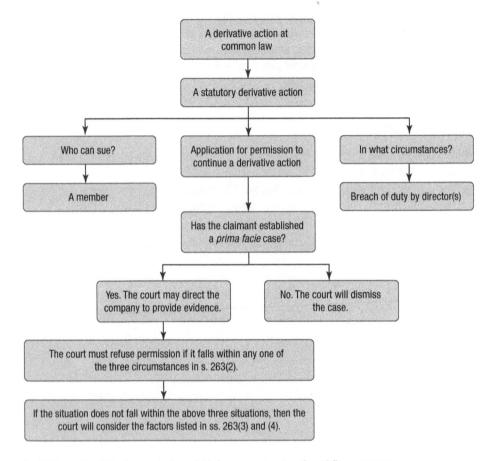

A printable version of this diagram plan is available from **www.pearsoned.co.uk/lawexpressqa**

Answer

[1] These opening sentences set the context for the analysis which follows and reassure the examiner that you know exactly what the essay is about in terms of subject content.

Derivative actions at common law were governed by the rule in **Foss v Harbottle** (1843) 67 ER 189 and the complicated rules effectively prevented vexatious suits. They were replaced by the statutory rules designed to provide a clearer procedure with more flexible criteria.[1] Whilst it can be asserted that they have modernised some aspects of derivative actions and removed some of the obstacles that existed previously, it is highly questionable as to whether the new procedures and criteria open floodgates for vexatious claims.

[2] These sentences outline the essential points of the main arguments and demonstrate that you clearly understand what is being asked in the question. They also demonstrate immediately your critical analysis of the statements.

[3] This quote shows your detailed knowledge of the important judgment in relation to the definition of fraud.

[4] These two sentences focus on whether directors' negligence amounted to fraud and demonstrate to an examiner your sound knowledge of derivative actions at common law.

[5] This paragraph shows your appreciation of the obstacles that a shareholder faced when bringing a derivative action at common law. It ties back to the question related to the obstacles at common law.

[6] The reference to the Law Commission's comments will gain you more marks because it demonstrates your wider understanding of the reform. This is also linked to the first two sentences in the question set.

[7] The brief comparison with the unfair prejudice remedy will gain you more marks as it demonstrates your awareness of the relationships between these two remedies.

It can be argued that there are still many obstacles in place and that any increase in the amount of litigation is debatable.[2]

This rule in **Foss v Harbottle** has two essential components: the majority rule and the proper claimant principle. This rule helps to prevent vexatious suits; however, it poses significant difficulties, especially when most or all of a company's directors have breached their duties. In order to protect the interests of minority shareholders, some exceptions were developed in **Edwards v Halliwell** [1950] 2 All ER 1064. Shareholders could bring an action in the case of an illegal or *ultra vires* act, or when there was a need for a special resolution, or when directors had committed fraud on the company. There was no clear definition of fraud; it was held in **Estmanco (Kilner House) Ltd v GLC** [1982] 1 WLR 2 that 'fraud in this context includes not only fraud and illegality at common law but also fraud in the wider equitable sense of an abuse or misuse of power by the directors'.[3] A mere negligent exercise of a director's powers did not constitute fraud if the directors had not benefited personally at the expense of the company: **Pavlides v Jensen** [1956] Ch 565. Nevertheless, it did amount to fraud if the directors had benefited from their negligence: **Daniels v Daniels** [1978] Ch 406.[4]

A shareholder also had to prove that the accused directors were in actual voting control of the company: **Prudential Assurance Co Ltd v Newman Industries Ltd (No. 2)** [1982] Ch 204. If an appropriate independent organ decided it was not in the commercial interests of the company to pursue the action, such a decision could prevent a derivative claim: **Smith v Croft (No. 2)** [1988] Ch 114. In addition, a derivative action would be barred if directors' breach of duties was only capable of ratification or had been actually ratified: **MacDougall v Gardiner** (1875) LR 1 Ch D 13.[5]

The Law Commission in 1997 concluded that the complex rules at common law were highly unsatisfactory and inadequate for minority shareholders.[6] In practice, there had been few cases, especially since the introduction of unfair prejudice remedies.[7] A new derivative procedure was recommended with more flexible and accessible criteria for determining whether a shareholder can pursue an action.

A shareholder can now bring a derivative action 'in respect of a cause of action arising from any actual or proposed act or omission involving *negligence, default, breach of duty or breach of trust by a director of the company*' (s. 260(3)). Compared with that of derivative actions at common law, the scope has been extended to cover a wider range of types of conduct including a director's mere negligence.[8]

Section 261 sets up a two-stage procedure for a derivative claim. At the first stage, the claimant is required to establish a *prima facie* case and the court considers only the application and evidence filed by the claimant. If it does not show a *prima facie* case the court must dismiss the application. If the court is satisfied at this stage, it may give directions for evidence to be filed by the company. In this way, the court can dismiss unmeritorious cases at an early stage without involving the defendant directors or the company.[9]

[9] This shows your understanding of the reasons for such a procedure which will gain you more marks.

At the second stage, permission will be refused under section 263(2) if the claimant in accordance with section 172 (to promote the success of the company) would not seek to pursue the claim, or if the misconduct has been authorised or ratified by the company. In other situations, the court can exercise its discretion and must take into account a number of factors under section 263(3), in particular, whether the claimant is acting in good faith and the importance that a person acting in accordance with section 172 would attach to continuing it. Other relevant circumstances include whether the cause of action would be likely to be authorised or ratified, whether the company has decided not to sue and whether the shareholder can pursue a personal action. Section 263(4) also states that the courts should consider the views of members who have no personal interests in the matter.[10]

[10] A clear and comprehensive discussion of the factors that the courts take into account is an essential aspect of statutory derivative actions.

The current rules on derivative actions offer some guidance for a court in the exercise of its wide discretion and therefore provide greater clarity and certainty compared with those at common law. The scope has been widened as it fills a gap regarding directors' mere negligence. Moreover, the claimant no longer has to prove fraud and wrongdoer control. It appears, therefore, that shareholders may find it easier to bring such actions and the floodgates for litigation may be opened.[11]

[11] This sentence relates your discussion back to the issues raised in the question in relation to the removal of obstacles at common law and easier access to derivative actions.

The court, however, is in control of litigation by way of the claimant's application for permission to continue the claim and, therefore, the amount of vexatious litigation can be controlled. The list of factors under section 263(2) and (3) also appears to be a set of hurdles that a claimant has to overcome. The Law Commission criticised the list of factors as a signal to adopt an over-restrictive approach and maintain a policy of not favouring a derivative action.[12] Effective ratification, for example, still bars a derivative action; the court must

[12] These two sentences highlight the difficulties in bringing a derivative action and they will impress your examiners.

also take into account the claimants' good faith, alterative remedies and the view of independent organ.

The Law Commission states that in all cases the new procedure will be subject to tight judicial control. These concerns are, to some extent, reflected in the judgments of *Mission Capital plc v Sinclair* [2008] BCC 866 and *Franbar Holding Ltd v Patel* [2008] BCC 885. In both cases the claimant's application for permission to continue the derivative claim was refused. The procedures and factors, as well as the recent restrictive judicial attitudes towards derivative actions, therefore act as sufficient filters for vexatious claims. Moreover, shareholders may be deterred by the costs of litigation and the free-riding problem, as any recovery goes back to the company and shareholders cannot benefit directly. Hannigan (2012) is of similar view that there is unlikely to be any significant increase in the number of derivative claims because of the restrictive judicial attitude, the majority rule and a lack of incentive for shareholders.[13] It is therefore concluded that the statutory derivative actions are unlikely to open the floodgates for vexatious litigation.

[13] This section evaluates the problems associated with the new procedure and demonstrates your critical analysis skills by reference to the Law Commission's Report, case law and academic opinion. It will make your answer stand out by demonstrating your up-to-date knowledge and sound understanding of the current issues on this topic.

✓ Make your answer stand out

- Discuss the difficulties that shareholders still face in bringing statutory derivative actions by reference to academic opinions, such as: Almadani, M. (2009) Derivative actions: does the Companies Act 2006 offer a way forward? 30 *Company Lawyer* 131; Keay, A. R. and Loughrey, J. (2008) Derivative proceedings in a brave new world for company management and shareholders. *JBL* 151; and Hannigan, B. (2012) *Company Law*. Oxford: Oxford University Press: pp. 437–8.

- Analyse the recent cases such as *Mission Capital plc* (2008) and *Franbar Holding Ltd* (2008) in greater detail. Explain why shareholders' application for permission to continue the derivative claim was refused in both cases.

- Examine the costs issue and the indemnity cost order as established in *Wallersteiner v Moir (No. 2)* [1975] QB 373.

- Evaluate the impact of the more popular unfair prejudice remedies on derivative actions. The court may refuse permission to continue a derivative claim when there is an alternative remedy available for shareholders.

- Consider more recent cases, such as *Kiani v Cooper* [2010] EWHC 557; *Stainer v Lee* [2010] EWHC 1539 (Ch); *Iesini v Westrip Holdings Ltd* [2009] EWHC 2526 (Ch); *Stimpson v Southern Landlords Association* [2009] EWHC 2072 (Ch); *Kleanthous v Paphitis and others* [2011] EWHC 2287 (Ch).

> **!** Don't be tempted to . . .
>
> ■ Focus only on the statutory derivative claim. You must also discuss the rule in *Foss* v *Harbottle* and the common law rules on derivative actions.
>
> ■ Confuse the codification of derivative actions with the codification of directors' duties. Although these are related issues, you should not discuss directors' duties in great length in this question.
>
> ■ Describe the detailed facts of some cases or apply case law which is not directly relevant. You should apply relevant case law, in particular, recent cases, in your answer.

? Question 2

Simon and Chris are directors of Cosham Bakery Ltd. They hold 30 and 60 per cent of its shares respectively; Donal holds the remaining 10 per cent of the company's shares. Sweet Bakery Ltd was opened near the company's premises recently. When talking to the employees of Sweet Bakery Ltd, Donal found out that it was wholly owned by Chris.

Donal wishes to bring a derivative claim against Chris.

Advise Donal in relation to the procedure and the merit of such claim.

Answer plan

→ Consider the procedure for derivative actions under sections 260–264 of the Companies Act 2006.

→ Discuss whether Chris breached any duty or duties as a director of Cosham Bakery Ltd.

→ Examine the factors that a court will take into account when it considers granting permission to continue the action.

Diagram plan

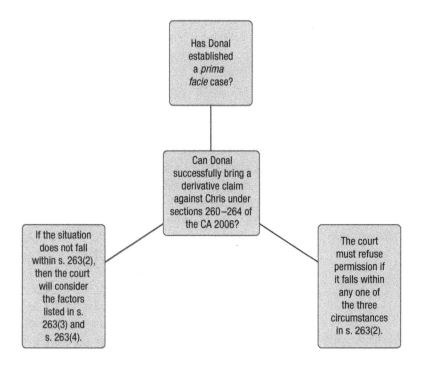

Has Donal established a *prima facie* case?

Can Donal successfully bring a derivative claim against Chris under sections 260–264 of the CA 2006?

If the situation does not fall within s. 263(2), then the court will consider the factors listed in s. 263(3) and s. 263(4).

The court must refuse permission if it falls within any one of the three circumstances in s. 263(2).

A printable version of this diagram plan is available from **www.pearsoned.co.uk/lawexpressqa**

Answer

[1] Your introduction should identify the key legal issues raised in the question.

[2] These two sentences explain derivative actions and their brief history. They demonstrate to an examiner that you are able to engage with the question and understand the context of a derivative claim.

In order to bring a successful derivative claim against Chris, Donal must establish that Chris has breached his duty a s a director of Cosham Bakery Ltd.[1] A shareholder may bring a derivative claim against directors' breach of duty under sections 260–264 of the Companies Act 2006 (CA 2006). It replaced derivative action at common law which was governed by the rule in **Foss v Harbottle** (1843) 67 ER 189 and its exceptions.[2]

Donal must apply to court for permission to continue the derivative claim and follow the two-stage procedure. At the first stage, the court considers only the application and evidence filed by Donal and decides whether a *prima facie* case is established. If so, the court may order the company or defendant to provide evidence at the second stage. Permission will be refused if a person acting in accordance with section 172 would not seek to pursue the claim, or if the misconduct has been authorised or ratified by the company (s. 263(2)). It can be argued that the person acting to promote the success of the company would seek to pursue the claim and recover any loss suffered by the company because Chris breached his duty as a director of Cosham Bakery Ltd.[3]

[3] Try to apply the law to the problem scenario whenever you can.

Chris as a director owes duties to the company: *Percival v Wright* [1902] 2 Ch 421 and section 170(1). As Chris set up his own business which competes with Cosham Bakery Ltd, it is argued that Chris breached his duties under sections 175 and 172.[4] A director must avoid a situation in which he has, or can have, a direct or indirect interest that conflicts, or possibly may conflict with the interests of the company (s. 175). Section 175 codifies the no-conflict rule and no secret profit rule at common law: *Aberdeen Railway Co v Blaikie Bros* (1854) 1 Macq 461 and *Regal (Hastings) Ltd v Gulliver* [1942] 1 All ER 378.[5] This duty is not infringed if the matter has been authorised by the directors and if nothing in this company's constitution invalids such authorisation. Authorisation is effective only when the matter was agreed without the votes of these directors (s. 175(6)). It appears that Chris' conflict of interest was not authorised by the board. Even if he tried to authorise it, authorisation would not be effective because Chris could not be counted towards the quorum and his votes would not be valid.[6]

[4] This sentence sets a clear structure for your discussion so your examiners know where you are going with your answer.

[5] Discuss the duty to avoid conflicts of interest by reference to case law and apply it to the question.

[6] These sentences show your sound understanding of effective authorisation. It adds more credit to your answer because it is a key aspect of the duty to avoid conflicts of interest under section 175.

According to section 172, a director must act in the way he considers, in good faith, would be most likely to promote the success of the company for the benefits of its members as a whole, and in doing so have regard to other stakeholders' interests. Section 172 codified the duty to act in good faith at common law (*Re Smith v Fawcett Ltd* (1942) Ch 304) and introduced the enlightened shareholder value. It adopts a subjective duty and emphasises what a director thinks. It may be difficult to prove a breach of this duty as Chris may argue that he acted in the way he considered to promote the success of the company.[7] The courts, however, have set some limits to the subjective test and will consider whether an intelligent and honest director could in the whole of the circumstances reasonably believe the transaction to be for the benefit of the company: *Charterbridge Corp Ltd v Lloyds Bank Ltd* [1969] 3 WLR 122.[8] It is unclear whether such an objective approach would be considered

[7] These sentences analyse the problems associated with section 172 and will gain you more marks.

[8] A discussion of the objective test by reference to case law makes your answer stand out more than a pure description of the statutory provision in section 172.

by the court in interpreting section 172; however, it appears that an intelligent and honest director could not reasonably believe setting up a competing business was for the success of Cosham Bakery Ltd.

Chris, as a majority shareholder of Cosham Bakery, may try to ratify his breach of duties at a general meeting. The resolution for ratification is passed only if the necessary majority is obtained disregarding votes in favour of the resolution by the director and any member connected with him (s. 239). Even though Chris holds 60 per cent of the company's shares, it was unlikely that an effective resolution to ratify his misconduct could be passed.[9] The court is therefore unlikely to refuse permission at this stage.

[9] A discussion of the law on ratification goes beyond a simple description of directors' duties and it will make your answer stand out.

The court must then take into account all the factors under section 263(3), in particular, whether the claimant is acting in good faith, the importance that a person acting in accordance with section 172 would attach to continuing it, whether it would be likely to be authorised or ratified, whether the company has decided not to sue and whether the shareholder can pursue a personal action. It also considers the views of members who have no personal interests in the matter (s. 263(4)).[10] It is likely that the court will take a restrictive approach as reflected in the judgments of two recent cases: **Mission Capital plc v Sinclair** (2008) and **Franbar Holding Ltd v Patel** (2008).[11] In both cases the court refused to grant permission to continue the derivative claims for two main reasons. First, the judge did not believe that the hypothetical director as mentioned in section 263(2)(a) or section 263(3)(b) would attach much importance to the claim. Secondly, all that the claimants were seeking could be recovered by means of an unfair prejudice petition. As Donal could bring an unfair prejudice remedy under section 994, it is most likely that the court would not grant permission to continue the derivative action against Chris despite his breach of director's duties.[12]

[10] This section highlights the factors that the court must take into account. It adds more credit to your answer because it is very important for the assessment of the success of the derivative claim.

[11] These recent case law demonstrates to an examiner your excellent understanding of the problems associated with the derivative actions, in particular, the restrictive judicial approach which will impress your examiners.

[12] In your conclusion, refer back to the question and clearly state your advice to Donal.

✓ Make your answer stand out

■ Comment on the judicial approach towards derivative actions by reference to most recent cases, such as *Hughes* v *Weiss* [2012] EWHC 2363 (Ch); *Kiani* v *Cooper* [2010] EWHC 577 (Ch); *Stainer* v *Lee* [2010] EWHC 1539 (Ch); *Lesini* v *Westrip Holdings Ltd* [2009] EWHC 2526 (Ch); *Stimpson* v *Southern Landlords Association* [2009] EWHC 2072 (Ch). ▶

- Refer to academic opinions on statutory derivative claims, such as Sykes, A. (2010) The continuing paradox: a critique of minority shareholder and derivative claims under the Companies Act 2006. *Civil Justice Quarterly* 205.
- Examine the costs problem and the possibility of obtaining an indemnity cost order.
- Briefly discuss the courts' wide discretion and flexible reliefs under unfair prejudice remedies.

! Don't be tempted to . . .

- Give a detailed description of different types of directors (*de facto*, *de jure* and shadow directors). This will add very little credit to your answer.
- Provide a narrative account of directors' duties at common law. You should apply the relevant case law to the codified duties.
- Describe all directors' duties in the Companies Act 2006. You should only focus on those duties which are relevant to this question.
- Concentrate on the director's breach of one duty. You should be aware that directors can breach more than one duty at the same time.
- Discuss in detail derivative actions at common law. Those rules at common law are replaced by the statutory derivative actions and therefore you should focus your discussion on the latter.
- Forget to relate your discussion back to the question. You should give specific advice to Donal as required by this question as to whether the derivative claim against Chris would be successful.

◙ Question 3

Discuss, by reference to case law, the application of unfair prejudice remedies in sections 994–996 of the Companies Act 2006.

Answer plan

→ Briefly explain the historical background of unfair prejudice remedy.

→ Discuss the meaning of 'conduct of company's affairs' and that of 'interests of members' in section 994 by reference to case law.

→ Evaluate what constitutes unfairly prejudicial conduct by reference to case law, in particular, *O'Neill* v *Phillips* [1999] 1 WLR 1092.

→ Consider the courts' wide discretion in granting relief in section 996, in particular, the purchase order.

Diagram plan

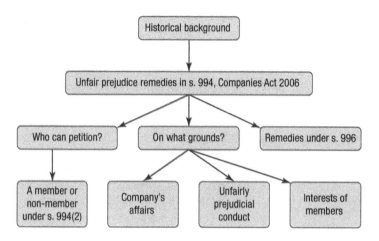

A printable version of this diagram plan is available from **www.pearsoned.co.uk/lawexpressqa**

Answer

Unfair prejudice remedy has evolved over a long period of time into an extremely valuable remedy for minority shareholders in England, particularly for those in small private companies. Whilst it has greatly enhanced minority shareholders' protection due to its broad scope of application and flexible reliefs, unfair prejudice remedy does have its own problems.[1]

Unfair prejudice remedy originated from the oppression remedy in section 210 of the Companies Act 1948, before the introduction of which aggrieved shareholders could either choose to bring derivative actions at common law or to petition for winding up the company on just and equitable grounds. Due to inadequacies of drafting and restrictive judicial interpretation of section 210, only two cases were successfully brought. The Jenkins Committee in 1962 recommended that a petition should be granted on the grounds of unfair prejudice rather than oppression. This was adopted in section 75 of the Companies Act 1980 and section 459 of the Companies Act 1985. This remedy is now restated in section 994 of the Companies Act 2006.[2]

[1] The introduction reassures the examiners that you know exactly what the question is about in terms of subject content.

[2] This paragraph demonstrates your clear understanding of the historical origins and the development of unfair prejudice remedy. It will add credit to your answer.

A petition under section 994(1) is made on the ground that the company's affairs are being, or have been, conducted in a manner which is unfairly prejudicial to the interests of its members generally or of some part of its members (including at least the petitioner), or that any actual or proposed act or omission of the company is or would be so prejudicial. It applies to a petition brought by a member or a person who is not a member of a company but to whom shares in the company have been transferred or transmitted by operation of law, for example, a personal representative and a trustee in bankruptcy.[3]

[3] The requirement for a section 994 petitioner is often ignored by students. Although it is a basic element of section 994, it is essential to include it in your answer.

There are three key elements in an unfair prejudice petition: conduct of a company's affairs, interests of a member and an unfairly prejudicial conduct.[4] First, the petition must relate to the conduct of the affairs of the company. It is not simply concerned with the conduct of an individual shareholder acting in a personal capacity: *Re Legal Costs Negotiators Ltd* [1999] BCC 547. It must be concerned with acts done by the company or those authorised to act as its organ.

[4] This sentence sets out a clear structure for the following discussion of the key elements of section 994. It also shows the examiners where you are going with your answer.

Secondly, the conduct complained of must be unfairly prejudicial to the interests of the petitioner *qua* member, which means the interests of the petitioner as a member as opposed to any other interests which the member might possess: *Re JE Cade & Son Ltd* [1991] BCC 360. It is recognised that the interests of members extend beyond their strict legal rights, which are usually contained in a company's constitution and the relevant company laws: *Re Blue Arrow plc* [1987] BCLC 585.

Lord Wilberforce in *Ebrahimi v Westbourne Galleries* [1973] AC 360 held that 'there are individuals, with rights, expectations and obligations *inter se* which are not necessarily submerged in the company structure'. His Lordship took the view that the strict legal rights of the parties could be subject to 'considerations ... of a personal character arising between one individual and another, which may make it unjust, or inequitable, to insist on legal rights or to exercise them in a particular way'. Hoffmann J in *Re A Company (No. 00477 of 1986)* [1986] BCLC 376 applied this reasoning to unfair prejudice petitions and recognised shareholders' legitimate expectations. This approach has strongly influenced the development of unfair prejudice remedy in a way that it has enabled the protection

[5] The sentence analyses
the impact of Hoffmann J's
judgment on the functions
of unfair prejudice remedies.
It is significant for the
understanding of this remedy
and will gain you more marks.

[6] O'Neill v Phillips is the only
House of Lords' judgment
on the scope of unfairly
prejudicial conduct. It should
therefore be discussed in
detail.

[7] This sentence sets the
context for detailed discussion
of unfairly prejudicial
conduct in different types of
companies.

[8] The reference to cases
demonstrates your excellent
understanding of the
application of unfair prejudice
remedies and it will add more
credit to your answer.

[9] The discussion of quasi-
partnership companies gains
you more marks because
it is important for your
understanding of equitable
considerations.

of members' wider interests and expectations beyond their strict legal rights.[5]

With regard to the unfairly prejudicial conduct, Hoffmann LJ in *Re Saul D Harrison & Sons plc* [1994] BCC 475 confirmed that the test of unfairness was objective in the sense that 'the focal point of the court's inquiry in determining whether conduct has been unfairly prejudicial is its impact and not its nature'. It was held in *O'Neill v Phillips* [1999] 1 WLR 1092[6] that a member would not ordinarily be entitled to complain of unfairness unless there had been some breach of terms on which the member agreed that the affairs of the company should be conducted, or some use of the rules in a manner which equity would regard as contrary to good faith. The application of equitable considerations depends on the nature of the company and the relationship among its shareholders.[7]

Where the company is purely a commercial relationship, as in a public company, the entire relationship of the parties is exhaustively determined by the constitution and there is no scope for equitable considerations to arise. Typical allegations include breach of company's articles of association, breaches of directors' duties involving misappropriation of corporate assets (*Re Little Olympian Each-Ways Ltd* [1995] 1 BCLC 636), improper allotments of shares (*Dalby v Bodilly* [2005] BCC 627) and allegations of mismanagement (*Re Macro (Ipswich) Ltd* [1994] BCC 781).[8]

Equitable considerations may make it unfair for those conducting the affairs of the company to rely upon their strict legal powers. This typically takes place in quasi-partnership companies, most of which are family-run businesses founded upon mutual confidence and trust.[9] Shareholders frequently play a role in the management of the company, based on the informal agreement that they should participate in management (*Re Saul D. Harrison & Sons plc*) and expect an investment return (*Re Kenyon Swansea* [1987] 3 BCC 259). The most common examples are exclusion from management in small quasi-partnership companies whereby the exercise of removal of directors under section 168 would amount to unfairly prejudicial conduct in the absence of a fair offer by the majority to buy the petitioner's shares: *Brownlow v GH Marshall Ltd* [2000] 2 BCLC 655.

If the court is of the opinion that the petition is well grounded, it has wide discretion in granting remedies under section 996 and may make such order as it thinks fit. Based on its survey of unfair prejudice cases, the Law Commission Report has concluded that the relief most commonly sought was the order for the purchase of the petitioner's shares by the company or the respondents. When a court makes such an order, it has a choice as to the date and basis of the valuation of shares and the key requirement is *fairness*: **Re Bird Precision Bellows Ltd** [1984] Ch 419.[10]

[10] An evaluation of the purchase order by reference to case law shows your sound knowledge and will gain you more marks.

The unfair prejudice remedy is widely used by minority shareholders due to its broad scope of application and flexible reliefs. It has been a more attractive remedy for minority shareholders, compared with the complex procedures in derivative actions and the extreme consequences of a winding-up order. The Law Commission (1996), however, criticised the fact that its broad scope enables petitioners to include facts that may be remotely relevant to the case, which leads to complex, costly and cumbersome litigation.[11] There is a risk that it may be used as a means of oppression by minority shareholders because of its easy access. Thus, the courts face the challenge of balancing their wide discretion to protect shareholders from unfairly prejudicial conduct on the one hand and preventing malicious lawsuits on the other.[12]

[11] The Law Commission's criticisms demonstrate your excellent understanding of the weakness of unfair prejudice remedies. They will make your answer stand out.

[12] This sentence highlights your sound evaluation of unfair prejudice remedy and shows your analytical skills. It will impress your examiner.

 Make your answer stand out

- Discuss in detail the nature of quasi-partnership companies which was identified by Lord Wilberforce in *Ebrahimi* (1973).

- Evaluate the problems associated with unfair prejudice remedies by reference to academic literature, such as Payne, J. (2005) Sections 459–461 Companies Act 1985 in flux: the future of shareholder protection. 64 *CLJ* 647; Hirt, H.C. (2003) In what circumstances should breach of director's duties give rise to a remedy under ss. 459–461 of the Companies Act 1985? 24 *Company Lawyer* 100.

- Discuss *Clark* v *Cutland* [2003] 4 All ER 733 and consider its implications on the scope of unfair prejudice remedies. In this case, it was held that shareholders could bring unfair prejudice petitions and seek corporate remedies where the company had suffered losses, thereby circumventing the procedural requirements of derivative actions.

- Comment on the interrelationships between unfair prejudice remedy and other types of remedies, such as the statutory derivative actions (ss. 260–264, Companies Act 2006) and the winding-up remedy (s. 122, Insolvency Act 1986).

> **❗ Don't be tempted to . . .**
>
> ■ Simply describe the provisions in sections 994–996. You must analyse the core elements of unfair prejudice remedies.
>
> ■ Forget to discuss *O'Neill* v *Phillips* [1999] 1 WLR 1092. This is the only House of Lords' authority on the scope of unfairly prejudicial conduct and therefore it is vital for your answer.
>
> ■ Fail to examine the courts' wide discretion and the flexible reliefs in section 996.

❓ Question 4

David, James and Emma incorporated Oriental Delight Ltd in 2009. They are all directors and hold 50, 30 and 20 per cent of company's shares respectively. David and James recently found out that Emma secretly directed Oriental Delight Ltd's contracts to another company which her husband controlled. They felt that it was impossible to work with Emma and a resolution was passed at a shareholder meeting to remove her from the board.

Emma is unhappy about her removal and is considering bringing an unfair prejudice petition so that she can sell her shares to David and James at a fair price.

Advise Emma as to the merits of her unfair prejudice petition.

Answer plan

➡ Discuss whether the shareholder resolution to remove Emma from the board of directors is unfairly prejudicial to her interests as a member.

➡ Evaluate Emma's breach of duties as a director and the implications of this misconduct on her unfair prejudice petition.

➡ Consider possible remedies that the court may grant under section 996.

Diagram plan

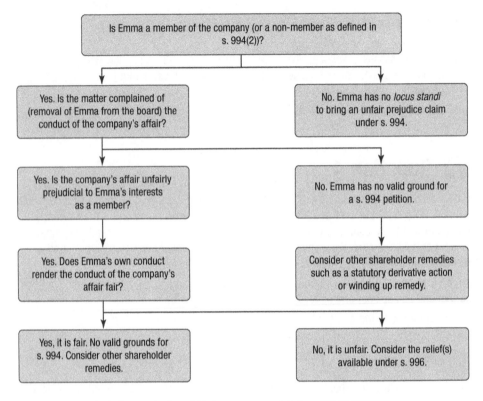

Is Emma a member of the company (or a non-member as defined in s. 994(2))?

Yes. Is the matter complained of (removal of Emma from the board) the conduct of the company's affair?

No. Emma has no *locus standi* to bring an unfair prejudice claim under s. 994.

Yes. Is the company's affair unfairly prejudicial to Emma's interests as a member?

No. Emma has no valid ground for a s. 994 petition.

Yes. Does Emma's own conduct render the conduct of the company's affair fair?

Consider other shareholder remedies such as a statutory derivative action or winding up remedy.

Yes, it is fair. No valid grounds for s. 994. Consider other shareholder remedies.

No, it is unfair. Consider the relief(s) available under s. 996.

A printable version of this diagram plan is available from **www.pearsoned.co.uk/lawexpressqa**

Answer

[1] This sentence identifies the key legal issues that are raised in this problem question. It demonstrates to your examiners that you are able to engage with the question.

[2] Although a word-by-word citation is not often required in an exam, you should show a good knowledge of the statutory provision of section 994.

The key legal issues here are whether Emma can successfully bring an unfair prejudice petition under section 994 of the Companies Act 2006 and whether the court will think it fit to make an order for David and James to buy Emma's shares at a fair price under section 996.[1] A petition under section 994 is made on the ground that the company's affairs are being or have been conducted in a manner which is unfairly prejudicial to the interests of its members generally or of some part of its members (including at least the petitioner), or that any actual or proposed act or omission of the company is or would be so prejudicial.[2]

In order to assess whether a section 994 claim would be successful, it is essential to consider three important questions: first, whether Emma is a member of the company; secondly, whether Emma's removal from the board is the company's affair; and finally, whether the removal is unfairly prejudicial to Emma's interests as a member.[3] It is clear from the scenario that Emma is a shareholder and therefore has the *locus standi* to bring a petition under section 994. The resolution to remove Emma from the board can be considered as a company's affair because it is connected with acts done by the general meeting of the company rather than the act of an individual shareholder acting in a personal capacity: *Re Legal Costs Negotiators Ltd* [1999] BCC 547.[4] It is then important to discuss whether the resolution to remove Emma is unfairly prejudicial to her interests *qua* member.

A company may by ordinary resolution at a shareholder meeting remove a director before the expiration of his period of office, notwithstanding anything in any agreement between it and him (s. 168).[5] As David and James hold 80 per cent of the company's shares, it is sufficient and legal to pass an ordinary resolution to remove Emma at general meeting. Whether this is unfairly prejudicial, nevertheless, depends on whether equitable considerations make it unfair to remove her.

Lord Wilberforce in *Ebrahimi* v *Westbourne Galleries* [1973] AC 360 held that 'there are individuals, with rights, expectations and obligations *inter se* which are not necessarily submerged in the company structure'. Hoffmann J in *Re A Company (No 00477 of 1986)* [1986] BCLC 376 applied this reasoning to unfair prejudice petitions and recognised shareholders' legitimate expectations. The interests of members therefore extend beyond their strict legal rights and include members' wider interests and expectations.

Such personal expectations are more likely to exist in quasi-partnership companies. As Lord Wilberforce stated in *Ebrahimi* (above), the personal relationship and mutual confidence form the basis of the business association in a quasi-partnership company; there is an understanding that all or certain shareholders will participate in management.[6] Hoffmann J in *O'Neill* v *Phillips* [1999] 1 WLR 1092[7] concluded that a member would not ordinarily be entitled to complain of unfairness unless there had been some use of the rules in a manner which equity would regard as contrary to good faith.

[3] This sentence sets the context and structure for your discussion of whether Emma's interests have been unfairly prejudiced by the decision to remove her.

[4] The discussion in relation to what constitutes a company's affair is often omitted in students' answers. Although this may appear a simple legal issue, you should discuss it by reference to case law.

[5] This sentence demonstrates that you understand the legal requirements for removal of directors under section 168. It will gain you more marks.

[6] The characteristics of quasi-partnership companies are important for your understanding of the concept of equitable considerations. The reference to Lord Wilberforce's classic definition of quasi-partnership companies will impress your examiners.

[7] This case is the House of Lords' authority on the scope of unfairly prejudicial conduct. Failure to discuss it in your answer will lead to a reduction of marks.

This typically takes place in quasi-partnership companies. Oriental Delight Ltd appears to be a quasi-partnership company and it can be argued that the exclusion of Emma from management by section 168 would amount to unfairly prejudicial conduct in the absence of a fair offer by David and James to buy her shares: ***Brownlow v GH Marshall Ltd*** [2000] 2 BCLC 655.

[8] The implications of the petitioner's own misconduct are significant legal issues which must be addressed because the court will take it into account when granting the remedy. They will make your answer stand out.

The court will take into account the petitioner's own conduct in determining whether the respondent's behaviour is unfair.[8] In ***Re A. Noble & Sons Ltd*** [1983] BCLC 273, the petitioner's own conduct led to his exclusion from management and therefore the respondent's conduct was considered as not unfair, although prejudicial. Moreover, the petitioner's conduct may be material to the court in framing its remedy, particularly in relation to fixing the appropriate valuation date or price for the purchase order under section 996(2)(e): ***Re London School of Electronics Ltd*** [1986] Ch 211.

Emma diverted the company's contracts away for her husband's company and therefore she breached her duties as a director in sections 172 and 175. Section 172 requires a director to act in the way he considers, in good faith, would be most likely to promote the success of the company for the benefit of its members as a whole: ***Re Smith & Fawcett Ltd*** [1942] 1 All ER 542. It appears that Emma did not act in the best interests of the company and therefore breached section 172. Moreover, a director under section 175 must avoid a situation in which he has, or can have, a direct or indirect interest that conflicts, or possibly may conflict, with the interests of the company. This applies to the exploitation of any property, information or opportunity: ***Cook v Deeks*** [1916] 1 AC 554. David and James may argue that Emma breached section 175 because there was a clear conflict between her personal interests in securing the contract for her husband and her duty to secure it for the company.[9]

[9] A clear understanding of directors' duties gains you more marks because Emma's breach of duties may affect the outcome of her unfair prejudice petition.

[10] This paragraph shows your sound understanding of the specific reliefs including the purchase order. It will add more credit to your answer because it is related to the second part of the question as to whether Emma can obtain such an order.

If it is satisfied that the petition is well founded, a court has wide discretion in granting remedies under section 996 and may make such order as it thinks fit. Without prejudice to the court's power, section 996(2) sets out in detail the types of order, including purchase order which is most commonly sought by petitioners. When a court makes a purchase order, it has a choice as to the basis of the valuation of shares but the key requirement is fairness: ***Re Bird Precision Bellows Ltd*** [1984] Ch 419.[10]

As Emma has breached her duties under sections 172 and 175, if *Re A. Noble & Sons Ltd* is followed, it is mostly likely that Emma's own conduct led to her exclusion from management and therefore her removal from the board was not considered as unfair. As such, Emma may not have valid grounds for section 994 petition and a purchase order. Even if the court is satisfied that the removal is unfairly prejudicial, Emma's own misconduct may have a negative effect on the price for the purchase order (*Re London School of Electronics Ltd*).[11]

[11] The conclusion should directly answer the question by providing specific advice to Emma. It should also include a reasoned assessment of the situation.

 Make your answer stand out

- Consider whether Emma may bring a personal action and claim damages for a breach of her service contract with the company if it is not complied with.
- Discuss the possibility of a winding-up order on the just and equitable grounds under section 122(1)(g) of the Insolvency Act 1986, although it would be very unlikely for the court to grant this order due to its serious consequences on the company.

! Don't be tempted to . . .

- Describe all directors' duties at common law and in the Companies Act 2006. You should discuss the relevant duties by reference to case law and apply them to the problem question.
- Simply state the provisions in sections 994–996 without case law illustrations. This is not an essay question so you need to analyse the problem scenario and apply the appropriate law, in particular case law, in your answer.
- Jump to the conclusion that Emma's removal is unfairly prejudicial and Emma can successfully bring a section 994 petition and obtain a purchase order. You must demonstrate detailed knowledge of the application of unfair prejudice remedies.

Question 5

'In the light of the introduction of statutory derivative actions, it is likely that the unfair prejudice remedies will be rendered redundant in the near future.'
Discuss.

Answer plan

→ Examine the changes introduced by the statutory derivative actions by comparing them with derivative actions at common law.

→ Compare the statutory derivative actions with unfair prejudice remedies in relation to:
- the scope of petitioners;
- the grounds for the petition;
- the procedure;
- the remedies available; and
- the issue of costs.

→ Evaluate whether the derivative actions will be more popular than unfair prejudice remedies and make them redundant.

Diagram plan

	Derivative action (ss. 260–264)	Unfair prejudice remedy (ss. 994–996)
Who can petition?	A member or a non-member to whom shares in the company have been transferred or transmitted by operation of law (s. 260(5)(c))	A member or a non-member to whom shares in the company have been transferred or transmitted by operation of law (s. 994(2))
On what grounds?	Directors' breach of duty(ies) (s. 260(3))	The company's affairs are being or have been conducted in a manner that is unfairly prejudicial to the interests of members generally or of some part of its members. (s. 994(1))
Procedure	A two-stage procedure for application for permission to continue a claim	Straightforward
Remedies	Sought on behalf of the company	Wide and flexible remedies under s. 996
Costs	Indemnity order – possible	Indemnity order – not applicable

A printable version of this diagram plan is available from **www.pearsoned.co.uk/lawexpressqa**

Answer

[1] Your introduction should outline the main arguments and show the examiners where you are going with your answer. This sentence also indicates that you will adopt an analytical approach instead of providing a narrative account of these shareholder remedies.

The statutory derivative actions are introduced in sections 260–264 of the Companies Act 2006 and they replace the common law rules governed by the rule in *Foss v Harbottle* (1843) 67 ER 189. Whilst it can be asserted that the statutory derivative actions have some advantages over the common law rules, it is debatable whether they are more effective for shareholders and whether they overshadow the unfair prejudice remedies under section 994.[1]

Prima facie, it is an excellent idea to have various rules on derivative actions at common law consolidated into the Companies Act 2006. There are certain obvious advantages in terms of procedure and scope of application. The new procedure may add certainty and clarity to the law. A claimant shareholder no longer has to prove fraud (**Burland v Earl** [1902] AC 83[2]) or wrongdoer control (**Prudential Assurance Co Ltd v Newman Industries Ltd (No. 2)** [1982] Ch 204). Neither the board's decision not to sue on behalf of the company (**Smith v Croft (No. 2)** [1988] Ch 114) nor the possibility of ratification of the breach of duty (**MacDougall v Gardiner** (1875) LR 1 Ch D 13) is a bar to derivative action. The court is in control of the litigation by way of the claimant's application for permission to continue the claim under section 261 and therefore the amount of vexatious litigation can be minimised and the management of a company is protected from such undue interference.[3]

The scope of derivative claims has been widened in the Companies Act 2006 as they fill up a gap at common law regarding the remedy for directors' negligence.[4] Section 260(3) clearly specifies the situations where derivative claims lie, which may help shareholders and their legal advisers make better assessments of the chances of obtaining permission to proceed. It is argued in *Gore-Browne on Companies Act 2006* that the new procedures introduce a 'welcome liberalisation' of the rules at common law.[5] Shareholders may be encouraged to use statutory derivative claims where possible, rather than the more expensive unfair prejudice proceedings under section 994.

It is, however, doubtful if statutory derivative claims are more effective weapons for aggrieved minority shareholders than those at common law.[6] Once a shareholder applies for permission to commence a derivative action, it is for the court to determine whether litigation can proceed by taking into account all the factors and circumstances and especially the list of criteria under section 263. Although the list provides some guidance for both the court and the shareholders, different interpretations of the factors such as 'good faith' and 'success of the company' may result in inconsistent exercise of judicial discretion. Most significantly, effective ratification still bars a derivative action (s. 263(2)). It is possible that the restricted judicial attitudes towards derivative actions at common law may remain. Moreover, shareholders may not have the incentives to bring derivative

[2] The reference to key cases demonstrates your sound understanding of the common law rules and will gain you more marks.

[3] This sentence evaluates the main features of the statutory derivative action and shows your analytical skills, which the examiners are looking for.

[4] Students often forget to compare the scope of application of the statutory derivative actions and that of the common law. Shareholders could not bring a derivative action against directors for pure negligence at common law. You will gain more marks by making this comparison.

[5] The reference to *Gore-Browne* will add more credit to your answer because it shows your broad knowledge of this subject.

[6] This sentence leads on to the discussion of the problems with the statutory derivative actions in this paragraph. An analysis of their ineffectiveness will make your answer stand out because it strengthens your arguments and supports your conclusion.

actions as any recovery goes back to the company. The difficulties and uncertainties in obtaining a costs indemnity order, along with the inconvenience and the lack of incentives, therefore still act as strong deterrents.

Some academics are sceptical of the success of the statutory derivative claims. As Payne (1998) has incisively argued, although the new procedure has removed the problems associated with the fraud exception, it seems unlikely to increase the use of the derivative actions in the face of the unfair prejudice remedy.[7] Both remedies are available to a member or a non-member to whom shares in the company have been transferred or transmitted by operation of law (s. 260(5)(c) and s. 994(2)). It is argued here that the unfair prejudice remedy is likely to remain the remedy of first choice because of its advantages over derivative claims in terms of scope of application, procedure, specific reliefs and the issue of litigation costs.[8]

In terms of scope of application, unfair prejudice remedies cover a potentially wider range of wrongful conduct than derivative actions. Section 994 applies to cases where the conduct is in breach of the company's constitution, or where the conduct is consistent with the constitution but breaches the petitioner's legitimate expectations based on some informal agreements (*O'Neill v Phillips* [1999] 1 WLR 1092). Moreover, it has become more popular in the wake of the Court of Appeal's judgment in *Clark v Cutland* [2003] 4 All ER 733. It is held that minority shareholders could make use of unfair prejudice remedies to obtain a substantive remedy for the company in relation to corporate wrongs without going through the procedures in derivative actions.[9] By contrast, the scope of derivative claims is relatively narrow because they are confined to a director's breach of duties (s. 260).

The procedures for unfair prejudice remedies are much simpler than those for derivative claims. A claimant has to go through the expenses and uncertainties of the two-stage procedure for a derivative action; by contrast, there are no such requirements for unfair prejudice claims. Moreover, the ratification principle and the decision of the independent organ do not apply to unfair prejudice proceedings.

[7] The evaluation of the academic opinion will impress your examiners because it shows your wider understanding of the derivative actions. The phrase 'incisively argued' also demonstrates your analytical skill.

[8] These phrases set a clear structure for the comparison between two remedies which are discussed in the next three paragraphs.

[9] The reference to *Clark* v *Cutland* and its implications on unfair prejudice remedies will make your answer stand out because it demonstrates your excellent understanding of the more complicated issues.

In terms of remedies, section 996 offers a more flexible remedy in that the court can exercise discretion to choose remedies. The purchase order is the most popular remedy as an exit mechanism. The court can also allow successful petitioners to bring civil proceedings in the name of the company. As the section 994 remedy is based on the infringement of personal rights, recoveries as a result of successful litigation go to the actual claimant and are not shared by other shareholders in the company (the remedy under s. 996(2)(c) would be an exception). The personal relief to the petitioners makes section 994 more attractive than derivative action where any relief goes back to the company and the claimant can only benefit indirectly. Unfair prejudice remedies are therefore powerful and preferable remedial tools for minority shareholders because of their wider scope, simpler procedures and especially the more flexible claimant-oriented remedies.[10]

Derivative actions, nevertheless, may be more attractive in certain circumstances:[11] for example, where the shareholder does not wish to sell his shares or leave the company, but needs a remedy for misconduct and the recovery of the company's assets. Moreover, the position in relation to indemnity costs orders remains slightly more favourable to shareholders in derivative actions (**Wallersteiner v Moir (No. 2)** [1974] 3 All ER 217). Despite this, it would be exceptional for a petitioner to proceed with a derivative action rather than by a section 994 petition. The Law Commission Consultation Paper (1996) argues that unless major changes were made to the unfair prejudice remedy, it would continue to offer advantages over derivative actions. Since the unfair prejudice remedy remains unchanged under the CA 2006, it can be argued that a derivative claim may not often be used in cases where an unfair prejudice remedy is available. In **Mission Capital plc v Sinclair** [2008] BCC 866 and **Franbar Holding Ltd v Patel** [2008] BCC 885, the claimant's application for permission to continue the derivative claim was refused. One of the main reasons is that the claimant could bring an unfair prejudice petition as an alternative remedy (s. 263(3)(f)). It is therefore unlikely that the unfair prejudice remedies will be made redundant by the statutory derivative actions in the near or far future.[12]

[10] This sentence summarises the main points that you have made in the previous paragraphs. It reinforces your arguments and also shows a neat structure.

[11] An evaluation of the few advantages of derivative actions over unfair prejudice remedies demonstrates your sound understanding of shareholder remedies. It will gain you more marks than simply emphasising the advantages of unfair prejudice remedies.

[12] A concise conclusion should refer back to the question and strengthen your arguments.

Make your answer stand out

- Discuss in detail the two-stage procedure for a statutory derivative action under sections 261–263.
- Evaluate the criteria that the courts will take into account when considering whether to grant the permission to continue a derivative claim under section 263.
- Consider the controversial debates as to whether derivative actions and unfair prejudice remedies should be assimilated into one.
- Make reference to academic opinions in relation to the above debates: Law Commission Report (1997), Para. 6.11; Payne, J. (2005) Sections 459–461 Companies Act 1985 in flux: the future of shareholder protection. 64 *CLJ* 647; Reisberg, A. (2005) Shareholders' remedies: in search of consistency of principle in English law. 16 *European Business Law Review* 1065; Hirt, H. C. (2003) In what circumstances should breaches of director's duties give rise to a remedy under ss. 459–461 of the Companies Act 1985? 24 *Company Lawyer* 100.

! Don't be tempted to . . .

- Simply describe the derivative actions at common law and the statutory rules. You need to compare them, analyse the changes and examine the strength and weakness of this reform.
- Discuss in detail the application of unfair prejudice remedies. This is not just a question on unfair prejudice remedies. It is essential to compare and contrast the derivative actions and unfair prejudice remedies and evaluate their differences.

www.pearsoned.co.uk/lawexpressqa

 Go online to access more revision support including additional essay and problem questions with diagram plans, You be the marker questions, and download all diagrams from the book.

Corporate insolvency

How this topic may come up in exams

Corporate insolvency is a complex area of company law. You are not required to show a detailed critical analysis but it is essential to have a clear understanding of the important statutory provisions in the Insolvency Act 1986 and apply them to problem questions. Exam questions often focus on the procedures for company voluntary arrangements, administration and liquidation. Distribution of a company's assets and the priority of creditors in an insolvent liquidation are popular topics for problem questions. Directors' liabilities in wrongful trading and fraudulent trading may also arise in corporate insolvency. This topic may overlap with directors' duties and company charges.

Before you begin

It's a good idea to consider the following key themes of corporate insolvency before tackling a question on this topic.

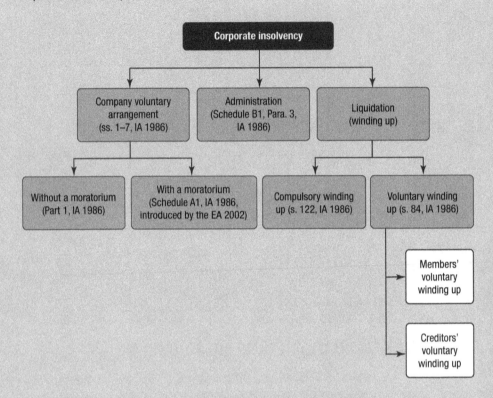

A printable version of this diagram is available from **www.pearsoned.co.uk/lawexpress**

❓ Question 1

Supreme Sofa Ltd specialises in manufacturing sofa and beds. Its sales have dropped significantly due to recent recession and it has not been making profit for the past six months. It also suffered serious cash flow problems due to rapid expansion. It is struggling financially and cannot pay off all its creditors. The directors hope that the company could be rescued by the company voluntary arrangement instead of going into administration.

Advise the directors as to the procedure required for a company voluntary arrangement without a moratorium.

Answer plan

→ Explain the definition of a company voluntary arrangement (CVA).

→ Consider the procedures for the meetings of the company and of its creditors to approve the proposal for CVA:

- Discuss the effect of the approval of CVA.
- Examine the ways of challenging the decision to approve a CVA.
- Discuss the procedures for the implementation of a CVA.

Diagram plan

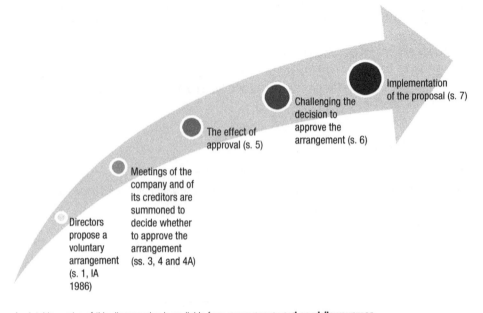

Implementation of the proposal (s. 7)

Challenging the decision to approve the arrangement (s. 6)

The effect of approval (s. 5)

Meetings of the company and of its creditors are summoned to decide whether to approve the arrangement (ss. 3, 4 and 4A)

Directors propose a voluntary arrangement (s. 1, IA 1986)

A printable version of this diagram plan is available from **www.pearsoned.co.uk/lawexpress**

Answer

¹ This sentence shows that you understand the question and, more importantly, appreciate the role of CVA.

Supreme Sofa Ltd is insolvent but its directors hoped that the company could be rescued: a company voluntary arrangement (CVA) which does not end the life of the company is therefore more appropriate than going into administration.¹ A CVA is defined as a composition in satisfaction of its debts or a scheme of arrangement of its affairs (s. 1(1), IA 1986). In *Commissioners of Inland Revenue v Adam & Partners Ltd* [2001] 1 BCLC 222,² a proposal set out the scheme that the preferential and unsecured creditors would not receive any payments while the company's main creditor would receive a better return. The Court of Appeal held that the proposal did not amount to a composition of the company's debts and therefore was not a CVA.

² The reference to case law explains the definition of a CVA. It will make your answer stand out because most students only focus on the statutory provisions.

³ Note that the directors can propose a CVA; neither the members nor the creditors can make such proposal.

The directors of Supreme Sofa Ltd may propose a voluntary arrangement (s. 1).³ The proposal must provide for a nominee to supervise the implementation of the CVA and the nominee must be a qualified insolvency practitioner. Directors shall submit to the nominee a document setting out the terms of the proposed voluntary arrangement and a statement of the company's affairs which contain the particulars of its creditors and of its debts and other liabilities and of its assets (s. 2(3)). A director commits an offence, if for the purpose of obtaining the approval of the members or creditors, he makes any false representation, or fraudulently does, or omits to do, anything (s. 6A).

[4] Pay attention to the time limit here.

[5] This phrase will gain you more marks because it shows that the prospect of the proposed arrangement is based on the nominee's opinion instead of an objective test.

The nominee shall, within 28 days after he is given notice of the proposal[4], submit a report to the court. The report should state whether, in his opinion[5], the proposed voluntary arrangement has a reasonable prospect of being approved and implemented, and whether meetings of the company and of its creditors should be summoned to consider the proposal, and stating the date, time and place for such meetings (s. 2(2)). Every creditor of the company of whose claim and address the nominee is aware shall be summoned to a creditors' meeting (s. 3(3)).

The meetings summoned shall decide whether to approve the proposed voluntary arrangement, with or without modifications (s. 4(1)). The proposal or modification shall not be approved if it affects the right of a secured creditor of the company to enforce his security or affects the preferential debt of the company, except with the concurrence of the creditor concerned or the preferential creditor concerned (s. 4(4)). After the conclusion of either meeting, the chairman of the meeting shall report the result of the meeting to the court, and, immediately after reporting to the court, shall give notice of the result of the meeting to such persons as may be prescribed (s. 4(6)).

[6] The mention of requirements in the Insolvency Rules 1986 in relation to voting and the passing of a resolution demonstrates your detailed knowledge. They will impress your examiners.

[7] The requirement for the passing of a resolution at a creditors' meeting is different from that at a members' meeting. A majority of three-quarters or more in value is needed rather than a majority of more than half in value.

At the members' meeting, members vote according to the rights attached to their shares by the articles; more than half in value of the ordinary shareholders is required in favour of the resolution (rr. 1.18 and 1.20, Insolvency Rules 1986).[6] At the creditors' meeting, a resolution to approve the proposal or a modification can be passed when a majority of three-quarters or more in value of those present and voting in person or by proxy have voted in favour of it[7] (r. 1.19, IR 1986). The decision to approve a proposed voluntary arrangement has effect if it has been taken by both the meeting of the company and the meeting of creditors. It also has effect if it has been taken by the creditors' meeting (s. 4A(2)). This means that if the decision taken by the creditors' meeting is different from that taken by the

[8] This sentence shows your excellent understanding of section 4A(2) with regard to a conflict of decisions at the members' meeting and the creditors' meeting. It will add more credit to your answer.

[9] You must pay attention to the effect of the approved voluntary arrangement. It is binding not only on the creditors who were entitled to vote at the meeting, but also those who did not vote either in person or in proxy.

[10] This sentence will gain you more marks because it demonstrates the extensive nature of the approved arrangement. It is even binding on the creditors who were not sent a notice or of whom the nominee was not aware.

[11] The basis for challenging the voluntary arrangement should be included in a good answer.

[12] The name of the specific judge shows your detailed knowledge of this case.

company meeting, the former shall prevail.[8] A member, however, may challenge this decision by applying to the court within 28 days of the creditors' meeting (s. 4A(3)). The court may order the decision of the company meeting to have effect or make such other order as it thinks fit (s. 4A(6)).

Once the voluntary arrangement is approved, it binds every person who was entitled to vote at the creditors' meeting, whether or not he was present or represented at it as if he were a party to the voluntary arrangement.[9] It also binds a creditor who did not receive notice of the meeting, or if he was unknown to the nominee and a notice was not sent to him (s. 5(2)).[10] After the conclusion of either meeting, the chairman of the meeting shall report the result of the meeting to the court within four days (s. 4(6)).

The voluntary arrangement may be challenged, upon an application to the court, by any person who is entitled to vote at either of the meetings or who would have been entitled to vote at the creditors' meeting if he had had notice of it (s. 6(2)). It can be made on the ground that a voluntary arrangement unfairly prejudices the interests of a creditor, member or contributory of the company; or that there has been some material irregularity at or in relation to either of the meetings (s. 6(1)).[11] In *IRC v Wimbledon* [2005] 1 BCLC 66, Lightman J[12] considered that the unfair prejudice complained of must be caused by the terms of the arrangement itself. In determining whether there is unfairness, all the circumstances should be considered. The existence of unequal or differential treatment of creditors of the same class does not of itself constitute unfairness. If the court is satisfied as to either of the grounds, it may revoke or suspend any decision giving effect to the CVA, or any decision taken by a meeting where there has been a material irregularity. It may give a direction to any person for the summoning of further meetings (s. 6(4)).

On approval of the CVA, the nominee becomes the supervisor (s. 7(2)) and he sets out the implementation of the CVA. He may apply to the court for directions if necessary (s. 7(4)). The supervisor often holds any funds in his possession on trust for the creditors following the terms of the voluntary arrangement: *Re NT Gallagher & Son Ltd* [2002] 2 BCLC 133. If any creditor of the company or any other person is dissatisfied by any act of the supervisor, he may

[13] Section 7(3) plays an important check on the supervisor's conduct and therefore it should be included in your answer.

apply to the court which may confirm, reverse or modify the act of the supervisor, give him directions, or make such other order as it thinks fit (s. 7(3)).[13] On completion or termination of the CVA, the supervisor must send notice within 28 days to all the creditors and members bound by the CVA together with a copy of a report which summarises all receipts and payments by him. Notice must also be given to the registrar of companies and to the court within the same time limit (r. 1.29, IR 1986).

✓ Make your answer stand out

- Briefly consider company voluntary arrangement with a moratorium which is governed by Schedule A1, IA 1986. It is not popular in practice mainly due to the complex procedures, the requirement for publicity and the onerous liabilities on the part of supervisors.
- Advise the directors that, if the company has failed to pay the creditors as required by the CVA, it may be necessary to terminate the agreement and the supervisor may petition for an administration order or winding up.
- Provide some examples of CVA. A few well-known businesses (such as Travelodge, JJB Sports, Fitness First) with big debts are rescued using company voluntary arrangements.

! Don't be tempted to . . .

- Focus on the procedures in relation to company voluntary arrangement with a moratorium. You must understand that there are two types of CVA and this problem question is asking you to discuss the CVA without a moratorium which is governed by Part 1 of the IA 1986.
- Make no reference to the statutory provisions. Although the subsection numbers are often not required, you should learn the main sections of the Insolvency Act 1986 in relation to a CVA.

🖎 Question 2

Critically analyse the main procedures for appointing an administrator by a holder of a floating charge, the functions of the administrator and how the administrator's conduct can be challenged.

Answer plan

→ Explain the role of administration by reference to the Cork Report 1982 and the Insolvency Act 1986.

→ Discuss who is entitled to appoint an administrator with particular reference to the holder of a qualifying floating charge.

→ Examine the objectives of an administrator.

→ Analyse the grounds for challenging the administrator's conduct.

→ Consider the effect of moratorium when the company is in administration.

Diagram plan

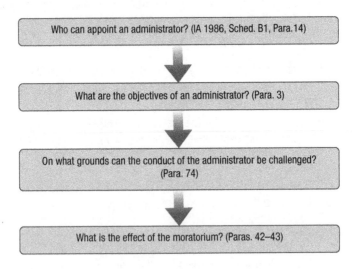

Who can appoint an administrator? (IA 1986, Sched. B1, Para.14)

What are the objectives of an administrator? (Para. 3)

On what grounds can the conduct of the administrator be challenged? (Para. 74)

What is the effect of the moratorium? (Paras. 42–43)

A printable version of this diagram plan is available from **www.pearsoned.co.uk/lawexpress**

[1] These sentences show your good understanding of the historical background of the administration procedure. They add more credit to your answer than only focusing on the current provisions in the IA 1986.

[2] This sentence helps you avoid repeating the reference to Schedule B1 to the IA 1986. It saves you some time in an exam.

Answer

The administration procedure was recommended by the Cork Committee on Insolvency Law and Practice Report (1982). It was designed primarily to facilitate the rescue of the viable parts of the company in financial difficulties.[1] The administration provisions have been revised by the Enterprise Act 2002 and are now set out in Schedule B1 to the Insolvency Act 1986 (IA 1986). The reference to the paragraphs in this answer is made to Schedule B1 to the IA 1986 unless otherwise stated.[2]

An administrator of a company must be a qualified insolvency practitioner who is appointed to manage the company's affairs, business and property (Para. 1). He owes his duties to the company and not to the creditors, individually or collectively: **Kyrris v Oldham** [2004] 1 BCLC 305.[3] An administrator may be appointed by an administration order of the court, or by the holder of a qualifying floating charge, or by the company or its directors (Para. 2). The holder of a qualifying floating charge may therefore appoint an administrator of the company out of court. A qualifying floating charge is created by an instrument which states that Paragraph 14 applies to the floating charge, or purports to empower the holder to appoint an administrator of the company (Para. 14(2)). A person is a holder of a qualifying floating charge if it relates to the whole or substantially the whole of the company's property (Para. 14(3)).

If the floating charge is not a qualifying floating charge, the holder can apply to the court for an administration order (Para. 12).[4] The court may make such order only if it is satisfied that the company is or is likely to become unable to pay its debts, and that the administration order is reasonably likely to achieve the purpose of administration (Para. 11). In **Re AA Mutual International Insurance Co Ltd** [2005] 2 BCLC 8 the insurance company had no new business and therefore no income: the court considered that it was more likely that the company's liabilities would exceed its assets within a short period of time and an administration may achieve a better result for the creditors than a winding up.

The administrator must perform his functions in the interests of the company's creditors as a whole, as quickly and efficiently as is reasonably practicable (Paras. 3–4). There is a hierarchy of purposes[5] which administration is supposed to serve in Paragraph 3. The administrator must perform his functions with the objective (a) of rescuing the company as a going concern, unless he thinks either that it is not reasonably practicable to achieve this objective or that objective (b) would achieve a better result for the company's creditors as a whole. Objective (b) is achieving a better result for the company's creditors as a whole than would be likely if the company were wound up without first being in administration. The third objective, (c), is realisation of property in order to make a distribution to one or more secured or preferential creditors. The administrator can only perform objective (c) if he thinks that it is not reasonably practicable

[3] This shows your good knowledge of the case law and will earn you more marks.

[4] Some students may forget to discuss the appointment of an administrator by a court order.

[5] This phrase is very important in demonstrating your excellent understanding of the objectives of the administration. It will add more credit to your answer.

6 You should understand not
only the three objectives but
also the conditions for the
performance of objectives
(b) and (c). The latter will gain
you more marks.

7 These sentences
evaluate the objectives
of administration and
demonstrate your analytical
skills. They will make your
answer stand out from those
which only focus on the
statutory provisions.

8 Many students forget to
discuss the requirement of
the notice of appointment.
You will lose some marks if it
is not included in your answer.

9 This paragraph examines the
powers of an administrator.
It is essential here because
it leads on to the discussion
in the next paragraph in
relation to how the conduct
of an administrator can be
challenged.

10 This ground for challenging
the administrator's conduct
is often missing in students'
exam answers. It should be
included in a sound answer.

to achieve either (a) or (b), and he does not unnecessarily harm the interests of the creditors of the company as a whole.[6] It should be noted that the above objectives are based on what the administrator thinks rather than what he reasonably believes. As the courts are generally reluctant to second-guess the commercial judgements of administrators, it is almost impossible for a court to interfere with the administrator's judgements as long as they are made in good faith: *Downsview Nominees* v *First City Corp* [1993] AC 295.[7]

The holder of a floating charge who appoints an administrator must file with the court a notice of appointment.[8] The notice must include a statutory declaration that he is the holder of a qualifying floating charge of the company's property, that the floating charge is or was enforceable on the date of the appointment, and that the appointment is in accordance with Schedule B1. The notice must identify the administrator; it must also be accompanied by a statement by the administrator that he consents to the appointment and that in his opinion the purpose of administration is reasonably likely to be achieved (Para. 18(3)). The appointment of an administrator takes effect when the above requirements as to the notice and documents are satisfied. The holder of a floating charge shall notify the administrator as soon as is reasonably practicable after the notice of appointment has been filed with the court (Para. 20).The administrator may do anything necessary or expedient for the management of the affairs, business and property of the company (Para. 59). In exercising his functions, he acts as the agent of the company (Para. 69). The extensive powers of an administrator are set out in Schedule 1 to the Insolvency Act 1986, including the power to take possession of, collect and get in the property of the company, sell or dispose of the company's property, raise or borrow money and grant security, bring and defend any legal proceedings, make payment and carry on the business of the company.[9]

A creditor or a member of the company may challenge the administrator's conduct (Para. 74). He may apply to the court claiming that the administrator is acting, or has acted, unfairly and harmed the interests of the applicant, or the administrator proposes to act in a way which would unfairly harm the interests of the applicant. He may also claim that the administrator is not performing his functions as quickly or as efficiently as is reasonably practicable (Para. 74).[10] The court has extensive discretion: it may grant relief, dismiss the

[11] A discussion of the effect of moratorium will make your answer stand out because it is a key feature of the administration procedure.

application, adjourn the hearing, make an interim order, and make any other order it thinks appropriate.

Once a company is in administration, it should be aware of the effect of the moratorium.[11] The moratorium provides a breathing space during which the company has an opportunity to make arrangements with its creditors and members. The moratorium takes effect so that no resolution may be passed or order made for the winding up of the company (Para. 42); no step may be taken to enforce security over the company's property and no legal process may be instituted or continued against the company or property of the company, except with the consent of the administrator or with the permission of the court (Para. 43).

✓ Make your answer stand out

■ Consider the main changes brought by the Enterprise Act 2002. It enabled a company to be placed in administration without the need for an application to the court and therefore simplified the administration procedure. Moreover, it abolished the right of a holder of a floating charge to appoint an administrative receiver and limited the administrative receivership procedure to exceptional cases.

■ Discuss the requirements in relation to the statement made by the administrator once he is appointed. The statement must set out proposals for achieving the purpose of administration (Para. 49). The proposals must be accompanied by an invitation to an initial creditors' meeting (Para. 51) and they can only be approved by a majority in value of the creditors present and voting, in person or by proxy.

! Don't be tempted to . . .

■ Write everything you know about administration. You are not required in this question to demonstrate detailed knowledge of the complex procedure in administration. You should only focus on the issues which are related to the question.

■ Assume that any holder of a floating charge can appoint an administrator. You must discuss whether the charge in question is a qualifying floating charge and whether the person is a holder of a qualifying floating charge.

![] Question 3

Evaluate the main distinctions between different types of winding up of a company.

Answer plan

→ Consider the members' voluntary winding up (ss. 91–96, Insolvency Act 1986), in particular, the requirement for the directors' declaration of solvency.

→ Examine the creditors' voluntary winding up (ss. 97–106, IA 1986), in particular, the requirement in relation to the meeting of creditors.

→ Analyse the compulsory winding up by the court (s. 122, IA 1986), in particular, the requirements in relation to the petitioner and the grounds for petition.

Diagram plan

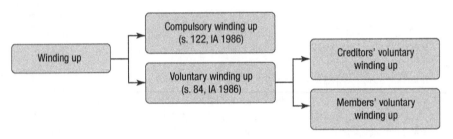

A printable version of this diagram plan is available from **www.pearsoned.co.uk/lawexpress**

Answer

[1] This sentence outlines the two main types of winding up and shows the examiners that you know what this question is about.

[2] This sentence demonstrates that you are aware of the two types of voluntary winding up. It also shows your analytical skills by briefly comparing the two and will gain you more marks.

Winding up refers to the process where the assets of the company are collected in and realised, its liabilities discharged and the net proceeds (if any) distributed to the persons entitled to it (s. 107, IA 1986). Winding up may be either voluntary or compulsory (s. 73(1)).[1]

Voluntary winding up is the most common form, whereby members pass a resolution at general meeting that the company be wound up (s. 84(1)(b)). It can be either members' or creditors' voluntary winding up: the main distinction lies in whether the company's directors are able to make a declaration of solvency.[2] Another difference is with respect to the appointment of liquidator. A liquidator, who must be a qualified insolvency practitioner, may be appointed by the company in general meeting in a members' voluntary winding up; the appointment may be made at creditors' meetings in a creditors' voluntary winding up.

In a members' voluntary winding up, the directors or a majority of the directors make a statutory declaration of solvency in the five weeks immediately preceding the date of the resolution to wind up the company, or on the date of the resolution but before it is passed.[3] The statutory declaration must state that the directors have made a full inquiry into the affairs of the company and have formed the opinion that the company will be able to pay its debts in full within 12 months from the date of the passing of the resolution for winding up (s. 89). Any director who makes a declaration of solvency without reasonable grounds for the opinion will be liable to imprisonment or a fine or both (s. 89(4)). If in fact the debts are not paid within the period specified in the declaration, it is presumed that a director did not have reasonable grounds for his belief (s. 89(5)). In the circumstances where the directors do not make a statutory declaration of solvency, it is a creditors' winding up. A meeting of creditors must be summoned to take place not more than 14 days after the members' meeting (s. 98).[4] A voluntary winding up is deemed to commence at the time the resolution is passed by the members in general meeting.

In a compulsory winding up, the court orders that the company be wound up following a petition by the company, its directors, creditors and contributories (s. 124(1)). In practice, most petitions are made by creditors of the company. In order to prevent individuals from purchasing shares for the purpose of winding up the company,[5] a contributory, including any present and past member of the company, can only make a winding up petition in one of the following four circumstances (s. 124(2)): first, the number of members is reduced to below two; secondly, the shares held by him were originally allotted to him; thirdly, the shares have been held by him for at least six months during the 18 months before the commencement of the winding up; finally, the shares have devolved on him through the death of a former holder. A contributory must also establish an economic interest in the winding up: for example, a partly paid-up shareholder remains liable to contribute the amount unpaid on his shares on winding up of the company. If the shares are fully paid up, it must be established that there is some prospect of assets available to him in the winding up.

The grounds for compulsory winding up are set out in section 122. The most common ground is that the company is unable to pay its debts. A company is deemed unable to pay its debts in one of the following four circumstances listed in section 123. First, a creditor to whom the

[3] Pay attention to the time limit for making the declaration of solvency.

[4] The requirement for the creditors' meeting must be clearly stated. You should also note the 14-day period.

[5] This phrase shows that you understand the rationale of the restrictions imposed on the petition by a contributory. It will gain you more marks than simply stating the law.

[6] Although you are
encouraged to use the precise
wording of the statutory
provision, it is often difficult
for most students to learn
them by heart if a company
law statute book is not
permitted in an exam. You can
interpret them in your own
words. Here, for example, you
can state that 'the creditor
of the company is owed
more than £750 and he has
demanded the payment due
in writing but the company
has failed to pay the sum
within three weeks'.

[7] The reference to case
law makes your answer
stand out from those which
only describe the statutory
provisions.

[8] Students are often confused
with this particular area of law.
Compulsory winding up starts
at the time of the presentation
of the winding up, not the time
when the court makes the
winding up order.

[9] This is an important
provision because it makes
any transaction which affects
the company's property void.
It will gain you more marks.

[10] This sentence explains the
rationale of section 127 of the
IA 1986. It shows your sound
understanding and will add
more credit to your answer.

[11] Make sure you get this
right. A liquidator does not
owe duties to individual
contributories or creditors.
You will lose some marks if it
is not correctly discussed.

company is indebted in a sum exceeding £750 then due has served on the company a written demand requiring the company to pay the sum due; and the company has for three weeks thereafter neglected to pay the sum or to secure or compound for it to the reasonable satisfaction of the creditor;[6] secondly, execution or other process issued on a judgment, decree or order of any court in favour of a creditor of the company is returned unsatisfied in whole or in part; thirdly, it is proved to the satisfaction of the court that the company is unable to pay its debts as they fall due; finally, it is proved to the satisfaction of the court that the value of the company's assets is less than the amount of its liabilities, taking into account its contingent and prospective liabilities.

The court has wide discretion as to whether or not to order winding up as it is a collective procedure for the benefit of creditors generally. The court may dismiss a petition if the company disputes the debt and the court accepts that the dispute is genuine: *Re MCI WorldCom Ltd* [2003] 1 BCLC 330.[7] The petition may also be dismissed if the company has a genuine and serious cross-claim for an amount which exceeds the petitioner's debt and which the company has been unable to litigate: *Re Bayoil SA* [1999] 1 BCLC 62.

Compulsory winding up is deemed to commence at the time of the presentation of the petition,[8] which takes place when the petition is delivered to the court for issue. Any disposition of the company's property, and any transfer of shares, or alteration in the status of the company's members, made after the commencement of the winding up, is void unless the court otherwise orders (s. 127).[9] This is designed to avoid the risk that the property which should be available to creditors is disposed of in the period between the presentation of the petition and the making of the winding up order.[10]

The court may appoint a liquidator after the presentation of a winding up petition. The liquidator's primary duty is to collect in and realise the assets of the company and then to distribute the proceeds amongst the creditors of the company and, if any surplus remains, to the shareholders (s. 143). A liquidator owes duties to the company and not to individual contributories or creditors: *Lomax Leisure Ltd v Miller* [2008] 1 BCLC 262.[11] He is in a fiduciary relationship with the company and must not place himself in a position of a conflict of interests: *Re Corbenstoke Ltd (No. 2)* [1990] BCLC 60. The exercise of power by the liquidator may be challenged by individual contributories or creditors (s. 167). Furthermore, any person aggrieved by an act or decision of the liquidator may apply to court which may confirm, reverse or modify the act or decision complained of and may make such order as it thinks fit (s. 168(5)).

✓ Make your answer stand out

- Consider that a solvent company may be wound up on the just and equitable ground under section 122(1)(g) of the Insolvency Act 1986 where the relationship between the members has completely broken down.
- Discuss the role of liquidation committee in a creditors' voluntary winding up. The creditors may resolve to form a liquidation committee, which may consist of up to five creditors and, if the creditors do not object, five members of the company (s. 165, IA 1986).

! Don't be tempted to . . .

- Use the word 'bankruptcy' to refer to winding up. Bankruptcy refers to the legal process by which the assets of an insolvent *individual or partnership* are realised and the proceeds distributed to the creditors.
- Only focus on the members' voluntary winding up. You must discuss both types of voluntary winding up in your answer.

? Question 4

Cake Ltd is in compulsory liquidation. The proofs of debts have been submitted by creditors in relation to the following claims. The expenses for winding up are £15,000 and the interests on all the debts which are proved amount to £8,000.

1   Sugar Ltd, which is the holder of a floating charge over the entire undertaking of Cake Ltd, is claiming £100,000. Sugar Ltd still owes £40,000 to Cake Ltd in a previous transaction.

2   Cake Ltd has three unsecured creditors who are claiming £5,000, £15,000 and £20,000 respectively.

3   Five employees of Cake Ltd are claiming £5,000 each for their salaries in the six months before winding up.

Advise the liquidator in relation to the priority of payment of the above claims.

Answer plan

→ Evaluate the rules on the proof of debts and the order of distribution of Cake Ltd's assets.

→ Consider the claims by the employees: are they preferential debts?

→ Examine the claim by Sugar Ltd in relation to the rights of set-off and the prescribed part of a floating charge.

→ Analyse the claims by the unsecured creditors by reference to the principle of *pari passu*.

→ Identify that the interests on the debts are deferred debts.

Diagram plan

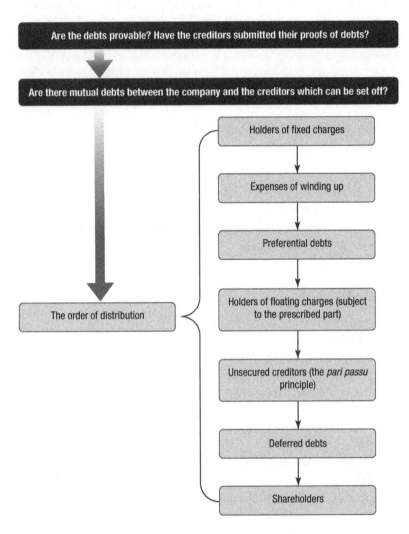

A printable version of this diagram plan is available from **www.pearsoned.co.uk/lawexpress**

Answer

When a company is in liquidation, only those debts which are provable in the insolvency and which are proved will receive payment.[1] All claims by creditors are provable as debts against the company whether they are present or future, certain or contingent, ascertained or sounding only in damages (r. 12.3, Insolvency Rules 1986[2]). The debt may arise at the date on which the company goes into liquidation, or after the company goes into liquidation provided that it is in respect of an obligation incurred before that date (r. 13.12). In a compulsory winding up, creditors must submit their proofs of debts in writing to establish their claims (r. 4.73).

1. The expenses of winding up[3]

All expenses properly incurred in the winding up, including the remuneration of the liquidator,[4] are payable out of the company's assets in priority to all other claims (s. 115, Insolvency Act 1986). The controversial issue is whether the company's assets include the property subject to a floating charge. The House of Lords in **Re Leyland Daf** [2004] 1 BCLC 281 held that the expenses of a winding up were not payable out of the assets comprised in a crystallised floating charge in priority to the claims of the charge holder.[5] This ruling was reversed by section 1282, CA 2006 and is now governed by section 176ZA, IA 1986,[6] which provides that the expenses of winding up have priority over any claims to property comprised in or subject to any floating charge created by the company and shall be paid out of any such property accordingly.

2. The claims by employees – preferential debts

The claims of salaries by the employees of Cake Ltd are regarded as preferential debts, which must be paid in priority to all other debts, except the expenses of winding up (s. 175, IA 1986). Preferential debts rank equally amongst them, and, if the assets are insufficient to meet them, they abate in equal proportions. The scope of preferential debts has been much reduced by the Enterprise Act 2002 (s. 251): for example, it has removed the preference afforded to claims by the Inland Revenue.[7] Preferential debts now only refer to contributions due by employers to certain pension schemes and the

---

[1] This shows your good knowledge of the rules on the proof of debts. It is the basis of payment of debts in corporate insolvency and should be the starting point of your discussion.

[2] Note that the reference here is not made to the Insolvency Act 1986 but the Insolvency Rules 1986. Some students may not notice this when they are revising.

[3] Try to structure your answer clearly and use headings so that it is easier for your examiners to follow.

[4] Students are often not aware that the remuneration of the liquidator is part of the expenses of winding up. Although this particular issue does not arise in this problem question, it may be examined in other questions.

[5] The reference to the case law and the House of Lords' decision makes your answer stand out.

[6] You should pay attention to the current law in section 176ZA of the Insolvency Act 1986. This sentence demonstrates your very good knowledge of the reforms in relation to this particular area of law.

[7] The reforms brought by the Enterprise Act 2002 will gain you more marks because they show your excellent understanding of the wider context.

[8] You should pay attention to the requirements of 'four months' and the amount of '£800 per employee' because they are relevant to the problem scenario.

limited amounts due such as remuneration of employees. Employees are entitled to claim as preferential debt salaries for services rendered in the four months before winding up but up to a maximum amount of £800 per employee (Paras. 9–12, Sch 6, IA 1986).[8] Thus the five employees of Cake Ltd can only claim their salaries in the four (instead of six) months before winding up and the amount is limited to £800 each.

3. The claim of Sugar Ltd

Whilst the holder of a fixed charge can look to their security for payment of the sums due, Sugar Ltd as the holder of a floating charge is subject to the prior claims of the expenses of winding up, the preferential debts and the prescribed part.

[9] This sentence identifies the legal issues in relation to the claim by Sugar Ltd. It shows where you are going with your answer.

As Sugar Ltd still owes £40,000 to Cake Ltd in a previous transaction, the issue arises as to whether the mutual debts of Cake Ltd and Sugar Ltd can be set off against each other.[9] Where, before the company goes into liquidation, there have been mutual credits, mutual debts or other mutual dealings between the company and any creditor of the company proving or claiming to prove a debt in the liquidation, the sums due from one party must be set off against the sums due from the other (r. 4.90, IR 1986). In **MS Fashions Ltd v BCCI SA (No. 2)** [1993] 3 All ER 769 the company's loan from a bank was guaranteed by a director who had a deposit account with the bank. It was held that the director, as a principal debtor, could rely on the right of set-off to reduce the debt owed to the bank by him and his company by the amount in his own account with the bank. Thus, Sugar Ltd and Cake Ltd must be set off their debts against each other and Sugar Ltd can only claim the balance of £60,000.[10]

[10] It is important to relate your discussion back to the question and apply the law to the problem scenario. You will lose marks if there is insufficient application to the question.

Another issue arises in relation to the prescribed part of a floating charge which should be set aside for unsecured creditors. The liquidator shall make a prescribed part of the company's net property available for unsecured debts. They shall not distribute that part to the holders of a floating charge unless it exceeds the amount required for the satisfaction of unsecured debts (s. 176A, IA 1986). The prescribed part of the company's net property shall be calculated according to Article 3 of the Insolvency Act 1986 (Prescribed

[11] The legal issue in relation to the prescribed part of the company's property is often missing in the exam answers. An excellent understanding of this area of law will make your answer stand out.

Part) Order 2003:[11] where the company's net property does not exceed £10,000 in value, 50 per cent of that property; where the company's net property exceeds £10,000 in value the sum of 50 per cent of the first £10,000 in value; and 20 per cent of that part of the company's net property which exceeds £10,000 in value, subject to a maximum of £600,000. The requirement for setting aside the prescribed part does not apply if the company's net property is less than £10,000, and the liquidator thinks that the cost of making a distribution to unsecured creditors would be disproportionate to the benefits (s. 176A, IA 1986). The claim of Sugar Ltd therefore may be subject to the prescribed part depending on the value of the company's net property.

4. The claims by the unsecured creditors

When the company goes into liquidation, its assets, after paying the expenses of the winding up and the preferential debts, form a common fund which is subject to a statutory trust for the benefit of all the creditors: **Webb v Whiffin** (1872) LR 5 HL 711. The unsecured creditors must be paid in accordance with the principle of *pari passu*, which requires that all creditors participate in the pooled assets in proportion to the size of their claim. Where the assets are insufficient to meet all the claims, they abate proportionately (s. 107, IA 1986).[12]

[12] The principle of *pari passu* is one of the most important rules in insolvency law. It must be included in a sound answer.

5. The interests on all proved debts – deferred debts

The interests on all proved debts from the company going into liquidation until the date of actual payment are considered as deferred debts. Deferred debts refer to the debts which are deferred by statute until all the other debts of the company have been paid (s. 189, IA 1986).

[13] Your conclusion should clearly address the question by summarising the order of payment in relation to the claims against Cake Ltd.

In conclusion, the assets of Cake Ltd should be distributed in the following order: the expenses of winding up, the employee's salaries (subject to the maximum amount), the claim of Sugar Ltd as the holder of a floating charge (subject to the rights of set-off and the prescribed part), the claims of the usecured creditors (according to the principle of *pari passu*) and the interests on all proved debts.[13]

Make your answer stand out

- Discuss the position of shareholders in an insolvent liquidation. If there are insufficient funds to pay the creditors in full, no funds will remain for the shareholders. You can point out that shareholders' losses are only limited to their capital and they are not liable to pay the creditors because of the principle of limited liability (the *Salomon* principle).
- Consider the no-deprivation rule which is also known as 'the rule in *Ex p Mackay*'. It provides that any contractual provision designed to defeat the *pari passu* distribution of the insolvent's assets is void.

! Don't be tempted to . . .

- Only focus on the claims by the creditors and employees. You must also discuss the expenses of winding up and the payment of interests on the proved debts.
- Get the order of priority of payment wrong. This is a very important area of law in corporate insolvency and is also a very popular exam topic. Make sure you know the order of payment of debts when the company is in liquidation.

❓ Question 5

John and Sam were directors of Fresh Fruit Ltd since January 2009. Fresh Fruit Ltd traded at a loss from May 2009 and its position gradually got worse. John and Sam did not take any professional legal or financial advice; instead, they falsified the company's accounts to show inflated profits in order to obtain additional overdraft facilities from the bank.

Fresh Fruit Ltd went into insolvent liquidation in December 2009. Two years later, both John and Sam were appointed directors of Tasty Fruit Ltd and directly took part in its management.

Advise the liquidator of Fresh Fruit Ltd in relation to the conduct of John and Sam.

Answer plan

→ Examine whether John and Sam are liable for fraudulent trading.

→ Analyse whether John and Sam are liable for wrongful trading.

→ Apply the law in relation to the prohibition on the re-use of company name.

→ Consider director's general duties in the Companies Act 2006.

Diagram plan

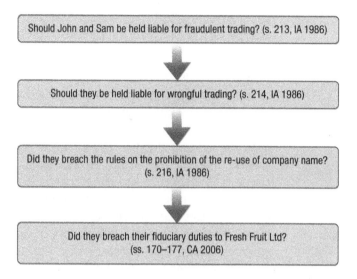

Should John and Sam be held liable for fraudulent trading? (s. 213, IA 1986)

Should they be held liable for wrongful trading? (s. 214, IA 1986)

Did they breach the rules on the prohibition of the re-use of company name? (s. 216, IA 1986)

Did they breach their fiduciary duties to Fresh Fruit Ltd? (ss. 170–177, CA 2006)

A printable version of this diagram plan is available from **www.pearsoned.co.uk/lawexpress**

Answer

[1] The introduction should identify the main issues that you are going to discuss in your answer. It also indicates that your answer is well structured.

The liquidator needs to consider the conduct of John and Sam as directors of Fresh Fruit Ltd in three main aspects:[1] first, whether they should be liable for fraudulent trading or wrongful trading; secondly, whether they breached the rules on the prohibition of the re-use of company name; and, thirdly, whether they breached their fiduciary duties owed to Fresh Fruit Ltd.

Civil liability may be imposed on John and Sam for fraudulent trading according to section 213 of the Insolvency Act 1986 (IA 1986). If, in the course of the winding up of a company, it appears that any business of the company has been carried on with intent to defraud creditors of the company or for any fraudulent purpose, the court, on the application of the liquidator, may declare them liable to make such contributions (if any) to the company's assets as the court thinks proper. The conduct must involve actual dishonesty: ***Re Patrick and Lyon Ltd*** [1933] Ch 786;[2] for instance, where directors allow a company to incur credit when they have no reason to believe

[2] The reference to case law adds more credit to your answer than simply stating the statutory provision in section 213.

[3] Students often forget to discuss the criminal offence for fraudulent trading in their answers.

[4] As this is a problem question, you need to apply the relevant law to the problem scenario.

[5] This is an important exception to the liability for wrongful trading and should be discussed in a good answer.

[6] You can point out here that the objective and subjective standards of care and skill for directors in section 214(4) of the Insolvency Act 1986 have been adopted in section 174 of the Companies Act 2006 (director's duty to exercise reasonable care, skill and diligence).

[7] You need to show your knowledge of the statutory provisions in section 214 of the Insolvency Act 1986 and, more significantly, analyse their application by reference to case law. The latter will gain you more marks.

that the creditors will ever be paid: *Re William C Leitch Bro Ltd* [1932] 2 Ch 71. Fraudulent trading is also a criminal offence under section 993, CA 2006.[3] As John and Sam falsified the company's accounts with the intention to defraud creditors, it is clear that they should be held liable for fraudulent trading.[4]

Section 214 of the IA 1986 on wrongful trading applies if the company has gone into insolvent liquidation and, at some time before the commencement of the winding up of the company, the director knew or ought to have concluded that there was no reasonable prospect that the company would avoid going into insolvent liquidation. The court, on the application of the liquidator, may declare that a director or shadow director is to be liable to make such contribution (if any) to the company's assets as the court thinks proper. The court shall not make such declaration if it is satisfied that the director took every step to minimise the potential loss to the company's creditors as he ought to have taken (s. 214(3), IA 1986): *Re Brian D Pierson Ltd* [2001] 1 BCLC 275.[5]

The director's obligation to predict insolvency is assessed both subjectively and objectively. The facts which a director ought to know or ascertain, the conclusions which he ought to reach and the steps which he ought to take are those which would be known or ascertained, or reached or taken, by a reasonably diligent person (s. 214(4), IA 1986). The reasonably diligent person should have the general knowledge, skill and experience that may reasonably be expected of a person carrying out the same functions as are carried out by that director in relation to the company, and the general knowledge, skill and experience that that director has.[6]

The crucial issue is how to establish that directors knew or ought to have concluded that there was no reasonable prospect of avoiding insolvent liquidation.[7] In *Official Receiver v Doshi* [2001] 2 BCLC 235 it was held that a director who knew that his company could only continue to trade as a result of fraudulent invoicing ought to have concluded that there was no reasonable prospect that the company would avoid going into insolvent liquidation. When Fresh Fruit Ltd was trading at a loss and the situation got worse, John and Sam ought to have concluded that there was no reasonable prospect of avoiding insolvent liquidation. The claim for wrongful trading, however, is unlikely to succeed where directors have acted

8 Try to refer back to the
problem question after
analysing the relevant area
of law.

9 The latter part of the
sentence will gain you more
marks because it shows your
sound understanding of the
purpose of section 216.

10 Note the requirement of the
period of '12 months' before
the liquidation.

11 The prohibited names in
section 216 include not only
the name of the company in
liquidation but also the name
which is similar to it. Students
are often not aware of the
latter.

12 You need to pay attention
to the requirement as to
the length of time for the
application of section 216
because it affects your advice
to the liquidator.

13 The reference to the case
law and the judgment of the
Court of Appeal shows your
excellent understanding of
section 216. It will improve
your grade.

responsibly: *Re Continental Assurance Co of London plc* [2007] 2 BCLC 287. It appears that John and Sam did not take necessary steps to minimise the loss by seeking professional advice or act responsibly and therefore it is mostly likely that they will be held liable for wrongful trading.[8]

The re-use of the name of the company which has been wound up is prohibited in section 216, IA 1986 in order to prevent any exploitation by the directors of any remaining goodwill in the insolvent company.[9] Where a company has gone into insolvent liquidation, a director of the company, who was in post at any time in the 12 months preceding the liquidation,[10] shall not be a director of any other company under a prohibited name, or in any way, whether directly or indirectly, be concerned or take part in the management of any such company (s. 216(3)). A prohibited name is a name by which the liquidating company was known in the 12 months preceding liquidation or *a name which is so similar to it as to suggest an association with that company*[11] (s. 216(2)). The prohibition on the use of the name lasts for *five years*[12] (s. 216(3)). If a person acts in contravention of this prohibition, he is liable to imprisonment or a fine, or both (s. 216(4)). In *Ricketts* v *Ad Valorem Factors Ltd* [2004] 1 BCLC 1 the defendant was a director of Air Component Co Ltd, which went into insolvent liquidation in February 1998. One month later he became a director of Air Equipment Co Ltd, which also traded in air compressors. The Court of Appeal compared both names in the context of all the circumstances in which they were actually used or likely to be used. It was held that the two names suggested an association and the second company's name was a prohibited name.[13]

These prohibitions do not apply where re-use of the name is permitted with the leave of the court or in the circumstances prescribed in the Insolvency Rules 1986 (rr. 4.228–4.230). John and Sam were directors of Fresh Fruit Ltd since January 2009, which is within the 12 months before it went into liquidation in December 2009. Thus, they shall not be directors of Tasty Fruit Ltd or take part in the management in it within five years of the liquidation because Tasty Fruit Ltd suggests an association with Fresh Fruit Ltd, unless the above exceptions apply.

In conclusion, it can be argued that John and Sam should be liable for fraudulent trading as they falsified the accounts with the intent to defraud its creditors. They should also be liable for wrongful trading as they ought to have concluded that there was no realistic prospect of Fresh Fruit Ltd avoiding an insolvent liquidation. The rules on the prohibition of the re-use of company name were infringed. Moreover, they have breached their fiduciary duties to promote the success of Fresh Fruit Ltd and to have regard to creditors' interests in case of insolvency (s. 172, CA 2006).[14]

[14] Your conclusion should specifically address the issues that arise in the question. Your answer will benefit from a sound conclusion.

✓ Make your answer stand out

- Consider that a director of an insolvent company may be disqualified under section 6 of the Company Directors Disqualification Act 1986 if the court is satisfied that his conduct as a director makes him unfit to be concerned in the management of a company.
- Discuss the exceptions to the prohibitions on the re-use of a company's name in the Insolvency Rules 1986. For instance, re-use of the name is permitted where the successor company acquires the whole or substantially the whole of the business from the liquidator and notice is given to the creditors that the director will be acting in that capacity of the successor company (r. 4.228).
- Comment on the practicalities of challenging directors' conduct for fraudulent trading and wrongful trading. The liquidator may face difficulties in trying to bring litigation against the directors due to a lack of funding.

! Don't be tempted to . . .

- Jump straight to the conclusion that John and Sam are liable for wrongful trading and fraudulent trading. You must analyse the relevant statutory provisions and then apply them to the problem scenario.
- Forget to discuss the prohibition on the re-use of the company's name. You need to show a good understanding of the key provisions in the Insolvency Act 1986 and the Insolvency Rules 1986.

❓ Question 6

Tomato Ltd specialised in the production of tomato soup. In May 2010, the directors of Tomato Ltd sold the company's computers to their family members at £2,000. The computers were worth £20,000. In July 2010, Tomato Ltd, which was solvent, sold its factory which was valued at £100,000 to Butternut Squash Ltd for £30,000. It was still able to pay its debts in consequence of this transaction.

In October 2010, Tomato Ltd went into compulsory liquidation. After the commencement of the winding up, the directors sold its remaining stock to Swede Ltd.

Advise the liquidator as to the validity of the above transactions.

Answer plan

→ Examine whether the sale of computers and the sale of the factory were transactions at an undervalue under section 238, IA 1986.

→ Discuss whether the sale of computers and that of the factory were transactions defrauding creditors according to section 423, IA 1986.

→ Evaluate whether the sale of the company's stock to Swede Ltd was valid after the commencement of winding up according to section 127, IA 1986.

→ Consider the misfeasance procedure in section 212, IA 1986.

Diagram plan

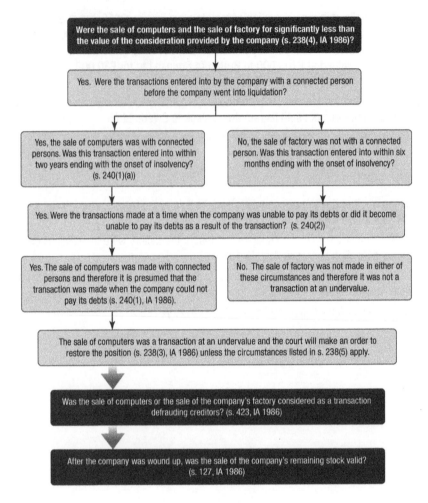

A printable version of this diagram plan is available from **www.pearsoned.co.uk/lawexpress**

Answer

[1] This paragraph identifies the legal issues that arise in the problem question. The last sentence shows that you understand the significance of the time when the transactions were made.

This question concerns the validity of three transactions: the sale of computers to the directors' family members, the sale of the factory to Butternut Squash Ltd and the sale of the company's remaining stock to Swede Ltd. The first two transactions took place before Tomato Ltd went into liquidation whilst the third took place after it went into liquidation.[1]

A liquidator can challenge a transaction previously entered into by the company at an undervalue under section 238 of the Insolvency Act 1986 (IA 1986). He may apply to the court for an order where the company has entered into a transaction with any person at an undervalue at a time in the period of two years (six months for unconnected persons) ending with the onset of insolvency,[2] which is defined as the commencement of the winding up. The transaction must have been entered into when the company was unable to pay its debts or it becomes unable to pay its debts in consequence of the transaction (s. 240(2)).[3] This requirement is presumed to be satisfied when the transaction was entered into by a company with a connected person. The court shall make such order as it thinks fit for restoring the position to what it would have been if the company had not entered into that transaction (s. 238(3)).

A transaction at an undervalue arises if the company makes a gift to that person or otherwise enters into a transaction with that person on terms that provide for the company to receive no consideration, or the company enters into a transaction with that person for a consideration the value of which is significantly less than the value of the consideration provided by the company (s. 238(4)). In *National Westminster Bank plc* v *Hones* [2002] 1 BCLC 55, the court, in determining whether the transaction was at an undervalue, identified the consideration of the transaction and compared the value obtained by the company and the value of the consideration provided by the company.[4] In *Re MC Bacon Ltd* [1990] BCLC 324 Millett J held that both the consideration provided and that received must be measurable in money or money's worth; both must be considered from the company's point of view; and a comparison must be made between two figures representing the actual value of the consideration. The court shall not make an order if it is satisfied both that the company which entered into the transaction did so in good faith and for the purpose of carrying on its business, and that at the time it did so there were reasonable grounds for believing that the transaction would benefit the company (s. 238(5)).[5]

As the company's computers were sold to the directors' family members, who were considered as connected persons under sections 249 and 435,[6] within two years of the commencement of the liquidation, it is presumed that the transaction was entered into when the company was unable to pay its debts or it became unable

[2] You should pay attention to the time limit here because it is one of the main conditions for the application of section 238.

[3] This is another key requirement for the transaction to be caught in section 238. You will lose some marks if it is not included in your answer.

[4] The reference to case law demonstrates your sound understanding of this area of law. It will gain you more marks than simply stating the statutory provision in section 238.

[5] Some students do not discuss the exceptions in section 238(5) in their answers. As they directly affect your conclusion as to whether the sale was a transaction at an undervalue, failure to discuss them will adversely affect your mark.

[6] The definition of the connected person demonstrates your detailed knowledge and adds more credit to your answer. Some students may take it for granted that family members are connected persons without any application of the statutory provisions.

to pay its debts in consequence of the transaction. Moreover, the transaction was made for a consideration which was significantly less in value. It is very unlikely that the directors could convince the court that the transaction was entered into in good faith or that the transaction would benefit the company. Thus, the court will make an order to restore the position it would have been in if the company had not entered into that transaction, for example, by ordering the property to be vested back in the company and ordering the directors' family members to make payments to the liquidator in respect of benefits received by them from the company: *Re Paramount Airways Ltd* [1992] 3 All ER 1.[7]

In relation to the sale of the factory, it was entered into with Butternut Squash Ltd (which was an unconnected person) within six months before the commencement of winding up and the value obtained by Tomato Ltd was significantly less than the value of the consideration provided by it. This transaction, however, was entered into when Tomato Ltd was able to pay its debts and it was still able to pay its debts after the transaction. It therefore was not considered as a transaction at an undervalue under section 238, IA 1986.

The court may also make an order under section 423, IA 1986 in relation to transactions at an undervalue.[8] If the court is satisfied that the transaction was entered into with the purpose of putting assets beyond the reach of the creditors or of prejudicing the interests of the creditors, the court may make such order as it thinks fit for restoring the position to what it would have been if the transaction had not been entered into, and protecting the interests of persons who are victims of the transaction. Section 423 covers a broader range of circumstances than section 238: for instance, it applies even when the company is not in liquidation or administration; there is no time limit in relation to the transaction in section 423, unlike the two-year limit in section 238.[9]

The transaction in relation to the company's remaining stock is governed by section 127 of the IA 1986 on the avoidance of property dispositions. In a winding up by the court, any disposition of the company's property, and any transfer of shares, or alteration in the status of the company's members, made after the commencement of the winding up[10] is, unless the court otherwise orders, void. Thus, the disposition of the company's remaining stock is void without the court's permission.

[7] The specific examples of the court orders help your answer stand out from those which only state that: 'The court will make an order to restore the position.'

[8] Some students are not aware of the provision in section 423. As the problem question is essentially concerned with transactions at an undervalue, a discussion of section 423 adds more credit to your answer.

[9] The comparison between sections 238 and 423 shows your excellent understanding of the relevant law with regard to transactions at an undervalue. It will make your answer stand out from those which only state the provisions of sections 238 and 423.

[10] Note that section 127 applies to transactions *after* the commencement of the winding up of the company. You will lose some marks if this legal issue is not clearly addressed.

[11] The misfeasance procedure in section 212 is another power that the liquidator may exercise against directors. A discussion of section 212 may impress your examiners.

The liquidator can also apply to the court according to section 212, which provides a summary remedy against delinquent directors.[11] The court may examine the conduct of the director if, in the course of the winding up of a company, it appears that the director has misapplied or retained, or become accountable for, any money or other property of the company, or been guilty of any misfeasance or breach of any fiduciary or other duty in relation to the company. The court may compel the directors of Tomato Ltd to repay, restore or account for the money or property or to make contribution to the company's assets as the court thinks just.

 Make your answer stand out

- Examine whether directors are liable for fraudulent trading (s. 213, IA 1986).
- Discuss whether directors are liable for wrongful trading (s. 214, IA 1986).
- Analyse briefly whether directors have breached their general duties (ss. 170–177, Companies Act 2006).

! Don't be tempted to . . .

- Provide a common-sense answer that the transactions were void without any application of the relevant statutory provisions. A good analysis of sections 238 and 127 of the IA 1986 is required.
- In your discussion of transactions at an undervalue under section 238, make no distinction between transactions with connected persons and those with unconnected persons. This distinction is important because a different time limits apply.

 www.pearsoned.co.uk/lawexpressqa

Go online to access more revision support including additional essay and problem questions with diagram plans, You be the marker questions, and download all diagrams from the book.

Bibliography

Abarca, M.L. de E. (2004) The need for substantive regulation on investor protection and corporate governance in Europe: does Europe need a Sarbanes–Oxley? *Journal of International Banking Law and Regulation* 419.

Almadani, M. (2009) Derivative actions: does the Companies Act 2006 offer a way forward? 30 *Company Lawyer* 131.

Armour, J. (2000) Share capital and creditor protection: efficient rules for a modern company law. 63 *Modern Law Review* 355.

Attenborough, D. (2006) The Company Law Reform Bill: an analysis of directors duties and the objective of the company. 27 *Company Lawyer* 162.

Bailey, P. (2013) Lifting the veil becomes a remedy of last resort after *Petrodel* v *Prest* in Supreme Court. Company Law Newsletter 1.

Berle, A.A. (1931) Corporate powers as powers in trust. 44 *Harvard Law Review* 1049.

Berle, A. and Means, G. (1932) *The Modern Corporation and Private Property.* New Brunswick, NJ: Transaction Publishers.

Boros, E. (1998) Altering the articles of association to acquire minority shareholdings, in B.A.K. Rider (ed.), *The Realm of Company Law.* London: Kluwer Law International, 116.

Boyle, A. and Birds, J. (2007) *Boyle & Birds Company Law* (6th edn). Bristol: Jordans.

Burke, P. (2003) The Higgs Review. 24 *Company Lawyer* 162.

Cadbury Report (1992) *The Financial Aspects of Corporate Governance.* London: Gee.

Capper, D. (2003) Fixed charges over book debts – the future after Brumark. 24 *Company Lawyer* 325.

Clark, T. (2004) *Theories of Corporate Governance.* London: Routledge.

Clarkham, J. and Simpson, A. (1999) *Fair Shares: The Future of Shareholder Power and Responsibility.* Oxford: Oxford University Press.

Company Law Reform – White Paper (2005)

Cork Committee (1982) Cork Committee on Insolvency Law and Practice Report (Cork Report), Cmnd 8558.

Davenport, B.J. (1993) What did *Russell* v *Northern Bank Development Corporation Ltd* decide? 109 *Law Quarterly Review* 553.

Dedman, E. (2002) The Cadbury Committee Recommendations on Corporate Governance – a review of compliance and performance impacts. 4 *International Journal of Management Reviews* 335.

Dignam, A. and Lowry, J. (2009) *Company Law* (5th edn). Oxford: Oxford University Press.

Dodd, E.M. (1932) For whom are corporate managers trustees? 45 *Harvard Law Review* 1145.

Drury, R.R. (1986) The relative nature of a shareholder's right to enforce the company contract. *Cambridge Law Journal* 219.

DTI (1999) *Modern Company Law for a Competitive Economy: The Strategic Framework.* URN 99/654, February.

DTI (2000) *Modern Company Law for a Competitive Economy: Completing the Structure.* URN 00/1335, November.

DTI (2000) *Modern Company Law for a Competitive Economy: Developing the Framework.* URN 00/656, March.

DTI (2001) *Modern Company Law for a Competitive Economy: Final Report.* URN 01/942 and 01/943, July.

DTI (2005) White Paper.

Ferran, E. (1994) The decision of the House of Lords in *Russell* v *Northern Bank Development Corporation Ltd. Cambridge Law Journal* 343.

Ferran, E. (2004) Corporate transactions and financial assistance: shifting policy perceptions but static law. *Cambridge Law Journal* 225.

Fisher, D. (2009) The enlightened shareholder – leaving stakeholders in the dark: will section 172(1) of the Companies Act 2006 make directors consider the impact of their decisions on third parties? *International Company and Commercial Law Review* 10.

Finch, V. (1992) Company directors: who cares about skill and care? 55 *Modern Law Review* 179.

Freedman, J. (1994) Small businesses and the corporate form: burden or privilege? *Modern Law Review* 555.

Gower and Davies (2008) *Gower and Davies Principles of Modern Company Law* (8th edn). London: Sweet & Maxwell.

Goldberg, R. (1985) The controversy on the section 20 contract revisited. 48 *Modern Law Review* 158.

Grantham, R. (2003) Can directors compete with the company? 66 *Modern Law Review* 109.

Greenbury Report (1995) *Directors' Remuneration.* London: Gee.

Gregory, R. (1981) The section 20 contract. 44 *Modern Law Review* 526.

Griffin, S. (1991) Holding companies and subsidiaries – the corporate veil. 12 *Company Lawyer* 16.

Griffin, S. (2003) Corporate collapse and the reform of boardroom structures – Lessons from America. 6 *Insolvency Law Journal* 214.

Griffiths, A. (1993) Agents without principals: pre-incorporation contracts and section 36 C of the Companies Act 1985. *Legal Studies* 241.

Gross, J. (1971) Pre-incorporation contracts. *Law Quarterly Review* 367.

Hampel Report (1998) *Committee on Corporate Governance: Final Report.* London: Gee.

Hannigan, B. (2007) Altering the articles to allow for compulsory transfer – dragging minority shareholders to a reluctant exit. *Journal of Business Law* 471.

Hannigan, B. (2012) *Company Law* (3rd edn). Oxford: Oxford University Press.

Harris, J. (2006) Law Society issues criticisms of company law Reform Bill at Second Reading. 27 *Company Lawyer* 95.

Hicks, A. (1997) Corporate form: questioning the unsung hero. *Journal of Business Law* 306.

Higgs Review (2003) *Review of the Role and Effectiveness of Non-executive Directors.* London: DTI.

Hirt, H.C. (2003) In what circumstances should breach of director's duties give rise to a remedy under ss.459–461 of the Companies Act 1985? 24 *Company Lawyer* 100.

Hirt, H.C. (2004) The scope of prohibited financial assistance after *MT Realisations Ltd v Digital Equipment Co Ltd.* 25 *Company Lawyer* 9.

Ho, L.C. (2003) Financial assistance after Chaston and MT Realisations. *Journal of International Banking Law Regulation* 424.

Kahn-Freund, O. (1944) Some reflections on company law reform. 7 *Modern Law Review* 54.

Keay, A.R. (2006) Enlightened shareholder value, the reform of the duties of company directors and the corporate objective. *Lloyd's Maritime and Commercial Law Quarterly* 335.

Keay, A.R. (2007) Section 172(1) of the Companies Act 2006: an interpretation and assessment. 28 *Company Lawyer* 106.

Keay, A.R. (2013) *The Enlightened Shareholder Value Principle and Corporate Governance* Oxon: Routledge.

Keay, A.R. and Loughrey, J. (2008) Derivative proceedings in a brave new world for company management and shareholders. *Journal of Business Law* 151.

Kiarie, S. (2006) At crossroads: shareholder value, stakeholder value and enlightened shareholder value: which road should the United Kingdom take? *International Commercial and Company Law Review* 329.

La Porta, R., Lopez-de Silanes, F. and Shleifer, A. (1999) Corporate ownership around the world. *Journal of Finance* 54.

Law Commission (1996) *Shareholder Remedies: A Consultation Paper* (No. 142). London: The Stationery Office.

Law Commission (1997) *Shareholder Remedies* (No. 246, Cm 3769). London: The Stationery Office.

Law Commission (1998) *Company Directors: Regulating Conflicts of Interests and Formulating a Statement of Duties* (Consultation Paper, No. 153). London: The Stationery Office.

Linklater, L. (2006) Piercing the corporate veil – the never ending story? 27 *Company Lawyer* 65.

Little, B. (1992) How far does shareholder's freedom of contract extend? – *Russell v Northern Bank Corporation Limited* and other recent cases. *International Commercial and Company Law Review* 351.

Lowry, J. (2008) Judicial pragmatism: directors duties and post-resignation conflicts of duty. *Journal of Business Law* 83.

Lowry, J. and Edmunds, R. (2000) The no conflict–no profit rules and the corporate fiduciary: challenging the orthodoxy of absolutism. *Journal of Business Law* 122.

Luxton, P. (1991) Financial assistance by a company for the purchase of its own shares – the principal or larger purpose exception. *Company Lawyer* 18.

Ma, F. (2011) Removal of directors: *Lord Morris in Bushell* v *Faith* [1970] AC 1099 in N. Geach and C. Monaghan (eds.) *Dissenting Judgments*: with a Foreword by Lord Nicholls of Birkehead. London: Wildy, Simmonds and Hill.

MacNeil, I. (2002) Shareholders, pre-emptive rights. *Journal of Business Law* 78.

MacNeil, I. and Li, X. (2006) Comply or explain, market discipline and non-compliance with the Combined Code. *Corporate Governance* 486.

Mallin, C.A. (2012) *Corporate Governance* (4th edn). Oxford: Oxford University Press.

Millett, Lord, Alcock, A. and Todd, M. (2007) *Gore-Browne on Companies Act 2006*. Bristol: Jordans.

Milman, D. (2007) Share capital maintenance: current developments and future horizons. *Company Law Newsletter* 1.

Modern Company Law for a Competitive Economy: Completing the Structure (URN 00/1335, 2000)

Moore, M. (2006) A temple built on faulty foundations: piercing the corporate veil and the legacy of *Salomon* v *Salomon*. *Journal of Business Law* 180.

Myners Report (2001) *Institutional Investment in the UK: A Review*. London: HM Treasury.

Ottolenghi, S. (1990) From peeping behind the corporate veil to ignoring it completely. 53 *Modern Law Review* 338.

Payne, J. (1998) Bigger and better guns for minority shareholders. *Cambridge Law Journal* 36.

Payne, J. (2005) Sections 459–461 Companies Act 1985 in flux: the future of shareholder protection. 64 *Cambridge Law Journal* 647.

Pennington, R. (2009) Recent developments in the law and practice relating to the creation of security for companies indebtedness. (2009) 30 *Company Lawyer* 163.

Poole, J. and Roberts, P. (1999) Shareholder remedies – efficient litigation and the unfair prejudice remedy. *Journal of Business Law* 38.

Prentice, D. (1974) The corporate opportunity doctrine. *Modern Law Review* 464.

Prentice, D. and Payne, J. (2004) The corporate opportunity doctrine. 120 *Law Quarterly Review* 198.

Reisberg, A. (2005) Shareholders, remedies: in search of consistency of principle of English law. 16 *European Business Law Review* 1065.

Reynolds, B. (1996) Shareholders class rights: a new approach. *Journal of Business Law* 554.

Riley, C.A. (1993) Vetoes and voting agreements: some problems of consent and knowledge. 44 *Northern Ireland Legal Quarterly* 34.

Riley, C.A. (1999) The company director's duty of care and skill: the case for an onerous but subjective standard. 62 *Modern Law Review* 697.

Rixon, F.G. (1986) Competing interests and conflicting principles: an examination of the power of alteration of articles of association. 49 *Modern Law Review* 446.

Rixon, F.G. (1986) Lifting the veil between holding and subsidiary companies. 102 *Law Quarterly Review* 415.

Savirimuthu, J. (2003) Pre-incorporation of contracts and the problem of corporate fundamentalism: are promoters proverbially profuse? *Company Lawyer* 196.

Scanlan, G. (2004) The Salomon principle. 25 *Company Lawyer* 196.

Sealy, L. (1997) Shareholders remedies in the common law world. *Company Financial and Insolvency Law Review* 172.

Sealy, L. (1992) Shareholders agreements – an endorsement and a warning from the House of Lords. *Cambridge Law Journal* 437.

Sharazi, G. (2013) To what extent does the section 33 contract differ from an orthodox contract? 34 *Company Lawyer* 36.

Sheehan, D. and Arvind, T. T. (2006) Prospective overruling and the fixed-floating charge debate. 122 *Law Quarterly Review* 20.

Smart, P. (2004) Fixed or floating? Siebe Gorman post-Brumark. 25 *Company Lawyer* 331.

Smith Report (2003) *Audit Committees Combined Code Guidance*. London: Financial Reporting Council.

Smith, A. (1776) *The Wealth of Nations*. London: Random House.

Sugarman, D. (1997) Reconceptualising company law: reflections on the Law. Commission's Consultation Paper on Shareholder Remedies: Part 1. 18 *Company Lawyer* 226.

Sykes, A. (2002) Overcoming poor value executive remuneration: resolving the manifest conflicts of interest. 10 *Corporate Governance: An International Review* 256.

Sykes, A. (2010) The continuing paradox: a critique of minority shareholder and derivative claims under the Companies Act 2006. *Civil Justice Quarterly* 205.

Times, The (1994) What a way to run the DTI. 1 November.

Turnbull Report (1999) *Internal Control: Guidance for Directors on the Combined Code.* London: Accountancy Books.

UK Corporate Governance Code (2014). London: Financial Reporting Council.

UK Stewardship Code (2010). London: Financial Reporting Council.

Walker Review (2009) *Review of Corporate Governance of UK Banking Industry.* London: HM Treasury.

Wedderburn, K.W. (1957) Shareholders rights and the rule in *Foss v. Harbottle. Cambridge Law Journal* 194.

Worthington, S. (2000) Corporate governance: remedying and ratifying directors breaches. *Law Quarterly Review* 638.

Yap, J.L. (2010) Considering the enlightened shareholder value principle 31 *Company Lawyer* 35

Index

INDEX

Tried and tested

What law students across the UK are saying about the **Law Express** and **Law Express Question&Answer** series:

'I personally found the series very helpful in my preparation for exams.'
Abba Elgujja, University of Salford

'Law Express are my go-to guides. They are an excellent supplement to my course material.'
Claire Turner, Open University

'This is the best law Q&A series in my opinion. I think it's helpful and I will continue to use it.'
Nneka H, University of London

'These revision guides strike the right balance between enough detail to help shape a really good answer, but sufficiently brief to be used for last-minute revision. The layout is user friendly and the use of tables and flowcharts is helpful.'
Shannon Reynolds, University of Manchester

'I find them easy to read, yet very helpful.'
Rebecca Kincaid, University of Kent

'The information is straight to the point. This is important particularly for exams.'
Dewan Sadia Kuraishy, University of Manchester

'In the modules in which I used these books to revise with, generally the modules I found the most difficult, I got the highest marks in. The books are really easy to use and are extremely helpful.'
Charlotte Evans, Queen Mary University of London